Cyber Resilience in Critical Infrastructure

Critical infrastructure sectors are those whose assets, systems, and networks, whether physical or virtual, are deemed so important to nations that their incapacitation or destruction would have a crippling effect on national security, national economic security, national public health or safety, or any combination of these. Each country might define their unique critical infrastructure. In this book, we compiled nine critical infrastructure sectors: Emergency Services, Energy, Finance, Food, Government, Health, Telecommunications, Transport, and Water. The continuity of services in these sectors is vital for the daily lives of societies and economies. This study introduces 49 case studies from various parts of the world.

This book investigates *Cyber Resilience in Critical Infrastructure* by paying attention to recommending a national-level cyber resilience framework for all nations to use. Furthermore, we present sectoral analysis and case studies for each infrastructure by going through an in-depth analysis. As military tensions grow in many parts of the world, nations are alarmed and focused on their national cyber resilience, especially the reliability of their critical infrastructure. We believe this book will be a popular reference and guidebook for a wide range of readers worldwide, from governments to policymakers, from industry to the finance sector, and many others.

Cyber Resilience in Critical Infrastructure

Sinan Küfeoğlu and Abdullah Talip Akgün

CRC Press
Taylor & Francis Group
Boca Raton London New York

CRC Press is an imprint of the
Taylor & Francis Group, an **informa** business

Cover Image Credit: Shutterstock

First edition published 2024
by CRC Press
6000 Broken Sound Parkway NW, Suite 300, Boca Raton, FL 33487-2742

and by CRC Press
4 Park Square, Milton Park, Abingdon, Oxon, OX14 4RN

CRC Press is an imprint of Taylor & Francis Group, LLC

ISBN: 9781032583051 (hbk)
ISBN: 9781032583068 (pbk)
ISBN: 9781003449522 (ebk)

DOI: 10.1201/9781003449522

Typeset in Sabon
by codeMantra

Contents

Acknowledgements

This study led by Dr Sinan Küfeoğlu has been completed as a non-profit and mutual benefit research collaboration between the University of Cambridge and the European Bank for Reconstruction and Development (EBRD) between September 2021 and November 2022. The authors wish to thank the Director of Cambridge Centre for Smart Infrastructure and Construction Dr Jenniffer Schooling, and (former) Head of Project Preparation and Implementation, Sustainable Infrastructure Group at EBRD Mr John Seed, for agreeing and initiating this research work.

The authors also would like to acknowledge the help and contributions of the following names in completing this book:

Görkem Balyalıgil

Ferhat Öğüt

Erdem Rençbereli

İrem Dağdeviren

Büşra Öztürk

Eray Açıkgöz

İlyürek Kılıç

Ali Kağan Önver

Arda Karacık

Fırat Akpınar

Hüseyin Akgün

Ahmet Baran Çekim

About the Authors

Dr Sinan Küfeoğlu is working as a Senior Policy Manager at the Office of Gas and Electricity Markets (Ofgem), HM Government. Previously he worked at the Oxford Institute for Energy Studies, University of Cambridge, and University College London. He led the research collaboration between Cambridge and EBRD in preparing recommendations for boosting the digital resilience of critical infrastructure. He was an adviser at the United Nations Institute for Training and Research (UNITAR) for integrating United Nations Sustainable Development Goals into university education and provided consultancy to the World Bank in the field of application of Machine Learning in electric power system.

Dr Küfeoğlu completed his D.Sc. and M.Sc. degrees in Electrical Engineering at Aalto University, Finland, in 2015 and 2011, respectively. He got his B.Sc. degree in Electrical and Electronics Engineering Department from Middle East Technical University, Ankara, Turkey in 2009. His research interests include energy futures, sustainable development, energy economics, and technology policy.

Abdullah Talip Akgün is a Treasury Associate at QNB Finansbank with a strong background in finance, consulting, sustainable development, and political science. He holds a B.A. degree in Political Science and International Relations from Boğaziçi University in Türkiye. Abdullah has demonstrated his entrepreneurial spirit by founding Educabee, an education consultancy startup that achieved remarkable success. His experience extends to contributing to several research projects, such as the *Emerging Technologies: Value Creation for Sustainable Development* initiative as part of the International Fellowship for Outstanding Researchers Programme.

Preface

The advent of the digital age has brought about an unprecedented level of connectivity and convenience for individuals and organisations alike. However, this same connectivity has also created a new frontier for cyber threats, particularly in the realm of critical infrastructure. From power grids to transportation systems, healthcare to finance, the functioning of our modern society relies heavily on the proper operation of these critical systems.

The consequences of a cyberattack on critical infrastructure can be catastrophic, with potential effects ranging from widespread power outages to disruptions in the delivery of essential services. As such, it is crucial that these systems are not only secure but also resilient in the face of ever-evolving cyber threats.

This book, *Cyber Resilience in Critical Infrastructure*, aims to provide a comprehensive overview of the challenges posed by cyber threats to critical infrastructure and the strategies and practices that can be employed to enhance their resilience by reviewing major cyber incidents threatening the critical infrastructure in 18 countries worldwide. Drawing on the expertise of these major incidents, this book covers a wide range of topics, from risk management and threat assessment to incident response and recovery.

Critical infrastructure sectors are those whose assets, systems, and networks, whether physical or virtual, are deemed so important to nations that their incapacitation or destruction would have a crippling effect on national security, national economic security, national public health or safety, or any combination of these. Each country might define their unique critical infrastructure. In this book, we explore the technical aspects of cyber resilience and then provide 49 case studies from nine critical infrastructure sectors: Emergency Services, Energy, Finance, Food, Government, Health, Telecommunications, Transport, and Water.

Ultimately, this book serves as a valuable resource for professionals, policymakers, academics, and students who are seeking to gain a deeper understanding of cyber resilience in critical infrastructure. It is our hope that the insights and knowledge presented in this book will contribute to the development of effective strategies and practices for securing the critical infrastructure that underpins our modern society.

Dr Sinan Küfeoğlu
Department of Engineering
University of Cambridge
Cambridge, United Kingdom

Chapter 1

Critical infrastructure and cyber resilience frameworks

Infrastructure can simply be defined as the basic physical systems, assets, and services that are necessary to sustain the societal and economic activities of countries, regions, or organisations. The protection and maintenance of these assets are essential for everyone. Some of these infrastructures might have higher significance than others in terms of continuity of the operation or national security, hence called "critical infrastructure." There are various definitions for critical infrastructure. The European Commission defines critical infrastructure as "an asset or system which is essential for the maintenance of vital societal functions" (EC, 2022). The United States (US) Cybersecurity and Infrastructure Security Agency's definition is "... sectors whose assets, systems, and networks, whether physical or virtual, are considered so vital to the United States that their incapacitation or destruction would have a debilitating effect on security, national economic security, national public health or safety, or any combination thereof" (CISA, 2022). On the other hand, the United Kingdom (UK) National Cyber Security Centre defines the critical infrastructure as "...elements of infrastructure (facilities, systems, sites, property, information, people, networks and processes), the loss or compromise of which would result in major detrimental impact on the availability, delivery or integrity of essential services, leading to severe economic or social consequences or to loss of life" (NCSC, 2022). The 16 sectors which are listed as critical infrastructure in the US are Chemical, Commercial and Facilities, Communications, Critical Manufacturing, Dams, Defence Industrial Base, Emergency Services, Energy, Financial Services, Food and Agriculture, Government Facilities, Healthcare and Public Health, Information Technology (IT), Nuclear reactors, materials and waste, Transportation Systems, and Waste and wastewater systems (CISA, 2022). On the other hand, the UK government lists 13 sectors as critical infrastructure: Chemicals, Civil Nuclear, Communications, Defence, Emergency Services, Energy, Finance, Food, Government, Health, Space, Transport, and Water (NCSC, 2022).

With the advance of information technologies and the Internet, economic activities are getting increasingly digitised every year. For example, according to the International Energy Agency, the number of Internet of Things

DOI: 10.1201/9781003449522-1

(IoT) connection points is estimated to reach 83 billion worldwide by 2024, and only 10% of the generated data in cities is currently being used (IEA, 2021). The number of IoT devices connected to our physical world will keep increasing, generating ever-increasing data to be stored and used. Along with the boosting digitalisation of economic and social activities, digitised virtual and physical assets have become targets for cyber threats. Numerous key players and stakeholders are involved in cyber resilience in critical infrastructure. To map the ecosystem, we need to follow the data transfers. Some/occasional and intensive/continuous data flow takes place among various key players. Figure 1.1 illustrates the critical infrastructure ecosystem with data flows as follows.

Critical infrastructure owners and operators own, operate, and maintain the assets. Businesses and entrepreneurs create new business opportunities by making use of infrastructure data. The industry provides necessary equipment based on the needs of the owners and operators by exchanging necessary data with them. Regulators collect critical service data and introduce or update regulations. Research institutions and academia make use of data to generate research work. Finance institutions make use of the data to make the assessment for funding and financing decisions. Customers/users provide continuous user data to the infrastructure owners/operators. In return, they receive a limited amount of data to fine-tune their consumption behaviour or for other purposes. Governments and authorities inspect both the physical assets and the operations of the infrastructure owners/operators as they are held responsible and accountable for their services. Physical

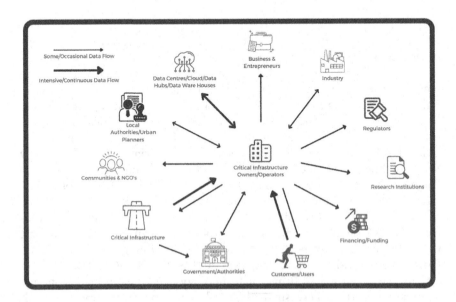

Figure 1.1 Critical infrastructure ecosystem.

assets are able to exchange data thanks to the ever-increasing number of IoT – compatible devices. This exchange is especially vital for condition monitoring. Communities and Non-Governmental Organisations (NGOs) demand some data to investigate the social and ethical value and societal benefits created by critical services. Local authorities and urban planners exchange data to improve efficiency and service quality and make future decisions and planning. Collected data are stored in data centres, the cloud, data hubs, or data warehouses. There is an excessive and continuous bilateral data flow between owners/operators and data storage facilities. Cyber threats should be considered seriously even when there is some/occasional data flow between stakeholders. However, the vulnerability increases in many folds when there is intensive/continuous data flow.

The continuity of services is vital, and disruptions in these critical assets could cause serious damage to economies and societies. Therefore, critical infrastructure cyber resilience is a significant concern for countries, organisations, and companies. In this book, we present a brief general introduction to cyber resilience and then provide 49 case studies from nine critical infrastructures: Emergency Services, Energy, Finance, Food, Government, Health, Telecommunications, Transport, and Water. Table 1.1 summarises these case studies and their locations.

1.1 CYBER RESILIENCE FRAMEWORK OVERVIEW

1.1.1 Governance and management

With the advancement of various technologies, the increase in digitalisation has brought new risks that might be faced in businesses, governments, and institutions in general. Furthermore, because such organisations are responsible for the data security of their customers, business partners, stakeholders, and their own, they must be far more cautious regarding cyber resilience.

Networks between computerised systems can impact vital infrastructures (Ten et al., 2010). Many software/hardware structures typically operate a network that can lean on area type (i.e., WAN or LAN). According to Reuters, the Russian Central Bank and private banks lost $31 million in a 2016 cyberattack (Reuters, 2016).

The Governance and Management of cyber resilience prioritise cybersecurity-related operations across various organisations and manages them accurately (Abraham et al., 2019). This step is one of the essential critical points within the framework. The general paradigm of cyber resilience is the flexibility of returning to a normal position from a negative situation. Governance of cyber resilience manages owned cyber areas and provides system normalisations and protection (Galinec & Steingartner, 2017). Protecting and normalisations include various methods and tools, e.g., non-thread actors.

Table 1.1 Summary of Cases

Emergency Services		Energy		Finance	
Case Name	Country	Case Name	Country	Case Name	Country
BlueLeaks	USA	Stuxnet Attack	Iran	Bitmart	USA
Baltimore's Emergency System	USA	The Shamoon Malware	Saudi Arabia	Coinbase	USA
D.C. Metropolitan Police Department	USA	Colonial Pipeline	USA	Dao Hack	Global
AAA Ambulance Service	USA	Oiltanking Deutschland Attack	Germany	Wormhole Token Hack	Global
		Ukrainian Power Grid Hack	Ukraine	Energobank	Ukraine
		COPEL and Eletrobras Cyber Attack	Brazil	Robinhood	USA
				Diebold Nixdorf	USA

Telecommunications		Transportation		Water	
Case Name	Country	Case Name	Country	Case Name	Country
Nortel Networks Corporation	Canada	Transnet	South Africa	Maroochy Municipal Sewage System	Australia
T-Mobile	Germany	Port of Antwerp	Belgium	Oldsmar Water Utility System	USA
NTT Communications Corporation	Japan	Rotterdam Port	Netherlands	Key Largo Wastewater Treatment	USA
LightBasin	Global	San Francisco Municipal Transport Agency	USA	Bowman Avenue Dam	USA

(Continued)

Table 1.1 (Continued) Summary of Cases

	Telecommunications		Transportation		Water	
Case Name	Country	Case Name	Country	Case Name	Country
Syniverse	USA	WannaCry Ransomware Attack	Germany	Onslow Water and Sewer Authority	USA
Orange SA	France	Cathay Pacific Airways Cyber Attack	China	–	–
Telefonica	Spain	–	–	–	–
Verizon	USA	–	–	–	–

	Food		Government		Health	
Case Name	Country	Case Name	Country	Case Name	Country
JBS	USA	SolarWinds	USA	Magellan Health	USA
Schreiber Foods	USA	2016 Clinton Campaign Data Leak	USA	United Healthcare Services	UK
JFC International	USA	Bundestag Hack	Germany	Broward Health	USA
Harvest Sherwood Food Distributors	USA	Aadhaar	India	Boston Children's Hospital	USA
Crystal Valley Cooperation	–	–	–	Texas Hospital Network	USA

The most significant advantage of establishing a strong governance and management system against risks and threats is to ensure that the prepared functions are implemented most effectively and to overcome calamities with minor damage to critical infrastructures and the fastest recovery (Heinimann & Hatfield, 2017). Cyber resilience management is crucial, as it is necessary for stable systems (Petrenko & Vorobieva, 2019). Governance of cyber resilience includes risks such as economic distress and vital problems. The World Economic Forum's definition of cybersecurity failures noted as "clear and present danger" in its 2021 report reveals how the seriousness and danger of the situation have increased (World Economic Forum, 2021). According to the Washington Post, an Indian nuclear power plant suffered a cyberattack (The Washington Post, 2019). The crucial point in this event was that the atomic plant network was LAN and not connected to the external network for cybersecurity protocols. This information shows that governance must be implemented straightforward, sensitive, and renewable way. In agreement with the administration of cyber resilience, the New Zealand Reserve Bank framework guidance indicates the three main parts, namely "Board and Senior Management responsibilities," "Cyber Resilience framework and strategies," and "Culture and awareness" (Reserve Bank of New Zealand, 2021). Generally, governance must be applied as a tree model with testable, renewable strategies.

Additionally, in the report published by Homeland Security and Representing Chief Information Officers of the States in the US in 2017, it is emphasised that management will take place in the following six areas: budget and procurement, risk assessment and mitigation, incident response, information sharing, workforce development, and education (Homeland Security, Representing Chief Information Officers of the States, 2017).

1.1.2 Identify

The factors that this subsection comprises range from developing an organisation-wide understanding of managing cybersecurity risks to identifying cyberattacks against systems, people, assets, data, and capabilities. Utilising the identify function is one of the essential functions required for the effective use of the framework (National Institute of Standards and Technology, 2018). Organisations need to understand the context of the work performed, identify the resources that support critical functions, and identify the cybersecurity risks that may occur in these areas (Conteh & Schmick, 2016). These definitions, if done correctly, allow an organisation to focus on and prioritise objectives consistent with its risk management strategy and business needs (RSI Security, 2019). The identify subsection covers several critical categories. These are risk management strategy, risk assessment, governance, business environment, and asset management (Infosec Institute, 2022):

1. **Risk Management Strategy:** It ensures that organisations' priorities, risk tolerances, and constraints are developed and specified (Boyens et al., 2015). The risk tolerance determination process is carried out

on a sectoral basis (Rehacek, 2017). Studies are carried out on particular risk analysis according to sectors and their role in critical infrastructures. These enhancements are used to aid decision-making when needed during operations.

2. **Risk Assessment:** Studies under this category include understanding the risks of cyberattacks on an organisation's operations, individuals, and assets (Zografopoulos et al., 2021). Identifying and reporting security vulnerabilities of assets owned by the organisation is performed in this section. Cyber threat information from knowledge-sharing forums and resources is documented. Internal and external threats that may occur are identified and documented. Potential business possibilities and impacts are also reported in this section. Threats, vulnerabilities, effects, and opportunities are used to understand the risks that may occur (Jouini et al., 2014). Responses to these risks are also determined, and the prioritisation process is carried out.

3. **Governance:** The studies carried out under this title are required for an organisation to monitor and manage its operational, environmental, regulatory, risk, and legal requirements (Hopkin, 2018). The company's cybersecurity policies are created within the scope of these studies. Cybersecurity roles and responsibilities align with internal functions, which include external partners. Cybersecurity legal and regulatory requirements are understood. In this context, studies are carried out on privacy and civil liberties.

4. **Business Environment:** This category defines the organisation's mission, stakeholders, activities, and objectives. The mission, activities, and goals of the organisation should be determined. The role of the institution in the sector and critical infrastructure should be selected. Essential functions and dependencies of the services offered should be defined, and flexibility requirements should be established according to these determinations (Alcaraz & Zeadally, 2015).

5. **Asset Management:** Studies under this category cover identifying facilities, systems, services, data, and personnel that the organisation uses to achieve its objectives. This topic includes identifying cybersecurity roles and responsibilities for the workforce, prioritising identified resources, categorising external information systems, organisational mapping communications and data flow, and defining physical systems, devices, and software inventories (Georgiadou et al., 2021).

1.1.3 Protect

Protection is a significant part of cyber resilience in critical infrastructure. As technology evolves, every device and infrastructure becomes a part of the cyber network (Alcaraz & Zeadally, 2015). While the network enlarges as more participants get included, the need for increased privacy measures and cybersecurity is heightened (Shaw et al., 2009). Specifically, data and infrastructure protection are critical (Moteff & Parfomak, 2004).

The National Institute of Standards and Technology (NIST) defines "protection" as the "Development and implementation of appropriate safeguards to ensure delivery of critical services" (NIST, 2018). It can be understood that a cyber network is a place that contains numerous participants. These participants could try to hack into the infrastructure system or be completely harmless. Either way, the system should be secured for any entrance that is non-authorised. To achieve that, organisations must improve the capability of limiting or mitigating the consequences of a future cybersecurity disaster within the protection principle.

The protection stage of the cyber resiliency framework is all about establishing and putting into place safeguards for vital facilities and services to lessen or contain the effects of an attack (Harrop & Matteson, 2014). The goal is to install first-line security programs that will restrict or control the effect of any potential threat and protect the organisation's infrastructure and data from malicious attacks to the best of its current abilities. While no amount of time or high technology cyber defence can guarantee success, the main objective is to minimise the chance of a breach succeeding (Vukalovic & Delija, 2015). Here, NIST suggests six protection functions to deploy the protection principle of a successful cyber resiliency framework (NIST, 2018):

1. **Identity Management, Authentication, and Access Control:** Physical and logical assets, as well as associated facilities, are only accessible to authorised individuals, processes, and devices, and access is strictly controlled.
2. **Awareness and Training:** The organisation's personnel and partners receive cybersecurity awareness training to conduct their cybersecurity-related activities.
3. **Data Security:** To ensure the confidentiality, integrity, and availability of information, information and records (data) are handled under the organisation's risk plan. High-tech cybersecurity technologies are essential and highly recommended in this situation.
4. **Information Protection Processes and Procedures:** To manage the security of information systems and assets, security policies, methods, and procedures are maintained and used.
5. **Maintenance:** Industrial control and information system components are maintained and repaired per policies and procedures.
6. **Protective Technology:** Technical security solutions are handled following applicable policies, procedures, and agreements to ensure the security and resilience of systems and assets.

All of these areas are important to the protection pillar. Most importantly, the necessary technology must be in place to safeguard organisations' critical infrastructures and assets (Hellström, 2007). Moreover, the technology must be integrated to provide the necessary intelligence to detect an attack quickly. Access to the network and data must be mobile and well-protected so that authorised users and employees can immediately identify and react to an emergency (Symantec, 2015).

The protection principle is very critical to creating a successful cyber resiliency framework. An organisation with a vital protection principle may have many benefits, such as fewer incidents, fewer fines and penalties, fewer risks of a breach, and an enhanced reputation. In conclusion, the protection principle is one of the most crucial parts of a successful cyber resiliency framework. Organisations with robust and secure protection pillars can realise many benefits from it.

1.1.4 Detect

The fourth principle of an assured cyber resilience framework is to detect abnormal data activity and potential data breaches before any critical damage occurs (Haughey, 2020). The detection principle concentrates on constructing and implementing strategies to identify malicious attacks or assess affected systems almost immediately (Symantec, 2014). Moreover, per NIST, the definition of the detect function is to "... develop and implement appropriate activities to identify the occurrence of a cybersecurity event" (NIST, 2018).

Most of the time, enterprises and organisations have no trouble adjusting their safeguards to protect their backrooms against possible cyber threats. However, when a successful cyber intrusion occurs, it takes much more than traditional defensive methods to detect this attack and determine which action plans to implement. In such a case, a company with a resilient system can overcome this problem by managing three different outcome categories included in the NIST Framework:

1. **Anomalies and Events:** The definition of this category, according to NIST (2018), is "anomalous activity is detected, and potential impact of events is understood." This means that enterprise security workers can detect abnormal events in network systems and intervene promptly before any damage or loss to the system.
2. **Security Continuous Monitoring:** According to NIST (2018), the definition of this category is "the information system and assets are monitored to identify cybersecurity events and verify the effectiveness of protective measures." The function of this category is to provide an approach for organisations to monitor information security controls, vulnerabilities, and other cyber threats on an atomic basis (Tunggal, 2021).
3. **Detection Processes:** The definition of this category is "detection processes and procedures are maintained and tested to ensure awareness of anomalous events." This is an approach based on continuous system testing and the implementation of necessary procedures for a sustainable security system.

1.1.5 Respond

The Respond Function entails actions that should be taken in response to a cybersecurity issue that has been detected. This function supports the capacity to contain the impact of a potential cybersecurity event. When a security flaw or breach is discovered, this function entails a comprehensive incident response plan that ensures business continuity in the event of a cyberattack. In other words, when a cybersecurity incident occurs, the function's objective is to ensure that business continues as usual or is minimally affected while providing appropriate action sets to execute. Moreover, organisations should undertake frequent team exercises and document outcomes for continuous improvements to complete this function effectively (Webb & Hume, 2018).

A function's categories are subdivided into groups of cybersecurity outcomes that are directly linked to programming needs and specific operations (NIST, 2018). Examples of a good result of this function include the following categories:

1. **Response Planning:** This category begins with the execution of reaction procedures, which follows the detect function. Ensuring a prompt response by following policies and processes that have been appropriately performed (Mylrea et al., 2017). Having a pre-defined action plan that everyone understands allows you to coordinate your response efforts more quickly and effectively than if you do not have one (Symantec, 2014). These response plans should be completed as soon as possible, either during or after the cybersecurity event.
2. **Communication:** The response category includes communication between external and internal stakeholders. Following the reaction plans, the organisation's relevant stakeholders must coordinate response efforts and, if necessary, seek assistance from law enforcement. The specifics of the cyber incident should be communicated to all parties inside and outside the company.
3. **Analysis:** Analysis comprises reviews carried out while response activities are performed to ensure proper procedures are followed. The research aims to ensure that effective reaction and recovery steps, including forensic investigation and determining incident effects, are taken. The process should include an assessment of the incident's impact and the organisation's ability to respond.
4. **Mitigation:** The activities preventing an occurrence from spreading while removing or neutralising its effects are risk mitigation. The threat's potential impact must be mitigated to the greatest extent possible.
5. **Improvement:** After a cybersecurity incident, it is essential to look back at earlier attacks and learn from them. These results should be improved to assist with future relevant occurrences. Before any cyber incident occurs, testing the strategy will nearly always show flaws that must be addressed. Maintaining up-to-date reaction plans as new information comes to light is critical (Mahn et al., 2021).

1.1.6 Recover

All the functions in the NIST Framework, such as identify, protect, detect, respond, and recover, are required for a complete defence. Nevertheless, at a more fundamental level, the recover function's capabilities have a severe effect across the organisation by providing data that can be used to improve other capabilities (Bartock et al., 2016).

An organisation's cyber recovery will aid in achieving effective and efficient cyber resilience. According to NIST (2018), the Recover function facilitates a quick return to regular operations to minimise the effects of a cyber incident. In other words, Onwubiko (2020) says that during and after a cyber incident, recover – recovering from a cyber incident and failure for cyber resilience – involves restoring all activities, functionalities, and services to their original state. This function can be divided into three main subsections, which are as follows: Recovery Planning, Improvements, and Communications (Staves et al., 2022). To briefly explain these subsections:

1. **Recovery Planning:** This category can occur during or after the event, depending on the timing of the incident. All affected systems should be detected, supported, and repaired, in a timely way, according to recovery plans.
2. **Improvements:** This category focuses on the cybersecurity event's lessons learned and how they might be incorporated into the organisation's security plans.
3. **Communications:** This entails coordinating activities among perturbed shareholders. To minimise the harm and maintain the organisation's reputation, all recovery plans and methods should be conveyed to all concerned persons, both internal and external.

1.2 IDENTIFY CRITICAL ASSETS, SYSTEMS, AND DATA

Nowadays, cyber resilience for critical infrastructures is a concern for every government or company in each sector. According to the NIST Framework, Belding (2020) states that identification is the most crucial step. To support the entire work builds, it is vital to identify the critical assets and prioritise them, focusing on their dependencies so that suitable defence can be provided to secure the assets (Kure & Islam, 2019).

Several critical infrastructure sectors rely on IT or operational technology (OT), such as health care, telecommunication, finance, and energy (Muray et al., 2017). The importance of the infrastructure increases as it encompasses a system, data, or asset that will affect other critical services. For example, water supply, power grids, and fuel pipeline supplies are critical infrastructures that will significantly impact several critical services when interrupted by any cause. The importance is also affected by the accessibility of multiple users, like cloud-based technology services. While resilience could be applied along with the whole system, being well-protected and

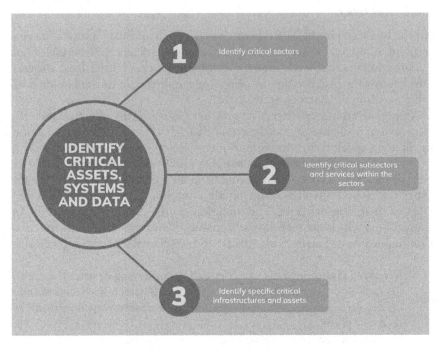

Figure 1.2 Identifying critical sectors, infrastructures, assets, and systems (Zaballos & Jeun, 2016).

ready at these points would decrease the amount of damage a cyberattack could do by preventing the dispersion to the whole system and infrastructure (Digital Regulation Platform, 2021).

As stated in Figure 1.2, the identification process carried out at the national level consists of three different stages. Thanks to these three stages, a general definition process is carried out from general to specific. Critical sectors should be determined in the identification processes carried out at the national level. Identifying critical sectors is carried out under the government's guidance. After the critical sectors are determined, it is necessary to determine the critical sub-sectors and services within these sectors. These determinations can be performed using a state-driven or operator-driven approach. In the state-driven approach, the responsibility, in most cases, rests with the ministries. In this approach, authorised government agencies carry out the processes of determining and protecting critical infrastructure. Operator-driven approach, on the other hand, is where critical infrastructure operators must perform operations. A critical assessment is required for this analysis to be performed correctly. This critical assessment is carried out by taking into account intra-sector and cross-border dependencies (Papastergiou et al., 2018; Herrera & Maennel, 2019). The so-called cross-border include interdependencies between critical sectors. Intra-sector, on the other hand, contains the interdependencies of the specified sector. After performing this classification, the critical infrastructures and assets hosted by the sub-sectors and services are determined. After these classifications are completed, it is necessary to identify the critical infrastructures and assets hosted by the sub-sectors and services. After this determination process is completed, the business processes of the determined infrastructures and assets are evaluated and defined. In addition, at this stage, the applications included in the sub-sectors and services considered critical for the system should also be defined (Zaballos & Jeun, 2016).

Furthermore, The US's Cybersecurity and Infrastructure Security Agency (CISA) defines critical infrastructures as the resources, fundamental structures, strategic systems, and networks – both physical and digital – that are so critical to a nation's survival that their incapacitation or destruction could have a crippling impact on physical security, financial continuity, or the national health service, or any combination thereof (CISA, 2022). The US Department of Homeland Security's CISA classified 16 industries as critical infrastructure, ranging from commercial enterprises to nuclear power plants. To qualify as critical infrastructure, these sectors must be regarded as so vital that their disruption would result in a recognisable socioeconomic catastrophe that would jeopardise a society's fundamental security. If these sectors are threatened, the resulting political, strategic, and security repercussions are nearly limitless (Eytan, 2021).

As for the identification processes within organisations, organisations must correctly identify the critical assets they own internally. The variety of assets owned by an organisation can be wide. These assets can include the people employed within the institution, the buildings they use, the products and services they provide, and the information the institution holds. Understanding which assets are vital to the organisation is crucial for protective measures. Answering various questions is essential to understand what these assets are. To specify these definitions, various questions must be answered by the institution. In this way, the identification process can be carried out. The questions created by the Center for the Protection of National Infrastructure for this are as follows (CPNI, 2020):

- Which unit of the organisation is responsible for the management of critical assets?
- Is a record kept of sensitive, high-risk, valuable sites, and assets owned by the organisation? Who or what within the organisation can access these critical assets if these records are kept?
- Are there effective communication channels between the people responsible for the management of the critical assets of the organisation and the personnel responsible for the organisation's security? If this communication channel does not exist, how can these communication channels be established?

- How often is the record of critical assets owned by the organisation or files owned by the organisation reviewed and updated?
- Has the organisation created and evaluated a scenario to see the impact if critical assets are lost or damaged?
- Does one of the organisation's collaborative contractors or suppliers have responsibility for the organisation's critical assets? If so, what assurances do you have that the organisation's assets are adequately protected?

1.2.1 Methods for identifying

Several categories are covered by the identify function as explained in the Cyber Resilience Progression Model Article (Carías et al., 2020). These functions show how to identify critical assets, data, and systems for critical infrastructure.

The governance domain is where policies and processes for maintaining cyber resilience can be found. It shows how much the organisation's management is included in the cyber resilience policy and whether the organisation is enough for the resilience risks. The main components of the governance domain are creating a cyber resiliency strategy and sharing it, complying with all regulations on cyber resilience, and assigning resources to build cyber resilience initiatives such as funds, people, and necessary tools.

The risk management domain contains the guidelines and procedures for systematically identifying, documenting, classifying, and mitigating/accepting the organisation's cyber risks. It includes identifying and documenting the organisation's cyber threats systematically, determining how to classify and prioritise the organisation's cyber risks, establishing a limit for cyber risk tolerance, and reducing the hazards that overstep the risk tolerance limit.

The asset management domain involves management devices, systems, software, services, and facilities for the organisation to actualise its purpose. The primary goals of this domain include listing the organisation's assets that catalogue and categorise them, as well as identifying the key assets, creating the basis for the configuration of the organisation's assets and documenting it, and creating a policy to keep track of asset configuration changes and for maintaining the company's assets regularly, and lastly identifying and documenting the assets of the organisation's internal and external dependencies.

Another domain is threat and vulnerability management, which includes identifying, prioritising, documenting, and finding protective procedures for risks and vulnerabilities based on the current system falls. Its components are identifying and documenting the threats and vulnerabilities that the organisation faces and reducing the risks and vulnerabilities that the firm faces.

The last domain is incident analysis. The investigative phase entails gathering as much information as possible from previous incidents and preparing for potential future attacks. It is imperative that after an occurrence, the entity should assess and document the damages and analyse the occurrences that occurred to get information about and learn more about the causes, strategies, goals, and entrance points. Moreover, it should also examine the organisation's response and response options in the aftermath of the occurrence and identify and implement methods to improve future responses, response options, and risk management based on lessons learned from previous incidents.

Although the identification process is built on certain foundations, differences can be seen in the transactions carried out from sector to sector. An example based on the identification process performed within the financial sector is provided to explain better the identification process mentioned above.

1.2.2 Identify process based on FMI example

Financial stability is likely to be adversely affected due to an operational problem that may occur in the financial market infrastructure (FMI). For this reason, the operations and supporting information assets within the FMI should be ranked according to their priorities. It should also be determined which one should be protected more against compromise. In this way, the infrastructure's internal situation and external dependencies are understood, enabling them to respond to the cyber threats that may occur.

1.2.2.1 Development

All critical functions, key roles, and processes involved in the FMI should be defined. In addition, the information that supports these functions should be identified and documented. These processes should be performed and updated at regular intervals. Furthermore, all processes associated with third-party service providers should be identified and documented. These should be linked together, and this information should be regularly checked and updated. An inventory of critical assets in the FMI should be established, and this inventory should be kept up to date. Infrastructure-critical assets, key roles, information assets, interconnections, processes, and third-party service providers are not included in this inventory process. Identification efforts should be integrated into other relevant processes, such as purchasing and change methods, facilitating regular inventory reviews. Within the framework of these infrastructure studies, it is necessary to identify risks, carry out regular risk assessments, and identify, classify and document all critical operations, key roles, procedures, information resources, outside service providers, and system connections. A simplified network map of network resources with an associated plan that supports critical functions of the FMI and defines connections to the outside world, addresses IPs, locates routing and security devices and servers should be created and maintained with the facility planning and analysis (FPA). Moreover, FMI should be used for risk assessment. In particular, risk analysis is required to identify potential threats and vulnerabilities before deploying updated technologies, products, services, and connections. If new information that is likely to affect cybersecurity is detected, the risk assessment should be updated. The cyber resilience strategy and framework are determined according to the results of this risk assessment. In this infrastructure, an inventory of all individual and system accounts should be found and maintained. In this way, awareness of access rights to information assets and supporting systems is ensured. This inventory in the infrastructure should be regularly reviewed and updated.

1.2.2.2 Advancement

Systems that enable the identification and classification of various assets in financial infrastructure systems can be made autonomous. These systems include critical functions, directors, information assets, and interconnections in the infrastructure system. One tool that provides this automation is the central asset inventory management tool. This tool is known as AIM, and it ensures that the inventory is updated accurately with the right timing, as well as sharing the results of these updates with the relevant personnel. Furthermore, systems that provide automatic identification and classification of roles, user profiles, and individual and system identification information in the infrastructure system should be used. An example of a system that can be used is the IAM tool, a central identity and access method. These systems automate the operations and thus ensure that the specified information is updated accurately and on time, as well as the transmission of new information to authorised persons. The FMI must maintain many information assets up-to-date and complete maps of data flows. These assets include network resources, interconnections and dependencies and partner connections, cloud services, Internet-facing services, and third-party systems. Risk assessment of critical dependencies is required for these systems as needed. It should use these maps to make this assessment and implement appropriate risk controls. Also, FMI should be updated regularly or whenever changes occur. This update process should cover new, relocated, reused, or sunset information assets.

1.2.2.3 Innovation

The automatic feeding systems above should be used to identify the risks in the FMI that may arise, make timely updates for risk assessments, make necessary improvements in line with the risk tolerances in this infrastructure, and take mitigation measures. AIM and IAM tools are examples of these systems. The FMI should also work in coordination with other institutions with which it is associated. They should identify the cyber risks that the organisations in their ecosystem carry or create for these organisations and maintain coordination on these issues. This coordination will enable the identification of common vulnerabilities and threats and increase overall system resilience. Thanks to the work to be done, appropriate measures can be taken collectively to increase the system's resilience.

1.3 PROTECT CRITICAL INFRASTRUCTURE SERVICES

The protection stage of the cyber resilience framework is concerned with planning, implementing, and constructing cyber defences for vital infrastructure and services to mitigate or limit the effect of an attack. The goal is to develop first-line security measures that mitigate the effect of any potential danger and, to a feasible degree, protect the organisation's infrastructure and data against malicious attacks (Abomhara & Køien, 2015). While no amount of time or sophisticated technology can guarantee success, the main goal is to lessen the probability of a breach. It has previously been addressed what characteristics an effective protective principle has, including the following (National Institute of Standards and Technology, 2014):

1. Identity Management, Authentication and Access Control
2. Awareness and Training
3. Data Security
4. Information Protection Processes and Procedures
5. Maintenance
6. Protective Technology

A robust cyber resilience plan must include the protection stage (Annarelli et al., 2020). Constructing a solid protective layer while developing a plan for safeguarding critical national infrastructures is necessary. Additionally, the protection concept must be founded on designing and implementing appropriate safeguarding controls, systems, and procedures that preserve the confidentiality, integrity, and availability of any vital national infrastructure's assets and services. According to a recent analysis from Forescout Technology (2021), hackers of all ability levels have turned their attention to critical national infrastructures worldwide. To exemplify many recent attacks:

- The "Energetic Bear" malware was discovered in over 1,000 energy businesses across 84 nations in 2014.
- In 2016, the US Department of Justice charged seven Iranian hackers with successfully hacking into the systems that managed the functioning of a dam in Rye Brook, New York, roughly 25 miles north of New York City.
- In 2017, the 'WannaCry' ransomware outbreak disrupted hospitals throughout the UK, resulting in the cancellation of patient appointments and surgeries.
- In 2018, Passenger ticketing systems for the Danish Railway were rendered inoperable by a distributed denial-of-service (DDoS) assault.
- In 2020, Iran attempted to contaminate the water supply of 12 million Israelis by boosting chlorine levels in the water delivered to their homes.

1.3.1 Enhancement of the protection of critical infrastructure

Several critical infrastructure procedures may significantly enhance cyber-security (Rinaldi et al., 2001). These vital principles simplify and streamline the protection of critical infrastructure. Dr Oren Eytan offers six crucial suggestions for enhancing critical infrastructure protection (Eytan, 2021):

1. **Regulation and Industry Compliance:** The compliance rate is dictated by industry-wide rules (such as the North American Energy Reliability Corporation's Critical Infrastructure Protection (NERC CIP) requirements) and the consequent penalties. The Critical Infrastructure Protection Plan of the North American Electric Reliability Corporation is a collection of regulations intended to regulate, enforce, monitor, and maintain the security of North America's Bulk Electric System (BES). These criteria are particular to BES's cybersecurity features. The CIP guidelines provide a cybersecurity framework for identifying and securing important assets that might jeopardise North America's BES's efficient and reliable power supply (Awati & Cole, 2021).

2. **Operational Network Isolation:** While isolating critical systems (e.g., health and national communications) from external systems reduces the attack surface, you must also consider how tedious and complex system-wide upgrades might become.

3. **Large-Scale Bottleneck of File Sanitisation:** With a range of important data sets and external storage devices and files incorporated into isolated networks, important national infrastructure sectors must implement a rigorous sterilisation technique to prevent malware and hazardous components infiltrating secure networks.

4. **Security Tools:** There is no shortage of technological methods for mitigating cyber risk. These solutions vary from layers of sandbox-based security solutions to network isolation, restricting user access to critical servers to different degrees of encryption. A network sandbox is a controlled testing environment that allows security teams to monitor, analyse, identify, and prevent problematic network artefacts. A network sandbox protects against previously undiscovered attack vectors (Vmware Inc., 2021). While each of the 16 critical infrastructure sectors has a distinct set of risks, integrating these standard security procedures may give the most outstanding technological basis for protection across several vital industries.

5. **Education:** With such a high proportion of cyber events attributable to a lack of staff knowledge or comprehension of prevalent phishing and ransomware strategies, one of the first steps towards securing critical national infrastructure must be to devote more time to companywide cybersecurity prioritising.

6. **Update and Apply Patches of All Software and Technology:** Stopping malware from reaching critical infrastructure requires the organisation's servers and endpoints to be updated and patched. Hackers are constantly developing new and more hazardous malware to unleash on various sectors; many are leveraging old malware kits with dramatic repercussions; to avoid this, it is critical to update and apply updates to the protective technology in use.

Lastly, it is noted that while some sectors have initiated various approaches to cybersecurity, mitigating risks and delineating sensitive areas, the vast majority of critical national infrastructure industries are willfully inadequate for the scope and breadth of cyberattacks that might compromise these essential systems (Eytan, 2021).

1.3.2 Zero-trust approach

The vast majority of industries are unprepared for the depth and breadth of cyberattacks that might damage their vital systems, even if some have adopted an active approach to cybersecurity, mitigating risk and defining vulnerable regions (McAfee Enterprise Security Solutions, 2021). From McAfee Security Solutions, Mo Cashman suggests that the zero-trust security approach can significantly strengthen the protection and safeguarding of critical national infrastructures. Cashman also offers four key starting points for adopting a zero-trust approach (Cashman, 2021).

1. To find changes, vulnerabilities, or strange user behaviour in mission-critical systems, the company must keep an eye out for possible hostile behaviour.
2. We can strategically examine threat information sources by integrating threat data throughout the enterprise's security environment and planning processes.
3. Allowing access to corporate resources regardless of location or network segment by eliminating trusted domains and micro-segment resources. Micro-segmentation between key business and security systems applies to workspace, industry networks, and remote management networks from vendors or employees.
4. Expanding asset identification and comprehension to include all data sources and computing services, namely cloud services.

In the past 20 years, the operation of all critical national infrastructures worldwide has started to go digital. The world has witnessed many cyberattacks on these critical national infrastructures. For example, the WannaCry attack targeted hospitals in the UK and prevented many patients from getting essential health services. These increasingly dangerous and hard-to-prevent cyber threats are becoming harder to fight, so it is vital to implement successful cyber resiliency practices with strong protection principles.

1.3.3 Protect process based on FMI example

These cyberattacks show that states must sensitively satisfy the protection principle's criteria to reduce and address the danger to vital infrastructures (Skopik et al., 2016). As a result, governments must detect and defend themselves from attacks with an effective cyber resilience plan and a methodology for resuming regular activities. Defending critical infrastructure demands a complete understanding of the interaction between hostile actors and the expanding attack surface. As an example, for the protection of FMIs, the Bank for International Settlements (2016) has developed the following proposal, which any critical national infrastructure institution may interpret and implement:

1. **Controls:** An FMI – or any other critical national infrastructure – should establish suitable protection measures that adhere to best practices for cyber resilience to reduce the chance and effect of a successful cyberattack on specified essential business operations, information assets, and data.
2. **Resilience by Design:** An FMI should design its systems, processes, and products with cyber resilience in mind. A strategy for designing resilience should include thoroughly testing supporting software, network settings, and hardware or connecting to critical systems against applicable security requirements.
3. **Strong Information and Communications Technology Control:** FMIs should continually maintain a robust information and communication technology to control the environment, including:
   a. **Protecting Information:** Implementing adequate controls to safeguard data.
   b. **Change Management:** Assuring that the system's change management strategy is comprehensive and explicitly integrates cybersecurity threats, both in terms of residual cyber threats detected previously and during a shift and any new cyberattacks discovered post-change. Assuring the presence of a method for discovering updates to devices and system assets, evaluating the criticality and risk of the patch, and testing and implementing the patch within a suitable time frame.
   c. **Security Settings Consistent with Levels of Protection:** Setting modern information and communication technologies (ICT) systems and devices with appropriate security settings. To guarantee that security settings are applied consistently across computer

networks, database management systems, network equipment, and mobile business devices in the ICT environment, FMIs should create baseline system security configuration standards.

4. **Layered Protection That Facilitates Response and Recovery:** The protective measures for an FMI should allow the monitoring and detection of aberrant behaviour across several levels of the FMI's architecture, which necessitates the establishment of a baseline profile of the system activity. If protective measures fail, controls should be installed in a manner that aids in monitoring, identifying, containing, and analysing abnormal activity. For instance, by including more segmentation, interim checkpoints, and intermediate reconciliations into processes, acceleration of detection, identification, and repair/recovery processes after a disruption may be achieved. Similarly, segmenting networks in such a way that systems and data with varying degrees of criticality are isolated from one another may have multiple benefits, both in terms of helping infrastructures in isolating systems in one segment and from security compromises in other segments and in terms of facilitating more efficient system recovery. The latter benefit is gained because, in a breach, only the compromised components of the IT infrastructure and all relevant data sets must be restored, rather than the whole IT infrastructure and all data sets.

Bank for International Settlements provides these cautions for processes or assets of critical infrastructure. In addition, the Bank for International Settlements shows that there are risks resulting from interconnections of the infrastructures or insider threats within the organisations. To protect the FMI from cyberattacks as a result of these risks, Bank for International Settlements suggests (Bank for International Settlements, 2016):

1. **Interconnections:** An FMI should have protective measures to limit risks posed by the entities that make up its ecosystem. The appropriate controls for each entity will vary according to the risk posed by the linked component and the nature of the connection with that component. Given its systemic significance and unique position within the financial system, an FMI should take adequate steps to limit the risk posed by its related components. Given its systemic significance and particular individual position in the financial system, an FMI should undertake effective risk mitigation strategies, such as the following:
   a. The standards for membership in an FMI should be structured in such a way that they sufficiently support its cyber resilience architecture.
   b. The structure under which the FMI manages its relationships with service providers should recognise and reduce cyber threats. At the very least, an FMI should guarantee that outsourced services have the same degree of cyber resilience delivered by the infrastructure.

Cybersecurity should be a critical component of the infrastructure arrangements for managing suppliers and vendor goods in contracting, productivity, partnerships, and risk management. Contractual agreements between the FMI and its system operators must ensure that the infrastructure and appropriate authorities get or have complete access to all information necessary to assess the services provider's cyber risk.

It is also possible that there are insider threats to critical national infrastructures. Bank for International Settlements states that getting the proper protection safeguards is essential and suggests four stages to successfully prevent insider threats (Bank for International Settlements, 2016).

1. **Security Analytics:** An FMI should adopt procedures to monitor and evaluate unusual activity by anyone accessing its systems. Data loss detection and prevention measures should be used to guard against the loss of private data from the infrastructure's network.
2. **Changes in Employment Status:** FMI – or other critical national infrastructure – should undertake screening/background checks on incoming workers to combat insider risks. Similar assessments should be undertaken on all employees consistently during their employment, corresponding with their access to vital systems. Additionally, infrastructures should implement procedures and controls to limit risks associated with individuals changing jobs or duties.
3. **Access Control:** Physical and logical access to systems should be restricted to authorised personnel, and authorisation should be confined to adequately educated and supervised individuals. FMIs should have safeguards that consistently limit such access to networks to individuals with a valid business necessity. Infrastructures must adopt tight controls against privileged system access, particularly by severely restricting and carefully overseeing employees with elevated system access entitlements. Securities such as role-based access, logging and auditing authorised employees' system performance, robust authentication, and anomaly detection should be established.

Finally, to prevent the impact of a potential cyber event and protect the infrastructures from it, Bank for International Settlements suggest training for cyberattacks (Bank for International Settlements, 2016):

1. **Staff:** All relevant workers, whether permanent or temporary, should receive training to acquire and maintain proper knowledge and competencies for recognising and resolving cyber threads.
2. **High-risk Groups:** Individuals with authorised system access or those responsible for completing sensitive operational tasks should be found and targeted for information, operating systems, and database security training.

1.4 DETECT SUSPECTED DATA BREACHES OR LEAKS

The detect function is the third step of having a solid cyber resilience environment. In the detection world, intrusion detection and prevention systems play a significant role at the enterprise level (Fuchsberger, 2005). It is essential for an organisation to be vigilant and have an educated staff since the increased level of knowledge on how phishing, doxing, and whaling kinds of breaches happen among employees, and board members will decrease the potential of cyber threats. Phishing, spear-phishing, doxing, and whaling are attacks aimed at collecting information (Bossetta, 2018). It all can be categorised under social engineering attacks. Cybercriminals could present themselves as customers, representatives, or different professional groups, use manipulation techniques to gain access, and try to collect scraps of information from organisations. An employee's carelessness can damage the organisation's functioning and critical infrastructure. All human resources must be provided with essential learning and development opportunities to ensure that all critical facilities of the organisation remain safe.

As a case example, the US's CISA provides various services and initiatives aimed at detecting cyber assaults and safeguarding critical national infrastructure. Among these is the Enhanced Cybersecurity Services (ECS). The ECS program helps ensure the security of IT networks by providing intrusion detection and prevention services through licensed service providers. All public and private enterprises with a physical presence in the US, including State, Local, Tribal, and Territorial (SLTT) organisations, are allowed to participate. ECS is an intrusion detection and prevention tool that operates in near real-time, not a threat feed. CISA offers ECS in collaboration with recognised service providers that have completed a rigorous system certification procedure. CISA approves these service providers to accept unclassified, sensitive, and classified cyber threat information and utilise it to safeguard their ECS clients (Cybersecurity and Infrastructure Security Agency, 2021a).

1.4.1 Methods for detecting

In terms of safety, the first step has a firewall. Some forms of firewalls, for example, pfSense, do not only block things from accessing but also engage in some level of intrusion detection and intrusion prevention by using notification systems. The routers organisations use to route data from the Internet should be set up by proper router and firewall notification systems activated when there is an unauthorised connection to the system. Suppose a foreign actor tries to log into the lockdown server. In that case, the firewall can send responsible organisation members a message to their phones indicating that an attempt was made. In such a plan of action, responsible parties can determine whether this unauthorised attempt was with malicious intent or not. Moreover, organisations should keep their firewalls up to date. Typically, firewalls make updates automatically, but if the update process is interrupted for any reason, organisations should confirm the accuracy of the data they send to the organisation.

Another instrument of the detection concept is leaning on third-party software providers. Microsoft 365, Google Workspace, SAML and Single sign-on can be given as an example to the software providers. These types of software enable organisations to utilise them to create secure access and monitoring through them. Therefore, enterprises can be notified when someone tries to log in from some foreign country when the state of the company is in another place.

Multi-factor authentication (MFA) is one of the basic security measures. MFAsets up layers to the sign-in process to protect critical network services (Johnson & Morillo, 2020). For example, when users access accounts, they encounter two or more identity verification, such as scanning a fingerprint or a user's voice and face. Another one is through encryption. According to the National Initiative for Cybersecurity Careers and Studies (NICCS), the extended definition of encryption is "Converting data into a form that unauthorised people cannot easily understand" (NICCS, 2013). When the user must enter their data into the organisation's networked computer system to accomplish a related task (Dan, 2022), encryption is essential in protecting and storing this information. Identity and Access Management (IAM) can also be considered another basic in the cyber domain. IAM allows IT administrators to following comprised of systems and processes:

- Assigning a single digital identity to each entity
- Authenticating them when they log in
- Authorising them to access specified resources
- Monitoring and managing those identities throughout their lifecycle (IBM, 2020).

After letting everyone in the organisation, from the board to the workers, know what precautions to take and how harmful the effects of a cyberattack can be, it is essential to talk about the time of the attack. Ways to reduce the damage that could happen in the cyber domain include quickly detecting attacks that an organisation is likely to face, responding to these attacks in near real-time, adapting the security system to current and changing conditions, testing the system against possible cyber threats scenarios, and keeping all of these processes going 24 hours a day, 7 days a week.

Lastly, another detect function instrument is based on logging and monitoring processes. The core of security (or protective) monitoring is the collection of logs, which is necessary to understand how systems are used. Good logging techniques will allow organisations to reflect on what happened and evaluate the impact of the occurrence in the event of concern or potential security incidents. Security monitoring goes a step further, involving the dynamic analysis of logging data to look for signals of known attacks or odd system behaviour, allowing businesses to detect occurrences that could be classified as security incidents and respond appropriately to minimise the impact (NCSC, 2021). Another instrument is penetration testing in the cyber domain. The systematic process of detecting and investigating vulnerabilities in your networks (infrastructure) and applications is known as penetration testing (pen testing or ethical hacking). It may also examine physical security procedures and pinpoint people's system vulnerabilities (social testing). It is a regulated type of hacking. The attackers uncover and test potential security vulnerabilities on your behalf. These may consist of the following:

- Employees' susceptibility to phishing and other social engineering attacks
- Inadequate or improper configuration
- Hardware or software defects
- Operational gaps in processes or technical countermeasures
- Inadequate or improper configuration (ITGovernance, 2020)

1.4.2 Detection process

For organisations from different sectors to integrate an effective cyber resilience policy into their systems, following resilience guidelines published and implemented outside of the industry allows them to identify specific application areas of the broad concept of cyber resilience. Here is a proposed detection guideline for FMIs from the Bank for International Settlements (2016), and it can also be interpreted and implemented by any critical national infrastructure institute.

1. **Continuous Monitoring:** An FMI should develop skills to monitor and detect unusual actions and occurrences in real-time or tight to real-time. A Security Operations Center is one instrument that can be used to accomplish this. These abilities should be maintained and tested adaptively.
2. **Comprehensive Scope of Monitoring:** An FMI must keep track of both internal and external factors, including administrative tasks and business line activities. The FMI should combine signature monitoring for known vulnerabilities with behaviour-based detection methods for both known and newly discovered flaws, including as so-called zero-day exploits. Detection tools should be used to deal with sophisticated malware behaviour, potential malicious insiders, and access abuse by service providers or other trustworthy agents. These operations should be coordinated and informed by a strong cyber threat intelligence programme.

3. **Layered Detection:** Effective containment and recovery depend on the early discovery of an invasion. The establishment of multi-layered detection measures involving people, procedures, and technology should be done by FMIs using a defence-in-depth strategy, with each layer acting as a safety net for the layers that came before it. Furthermore, an effective intrusion detection capability could help FMIs identify and fix security system flaws.
4. **Incident Response:** The monitoring and detection capabilities of an FMI should help with incident response and data collection for the forensic investigation process.
5. **Security Analytics:** Measures to capture and analyse aberrant behaviour by personnel with access to the business network should be implemented by an FMI within relevant legal constraints.

1.4.3 Detect process based on FMI example

Another detection guideline for FMIs from the Reserve Bank of New Zealand was released in April 2021:

- The entity should collect regular reference points for its selected critical services and underlying infrastructure so that any change from the baseline may be observed and odd actions and occurrences may be marked for future inquiry.
  - The organisation should ensure it has the proper people, processes, and technology to monitor and detect deviations from typical system behaviour.
  - When aberrant behaviours occur, the entity should have criteria to trigger notifications. Thresholds for initiating a cyber event alert and response mechanism should also be included.
  - To ensure accuracy in cyber risk screening and remain consistent with the entity's cyber threat scenario, the entity must guarantee that these detection and monitoring abilities, system performance baselines, trigger conditions, and alerts are evaluated, tested, and updated routinely.
- The organisation should activate and enhance its incident response mechanism. The corporation should specify alert thresholds for its monitoring and detection solutions.
- The entity should ensure that all relevant employees are trained to recognise and report usual activities, events, and incidents and that this training is updated regularly to keep up with any changes in the institution's cyber threat environment.
- People, processes, and technology should all be included in the entity's detection controls, and these controls should be capable of detecting cyberattacks and isolating the point of corruption.

- The business should ensure that its detection and monitoring capabilities allow enough data collection to assist forensic investigations of events and incidents.
  - Information, system, and data logs should be backed up to a secure location, and procedures should be in place to ensure that the logs stay accurate, unaltered, and unaffected.
- The entity should ensure that the information gathered from the system and user activity monitoring is analysed as soon as possible and that the results of this analysis are used to improve its detection capabilities, strategies, and incident response process.
- The organisation should run security checks on their systems and networks to find flaws that cyberattacks could exploit or expose them to a cyber disaster.
  - The tests should be performed regularly and whenever the entity's cyber threat status changes significantly, such as when new systems or technologies are implemented.
  - If necessary, the testing should include all critical internal workers and departments that are crucial to the entity's cyber resilience and relevant third parties.

1.5 RESPOND TO A DETECTED SECURITY BREACH

The concept we call a cybersecurity incident is a set of events that threaten information privacy and affect the accessibility of information resources. These incidents can have varying levels of impact. Responding to cybersecurity incidents can be challenging for organisations as it may cause disruptions within their operations, whether on a small or large scale. According to the research conducted by the international accreditation institution The Council for Registered Ethical Security Testers (CREST), institutions are experiencing great confusion about which paths to follow and which documents to use in the face of a cybersecurity incident (Creasey & Glover, 2013). First and foremost, Incident Response Teams and team types, which are the most crucial need for responding to cyberattacks and keeping critical infrastructures safe, will be discussed in this section. Following that, the Response Plan will be outlined, which is critical in responding to and preparing for attacks. Furthermore, the Common Sorts of Cyberattacks will be covered so that organisations can decide how to respond to incoming threats and prioritise their response plans. Moreover, Response Types will be covered to understand better how organisations should operate. Following that, the topic of Incident Response Life Cycles will be explained, which will go over the procedures organisations should take in the face of a cyberattack. As a first step, an emergency response team should be established.

1.5.1 Incident response teams

One of the first steps in building a response strategy is to form incident response teams. A cybersecurity incident response team (CIRT) consists of professionals that have sufficient knowledge of the skill sets required against different types of attacks, such as malware capture, containment, and reporting; network administration, intrusion detection methodology; firewall and system administration; packet-level analysis; cryptography, data collection, and artefact preservation; and data storage and recovery (Shoemaker et al., 2016).

Furthermore, according to the American Public Power Association, the size of CIRT should be determined by the incident's needs. It is also noted that a hierarchical structure allows for a more flexible approach (American Public Power Association, 2019). The proposed hierarchies are First Response Team, CIRT Steering Committee and Full CIRT.

- First Response Team conducts initial investigations, declares cyber incidents, and supervises plan creation and revisions following an incident.
- The CIRT Steering Committee assists in determining the composition of the full CIRT by assessing and confirming that the first response team coordinates the investigation, reaction, and reporting of incidents, escalates the situation and alerts the C-suite and Board of Directors in the case of a significant incident.
- The Full CIRT comprises legal counsel, human resources, logistics lead, and finance/procurement representative. Full CIRT's roles may be occupied by utility or municipal workers and third-party service providers.

Following is the list of feasible solutions for an incident response team, according to NIST: Central Incident Response Team, Distributed Incident Response Teams, and Coordinating Team (Cichonski et al., 2012).

- **Central Incident Response Team:** Across the whole organisation, a centralised incident response team deals with hazards. This paradigm works well for small businesses and those with slight regional variations in computer capabilities.
- **Distributed Incident Response Teams:** Several incident response teams exist inside the corporation, each in charge of a different company division. This concept works well for big companies and companies with many computer capabilities across the state. Nevertheless, the teams should become members of a specific unified body to verify that the organisation's incident response methodology is consistent and that communication takes place throughout teams. This is especially significant since different teams may view different aspects of the same situation or deal with similar incidents.

- **Coordinating Team:** An incident response team assists other teams while keeping zero control over them. It is critical to acquire the complete support of top management for teams to conduct their research and actions. During cyber incidents, the degree of authority of the teams responsible for responding to these incidents in different countries varies. To illustrate, the Cyber Emergency Response Team of Estonia (CERT-EE), working under the Republic of Estonia Information System Authority (RIA), is in the highest position of responsibility and authority. Furthermore, in Israel, the Israeli Cyber Emergency Response Team (IL-CERT) deals with cyber incidents by proactively addressing events and activities before they occur (Lewis, 2016). Moreover, The Korea Computer Emergency Response Team Coordination Center (KrCERT), operating under the Korean Internet & Security Agency (KISA), is the most authoritative body for response to cyberattacks in South Korea. KISA works with the private sector, while KrCERT deals with government agencies.

1.5.2 Response plan

The Response Plan is an essential part of a cyber incident response for ensuring that business runs as usual during an attack. Therefore organisations should determine their own specific needs and plans that must be tailored to the organisation's mission, scale, layout, and activities inside the incident response plan. A response plan is composed of a series of approaches and methodologies. It is recommended that enterprises offer a centralised team that serves as the focal point for reporting any suspicious behaviour from a procedural aspect. This team is frequently the helpdesk, which has a public phone number that users are acquainted with and is operated every day of the week, 24 hours a day (Shoemaker et al., 2016). Response incident teams must immediately begin the response plan procedures. Response procedures are identified before incidents. Hence, they are pre-defined action plans. These procedures should be based on the most common cyberattacks rather than all possible attacks.

1.5.3 Common sorts of cyberattacks

Most cyberattacks occur in the following types: Insider attacks, social engineering, exploitation malware, extortion, and blackmail (Farhat et al., 2017). The rising interconnectedness of vital infrastructures via IoT technologies, as well as the rise of coordinated cyberattacks worldwide, is a concerning issue (Gündüz & Daş, 2019). There are different types of attacks. While some of them are simultaneously IoT-based attacks, some of them are not. Therefore, IoT causes extra vulnerability to systems. Since the IoT is the evolution of Machine-to-Machine communication, and it uses embedded electronics to link everyday things to the Internet, with minimum human effort, these linked items can exchange and gather data (Gündüz & Daş, 2018). Digital systems can record, monitor, and alter each interaction between linked items in today's hyper-connected environment (Oracle, n.d.). Although IoT is a beneficial breakthrough and has become widespread, it is vulnerable to cyberattacks.

If devices connect to the Internet, they are considered within the IoT concept. This way, practically all cyber incidents in IP-based systems may affect IoT devices. For example, a teen hacked Lodz city's tram system with a homemade transmitter and rerouted trains. This is the first cyber kinetic attack that has resulted in injuries (Kimani K. et al., cited in Gündüz & Daş, 2019). To provide another example, the attackers infiltrated a water utility's SCADA system and manipulated the system to change the number of chemicals used. Thus, they intervened in water treatment and production (Sanchez HS. et al., cited in Gündüz & Daş, 2019).

1.5.3.1 Insider attacks

Insider attacks occur when workers use their positions to get access to the company's computers or breach its IT systems in various ways. In this case, important information may be lost due to the misuse of the position and authority of the employees within an institution. When such an event occurs, the first question that institutions should ask should be: "What data or systems appear to be affected by the attack?" (Farhat et al., 2017). The potential harm the insider can cause the company should also be analysed. The technological abilities of the insider will also be essential information for predicting the damage that may be caused to the company. The higher the attacker's position and the more parts they have access to within the organisation, the greater the potential damage they can inflict. Furthermore, it should be determined immediately which systems and data the insider have access to. The Capital One Data Breach case, which took place in 2019, is one of the most important examples of the insider attack type. The perpetrator of the attack, a woman named Paige A. Thompson, was a former Amazon employee. The servers where the attack occurred were in the Amazon Web Service (AWS) cloud computing infrastructure (Neto et al., 2020).

1.5.3.2 Social engineering

Employees and customers are persuaded into providing their credentials, which are then used to obtain network and account access through social engineering (Conteh & Schmick, 2016). Determining who the targets are in the social engineering attack case is crucial. What information is captured and how the attack is detected are critical factors in determining the actions that will be taken. To be prepared for such situations, employees must be trained about suspicious emails. Most importantly, it must be determined in which part of the institution the weakness causes this situation. In 2014, Sony Pictures Entertainment was the target of a social engineering cyberattack in which confidential data was disclosed, and the firm was severely harmed because it refused to stop a comedy show despite the North Korean government's request (DeSimone & Horton, 2017). Employees may have mistakenly clicked on phishing emails containing harmful links, resulting in the attack. Hackers obtain access through malware downloads and weak system protection (Maryann, 2021). As a precaution, the IT business reportedly shut down its computer network and informed staff that the matter might take anywhere from one day to three weeks to resolve (BBC, 2014).

1.5.3.3 Malware attacks

Malware attacks, in definition, is a set of commands placed into application software to jeopardise the system's safety without the owner's permission (Uppal et al., 2014). Malware is developed, distributed, and sold for several objectives, the most typical of which is to steal personal, financial, or business data. Organisations need to know how to respond to malware attacks. After a malware attack, the first thing to do is to investigate whether the attackers have stolen any information. In addition, forensics analysis must be performed before the computers of the attacked institution are cleaned of malware (Farhat et al., 2017). One of the most important examples of such attacks is the WannaCry virus which the world knew more closely in May 2017, which is one of the most famous cases of cyberattacks using malware. The virus, which affected more than 150 countries worldwide, demanded ransom by locking users' keyboards. Among those affected by this malware are the UK National Health Service, US FedEx, Spain's Telefónica, Russian MegaFon, and more (Trautman, 2018). After the damage done by the WannaCry virus, Chief Information Officer for Health and Social Care Smart W. suggested that the SHSC (Sheffield Health and Social Care), NHS (National Health Service) England, NHS Improvement, and NHS Digital should work together to produce clear and consistent standards for providing updates, advice, and assistance to local organisations, as well as for local reporting. Working with local organisations and related networks to establish alternate communication routes if normal channels are unavailable should be part of this process (Smart, 2018). All stakeholders should communicate clearly and precisely on issue resolution and control improvement. It should identify any remaining gaps and recommend how to close them (Creasey & Glover, 2013). Therefore, communication also has a significant impact on responding to an incident. To illustrate, the cyberattack experienced by Estonia in 2007 had a huge impact. Websites of ministries, banks, media outlets and political parties shut down. The basis of attack was based on Distributed Denial of Service (DDoS). The response step against this cyberattack was taken by the Computer Emergency Response Team (CERT). This step started by closing the websites under attack to foreign traffic and enabling them to be used only locally. To restore the regular cyber network situation, the CERT received support and intelligence from cybersecurity professionals from several European nations and further assistance from NATO CERTs and the European Union's European Network and Information Security Agency (Meer, 2015).

1.5.4 Response types

Sutcliffe & Co (2020) reported that there are four types of responses. These are Technical Response, Management Response, Communications Response, and Legal Response.

1.5.4.1 Technical response

Technical Response focuses on cybersecurity personnel's tasks. Technical response teams, in particular, are the people who can deal with a particular cyber threat. Since responding to a threat can be complicated, a technical response may involve numerous organisations or departments. The technical response is crucial for returning organisational systems to a good position after a data incident.

1.5.4.2 Management response

Any activity requiring high-level intervention, notification, interaction, escalation, or approval is a management response. This is an example of managing communication and cooperation, handling finances, ordering audits, and ensuring regulatory compliance. Management personnel at smaller organisations cooperate with third-party service providers to guarantee that cyber-continuity and incident response programs are correctly performed.

1.5.4.3 Communications response

When minimising negative publicity, correctly communicating cybersecurity issues can make a massive difference. Every company should have a designated line of communication with the media, such as a public relations professional skilled in developing accurate and robust news releases. Public relations professionals should have communication scripts to deal with various incident cases. Over all else, the company's commercial interests must be balanced with public transparency by communications response personnel.

1.5.4.4 Legal response

You should seek qualified legal guidance or advice when responding to a cyber incident. Legal professionals can offer guidance and collaborate with outside regulators, third parties, and other stakeholders to address potential legal issues. Additionally, communication channels might require legal assistance to ensure compliance with corporate laws and policy obligations. Legal specialists ensure that your organisation takes proper precautions, especially when dealing with confidential information, evidence, and documents.

1.5.5 Incident response lifecycle

The primary steps of the incident response process are explained in this section. There are four stages in the NIST incident response lifecycle (Cichonski et al., 2012).

1. Preparation
2. Detection
3. Containment, Eradication and Recovery
4. Post-Incident Activity

Similarly, according to the American Public Power Association report, the incident response procedure involves multiple stages. These stages are Detection, Containment, Eradication, and Recovery (American Public Power Association, 2019). The output of the second stage is the third stage's input (and vice versa). The fourth stage's output is used as the first stage's input. Figure 1.3 explains these stages.

In addition, NIST, SANS, ISO, and other organisations publish incident response life cycles, which aid in the protection of their associations. Different life cycles created according to different frameworks can be seen in Figure 1.4.

1.5.5.1 Preparation

Everything an organisation does to prepare for incident response, such as putting in place the appropriate tools and resources and training the team, comes under the Preparation phase. The efforts in this phase are targeted at preventing incidents from occurring. As a starting point, if one communication or coordination mechanism fails, an organisation should have numerous communication and coordination systems in place (Cichonski et al., 2012). Cichonski suggested many handler communications and facilities such as encryption software utilised for internal and external communications among team members, as well as inside the corporation; smartphones which will be carried for after-hours assistance and onsite communication; war room for central communication and coordination. In this phase, ensure your employees are adequately prepared in their incident response roles and responsibilities in the event of a data breach. In addition, to test your incident response plan, design exercise scenarios for incident response, and run virtual data breaches on a routine basis when rehearsed and tested regularly, an adequate incident response plan will implant portions of the reaction flow into your team's muscle memory (Wiese & Aanenson, 2020). This will enable them to bring order to any response's confusion more effectively.

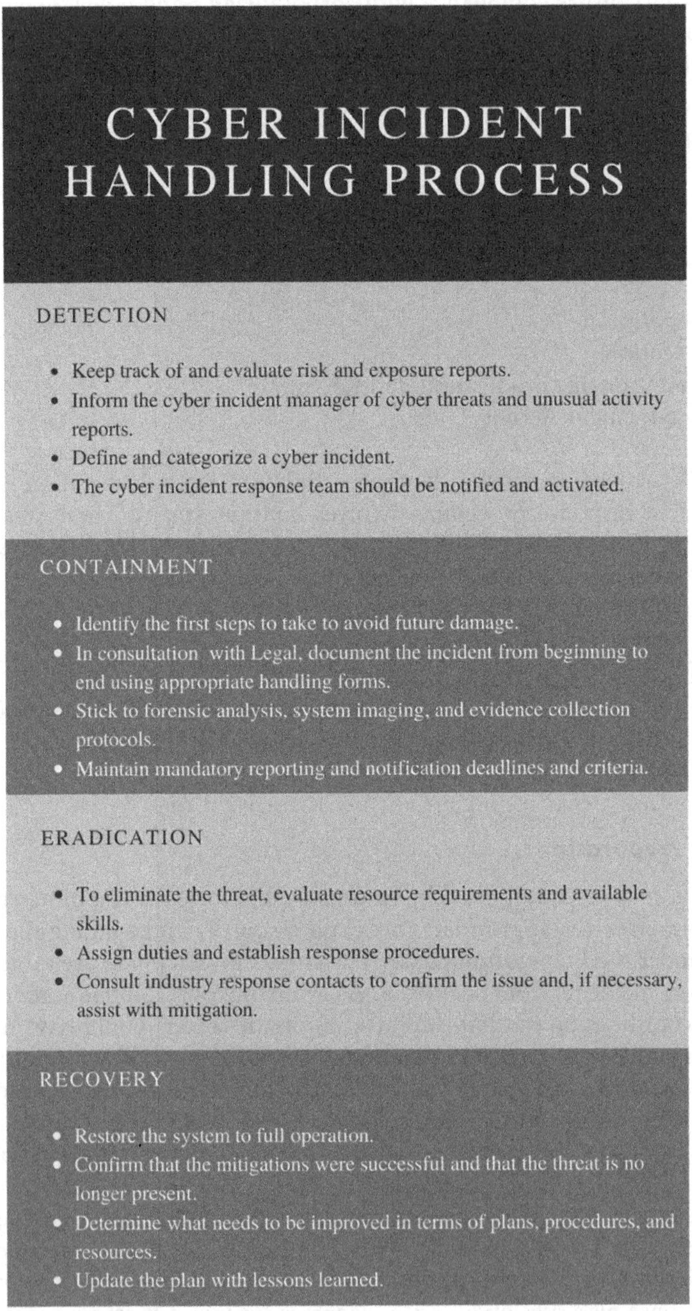

CYBER INCIDENT HANDLING PROCESS

DETECTION

- Keep track of and evaluate risk and exposure reports.
- Inform the cyber incident manager of cyber threats and unusual activity reports.
- Define and categorize a cyber incident.
- The cyber incident response team should be notified and activated.

CONTAINMENT

- Identify the first steps to take to avoid future damage.
- In consultation with Legal, document the incident from beginning to end using appropriate handling forms.
- Stick to forensic analysis, system imaging, and evidence collection protocols.
- Maintain mandatory reporting and notification deadlines and criteria.

ERADICATION

- To eliminate the threat, evaluate resource requirements and available skills.
- Assign duties and establish response procedures.
- Consult industry response contacts to confirm the issue and, if necessary, assist with mitigation.

RECOVERY

- Restore the system to full operation.
- Confirm that the mitigations were successful and that the threat is no longer present.
- Determine what needs to be improved in terms of plans, procedures, and resources.
- Update the plan with lessons learned.

Figure 1.3 Cyber incident-handling process.

NIST SP 600-61 r2	SANS	ISO
Preparation	Preparation	Prepare
Detection & Analysis	Identification	Identify
Containment, Eradication & Recovery	Containment	Assess
	Eradication	Respond
	Recovery	
Post-incident Activity	Lessons Learned	Learn

Figure 1.4 Incident response life cycle variations.

1.5.5.2 Detection

The primary objectives of this phase are to verify that the incident is indeed happening and to examine the characteristics of the occurrence. These may be complex operations. Precursors and indicators are the two types of signs that occur during an occurrence. A precursor is an indication that something terrible is about to happen. While precursors are unusual, indicators are far more widespread. Indicators include the following (Cichonski et al., 2012):

- When a buffer overflow attempt is made against a database server, a network intrusion detection sensor sends an alarm.
- When antivirus software discovers malware on a host, it sends an alert.
- A system administrator discovers a filename containing odd characters.
- An auditing configuration modification is recorded in a host's log.
- An application logs multiple unsuccessful login attempts from an unknown distant system.
- An email administrator sees a considerable number of bounced emails with dubious content.
- An odd divergence from conventional network traffic flows noticed by a network administrator.

According to the cyber resilience firm UnderDefense, your infrastructure may already be contaminated with Trojans, malware, spyware, and other malicious tools if your company has over 50 workstations and a few servers (UnderDefense, 2020). UnderDefense states the essential components of incident detection and analysis:

- **Network Monitoring:** It is critical to keep track of your users' and devices' activities on your network if you want to establish a robust cybersecurity defence. Most controls, such as corporate firewalls or Intrusion Detection Systems, are now disabled since the centralised corporate infrastructure protection and monitoring systems became ineffective due to the lockdowns.
- **Endpoint Monitoring:** When infected devices connect to the corporate network, modern antivirus and monitoring solutions use the power of behavioural big data analytics to detect them. This protects your digital assets and bridges the cybersecurity gap produced by the growing use of remote office connections.
- **Dark Web Monitoring:** Your system access credentials and business-critical information may already be for sale on the dark web if your systems have already been compromised. Cybersecurity professionals can keep an eye on the industry, alert you if an issue emerges, and provide solutions (UnderDefense, 2020).

The usage of alerting is also required for timely incident response processes. This decreases fear, speeds up the identification of malicious behaviour, and cuts the time it takes to control and neutralise the attack. According to American Public Power Associations (2019) and National Institute of Standards and Technology (2014), incidents should not be dealt with in a first-come first-served manner but instead prioritised based on the incident's functional effect, information impact, and recovery capability.

Functional Impact: IT system incidents frequently significantly impact the business functionality supplied by those systems, negatively impacting their users. Incident handlers should evaluate the immediate functional impact of the incident and the possible future functional impact if it is not contained soon (Cichonski et al., 2012).

An organisation can determine the effect of the incidents by categorising them. There are four types of ratings for incidents.

- **None:** The organisation's ability to provide all clients services remains unchanged.
- **Low:** Minimal effect; the organisation can continue to provide all essential services to all customers, but efficiency has weakened.
- **Medium:** The ability of an organisation to offer an essential service to a subgroup of users of the system has been lost.
- **High:** Some key services are unavailable to consumers because the organisation can no longer supply them.

Information Impact: Incidents may compromise the organisation's information's confidentiality, integrity, and availability. Incident responders should consider how this data theft would affect the organisation's ultimate objective. If any data in question belonged to a partner business, an event that results in the exfiltration of sensitive material might have implications for other firms (Cichonski et al., 2012). It is possible to use information impact criteria to define the breadth of the information loss during the event. There are four categories:

- **None:** There is no data modified, destroyed, or otherwise manipulated.
- **Privacy Breach:** Individuals' personally identifiable information was accessed or stolen.
- **Proprietary Breach:** Sensitive critical infrastructure data, such as unclassified privileged data, was accessed or stolen.
- **Integrity Loss:** Information that was critical or confidential was altered or erased.

Recoverability from the Incident: The scope of the incident and the sorts of resources it affects determine the amount of time and resources needed to recover from it. In some cases, recovering from an incident is impossible (for example, if sensitive information's confidentiality has been damaged), and it would be wasteful to devote limited resources to a long and complex incident-handling cycle unless the effort was focused on preventing a repeat of the incident. In other cases, an incident may necessitate much more resources than a company presently has. Event controllers should weigh the effort necessary to recover from an incident against the advantage that the recovery effort will provide and any incident-handling regulation (Cichonski et al., 2012). The following recoverability effort categories can be used to reflect the amount and type of resources necessary to recover from incidents:

- **Regular:** With existing resources, the time to recover is foreseeable.
- **Supplemented:** The time to recover is expected with more resources.
- **Extended:** Recovery time is unpredictable; extra resources and outside help are needed.
- **Not Recoverable:** If recovery from the event is impossible (confidential material, for example, has been leaked and made public), an inquiry should be launched.

The business effect of an event is calculated by integrating the functional impact on the organisation's systems and the impact on the organisation's information. An attack on a public web server, for example, may temporarily reduce the functionality for users attempting to access the server, whereas unauthorised root-level access to a public web server may result in the data leakage of personal information, which could have a long-term effect on the organisation's reputation (Cichonski et al., 2012). Moreover, the software company Rapid7 suggests not automating the prioritising incidents because it necessitates much human involvement and decision-making. It may also necessitate involvement from those not part of the incident response team (Rapid7, 2017).

Severity is separated into six segments, and colour codes are used to define them in Figure 1.5. The explanation of these severity levels and colour codes by CISA (2022) is as follows:

- A Baseline (White) priority incident is unlikely to significantly impact critical infrastructures such as public health or safety, homeland security, economic security, international relations, individual freedoms, or public confidence.

OT and Business Impact	Level 5	A cyber event that has a direct effect on critical infrastructure	The utility won't be able to supply critical operating services to all or a part of their customers	Information regarding critical infrastructure was accessed	Due to the unpredictable nature of the situation, additional resources, and outside assistance may be required	Poses a serious risk to the delivery of critical infrastructure operations on a large scale.
	Level 4	A network or system has been compromised, which could result in significantly dreadful conditions at one or more utilities.	The utility is no longer capable of providing a vital business service to all users or a crucial operational function to a group of users	Information regarding critical infrastructure was accessed	Due to the unpredictable nature of the situation, additional resources, and outside assistance may be required	Critical infrastructure services are likely to be significantly impacted
IT Impacts	Level 3	A critical company system or service is harmed or inaccessible.	A group of system users can no longer receive a crucial business service from utilities	Sensitive data was accessed, modified, deleted, or become unusable	Due to the unpredictable nature of the situation, additional resources, and outside assistance may be required	Critical infrastructure services are likely to be demonstrably impacted
	Level 2	Non-critical systems suffer from a security breach	The service can still supply all vital business operations to all customers, but efficiency has been lost or some non-critical operations have been damaged	Information that belonged to a company was accessed or stolen	With present or improved resources, predictable	Critical infrastructure services are likely to be impacted
	Level 1	Suspected threat or incident with relatively insignificant effect	Minimal impact; the utility can still deliver all vital services to all customers, although efficiency has decreased	Sensitive data is in danger, but it has not been compromised.	Predictable with existing or additional resources	Critical infrastructure services are unlikely to be impacted
	Level 0	Inappropriate behaviour is reported.	The organisation's capacity to deliver all services to all users is unaffected	There is no data that exfiltrated, altered, or destroyed		Unproven or insignificant incident

Figure 1.5 Sample cybersecurity incident severity levels (CISA, 2022).

- Critical infrastructure is unlikely to be harmed by a Low (Green) priority incident.
- A Medium (Yellow) priority incident may affect public health or safety, national security, economic security, foreign relations, civil liberties, or public confidence.
- A High (Orange) priority incident will likely have measurable consequences for critical infrastructure.
- An incident with a Severe (Red) priority is expected to impact critical infrastructures significantly.
- An Emergency (Black) priority incident significantly threatens critical infrastructure services on a large scale.

1.5.5.3 Containment, eradication, and recovery

The containment phase aims to stop an attack from overwhelming resources or to cause harm. The first and most important point to note about this stage is that during a particular incident response timeframe, the detection may have numerous input–output cycles. UnderDefense states that team members may take several actions that may have a beneficial (or harmful) effect on how the attack is handled, and they will need to keep an eye on the system's reaction. If they wait for confirmation from their superiors for each move, significant time will be squandered, and the malicious breach will succeed. However, if each team member does what they want while the stakeholders are kept in the dark, the result will be chaotic and potentially catastrophic. Furthermore, decision-making is an essential aspect of containment. The Cyber Incident Response Manager and technical staff from the cybersecurity team will assess the incident and determine the first step that must be taken to control it and prevent it from spreading. Before making any move, the team should consider the effects of their activities on the investigation. When a breach is first discovered, for example, an initial action might be to wipe everything clean so that you can get rid of it. However, you will potentially hurt yourself in the long run since you will be destroying robust findings that you will need to find out how the breach was initiated and devise a plan to prevent this from happening. American Public Power Association experts' advice against taking quick steps that might harm the investigation or recovery process, such as:

- Shutting down servers and systems clears temporary memory, which might provide essential details about the occurrence.
- Disconnecting a server from the Internet; if the server is removed from its control server, it may be impossible to identify the degree of the compromise.

- Restoring impacted systems from a backup until the team can confirm that backups are not tampered with.
- Reinstalling on the same server or device without a forensic copy or image might delete or overwrite crucial evidence (American Public Power Association, 2019).

Organisations should identify acceptable risks and establish solutions appropriately in dealing with events. The type of event affects the containment strategy. A network-based DDoS attack, for instance, requires a different approach than an email-based malware infection. Every major event category should have its containment plan, with standards explicitly established to make decision-making easy. The following are some of the factors to consider while deciding on the best strategy: evidence preservation requirements, service accessibility, time and resource requirements for strategy implementation, effectiveness of strategy, and duration of solution (Cichonski et al., 2012).

Cichonski et al. (2012) state that another concern with containment is that some attacks may do more destruction while being contained. A hacked host, for example, may execute malicious software that frequently pings another host. Pings will fail if the incident responder tries to confine the problem by unplugging the hacked server from the network. The malicious software may rewrite or encrypt all of the data on the host's hard disk due to the failure. Handlers should not believe that simply because a host has been unplugged from the network, it has been protected from further damage. Furthermore, before incident elimination, the cyber event IT support team should begin executing a complete forensic investigation under the guidance of legal counsel. This is required for the utility to fully comprehend the nature and scope of an event, identify probable intruder channels and activities, and determine how to eliminate the danger. During this investigation, law enforcement must preserve, secure, and document evidence to investigate and punish criminal assaults that steal sensitive data or harmful attacks that target energy operations.

Although gathering evidence during an event is primarily to resolve the situation, it may also be required for legal procedures. In such circumstances, it is critical to record how all proofs are maintained, even hacked systems. For any evidence to be accepted in court, evidence should be gathered by processes that comply with all applicable rules and regulations, as determined by prior consultations with legal personnel and other law enforcement authorities. Furthermore, evidence should be tracked at all times; if it is transferred from one person to another, transfer custody papers should be used to document the transfer and contain signatures from all parties involved. All evidence should be preserved in a thorough log, which should include the following: identifying information (such as IP addresses and location), time and date, location of the stored evidence and each person who gathered or handled evidence throughout the investigation was given their name, title, and phone number.

Moreover, the Eradication is the process of removing malicious software, credentials, and unauthorised access. Restoring security holes that could be the source of the breach is also part of the eradication process. A complete reinstallation of the OS and programs is strongly encouraged at this time (Virginia Tech, 2016). Moreover, it is critical to detect all afflicted admins inside the organisation during eradication, according to NIST so that they can be remedied. Eradication also is not required or undertaken during the recovery process for some incidents (Cichonski et al., 2012). The eradication stage of the incident response involves five basic broad steps:

- Establish eradication targets.
- All compromised vulnerabilities should be identified and mitigated.
- Malware, illegal elements, and other subassemblies should all be removed.
- If more impacted hosts are detected, repeat the Detection phase to identify them all, then confine, and eradicate the event for them.
- Reinstall the OS, apply updates, and reinstall apps.

Lastly, the Recovery phase aims to carefully reintegrate affected systems into the production system so that another incident does not occur. It is critical to test, analyse, and validate systems before they are placed back into production to ensure they are not infected with malware or exploited in any other way. During this stage, some significant decisions have to be made. To begin with, the time and date for the system's restoration must be determined. Elsewhere, methods for ensuring that the tainted systems are clean and fully functional through testing and verification have to be decided. Moreover, the amount of time monitoring to see any abnormal online system behaviours should also be determined. Last, choosing the right tools for testing, monitoring, and validating the system's behaviour is essential. Following an incident, there are several options for restoring a system. Each option includes pros and cons:

- Remove the harmful traces and replace the corrupted files with clean versions.
  - **Pros:** Fast recovery time and cost-effective.
  - **Cons:** May leave obscured traces behind.
- Restore from a backup.
  - **Pros:** Almost-good recovery time and cost-effective.
  - **Cons:** Not possible if a known backup is affected.
- Rebuilding system.
  - **Pros:** If backups are impacted, rebuilding is the only option to fix the problem.
  - **Cons:** Slow recovery time and very costly.

1.5.5.4 Post-incident activity

Learning from incidents is among the most critical aspects of incident response. Possible risks, technological improvements, and lessons learned should all be considered by each incident response team. Organising meetings regarding lessons learned after a catastrophic event is essential for informing the teams about past mistakes and warning them about potential future threats. The lessons learned meeting should be held as soon as feasible following the incident; a decent rule of thumb is within two weeks, if possible (Kral, 2021). Having a presentation that highlights the following material is an excellent demonstration of executing lessons learned:

- When was the problem initially identified?
- Who identified the problem?
- How did management and employees handle the situation?
- What steps can be taken to avoid such events in the future?
- Which areas need to be improved?

Lessons learned: Meetings have other advantages for organisations. These meeting reports can be used to instruct new personnel by demonstrating how more experienced staff respond to events. Preparing a follow-up report for each event is another crucial post-incident task that may be very useful in the future. Subsequent assessments for incidents are one of the most important things to do after an incident. An incident response audit should, at the very least, compare the following things to applicable rules, policies, and best practices:

- Policies, strategies, and processes for responding to incidents
- Documentation and reporting on incidents
- Model and structure of a team

Furthermore, Figure 1.6, published by NIST, lists the practical procedures to take while dealing with an event. It is important to note that the procedures taken will differ depending on the occurrence and the type of individual incidents.

1.6 RECOVER TO RESTORE DURING A CYBERSECURITY INCIDENT

Recovery, another vital function of a complete cyber resilience framework, can be defined as a rapid return to regular operations by restoring all activities, functionalities, and services after a cyber incident. It entails a thorough examination of the incident for procedural and policy consequences, the collection of data, as well as the application of "insights

	Action
	Detection and Analysis
1.	Check to see whether there has been an incident
1.1	Examine the indicators and precursors
1.2	Search for information that is related
1.3	Perform research (e.g., search engines, knowledge base)
1.4	Initiate documenting the inquiry and collecting evidence as soon as the handler suspects an incident has happened
2.	Determine the incident's priority based on the relevant factors
3.	Notify the necessary internal and external staff members about the event
	Containment, Eradication, and Recovery
4.	Gather, protect, and document evidence
5.	Contain the incident
6.	Eradicate the incident
6.1	Identify and mitigate any exploited vulnerabilities
6.2	Eliminate malware, unauthorized materials, and other components
6.3	If more impacted hosts are identified, repeat the Detection and Analysis stages to identify them all, then contain and eradicate the incident for them
7.	Recover from incident
7.1	Return the afflicted system to a ready-to-use state
7.2	Verify that the affected systems are fully operational
7.3	Conduct further monitoring if necessary to check for future similar activities
	Post-Incident Activity
8.	Prepare a report as a follow-up
9.	Organize a meeting to discuss the lessons learned

Figure 1.6 Incident-handling checklist (Cichonski et al., 2012, p. 42).

gained" to upcoming response actions and training (Carnegie Mellon Information Security Office, 2014). The recover function of a cyber resilience framework can be divided into three essential subsections, which are as follows:

1. Determining a Recovery Strategy
2. Recovery Plan Creation
3. Plan Testing

1.6.1 Determining a recovery strategy

A recovery site for your company's information is crucial in a crisis. When the worst-case situation happens, having an offsite facility to recover data and resume operations is critical to maintaining business continuity and preventing data loss (Sullivan & Betan, 2018). It should be a crucial component of any disaster recovery (DR) plan. There are various solutions to examine when it comes to applying the strategy for recovery. The solution that best suits the business objectives and security standards is the ideal choices (Canadian Centre for Cyber Security, 2021). There are three types of recovery sites which are categorised as hot, cold, and warm sites.

1.6.1.1 Hot site

A Hot Site is a DR site set up and ready to operate. All core data centre services will be copied and maintained offsite, and when you walk in, a hot backup location will have equipment set up with your current data available (Sullivan & Betan, 2018). In other words, it uses the same servers and equipment for your backup site as you do for your primary site. It performs the same functions as your primary site and is always available during downtime. Synchronisation of the data takes minutes to hours. Thus there is less chance of data loss (Canadian Centre for Cyber Security, 2021).

A hot site is preferable for critical mission data because all the systems/operations are supposed to run every moment. While having a DR site up and running in addition to a significant data centre is expensive, it pays off in terms of providing redundancy when tragedy strikes. This urgency varies by industry, but hot sites are becoming more attractive options in an age where downtime is unacceptable. A hot site has duplicates of all essential servers and personnel to manage and monitor the equipment.

An example of a hot site is called "Disk Mirroring." The data is replicated on two or more hard disks using disk mirroring. When your central system has unforeseen downtime, disk mirroring automatically shifts your vital data to a standby server or network. You can utilise the mirror copy if you cannot restore your systems. It is critical to back up the mirrored copy to a separate location or server that is not affected by the outage (Tkachenko, 2011).

1.6.1.2 Cold site

A cold site is an essentially available space with little, if anything, set up in it, in contrast to a hot site, which is ready for use and operational 24 hours a day, 7 days a week. When you arrive at a cold backup site, you must set up the equipment, make all connections, load the software, and perform various startup operations. Only the IT system's elemental power, communication, and environmental controls are installed until DR services are engaged. In other words, backup sites with little equipment are known as cold sites. Setting up and restoring commercial activities takes additional time and resources. Because servers must be transferred from your main site, data synchronisation can be complicated and time-consuming, with a more significant chance of data loss.

Until a calamity strikes, cold places are underutilised. There is usually a plan for quickly establishing a cold DR site, but there are no resources physically in place or actively running before a crisis. Periodic backups are frequently performed in preparation for a cold DR site, so that data may be recovered once the site is operational.

Cold sites keep expenses down due to their bare-bones infrastructure. They are rarely utilised for mission-critical data that requires immediate access. While a hot site often only requires essential employees to ensure that equipment is operational, technical personnel is required to set up a cold site.

To better understand, an example of a low-cost cold site DR is as follows: It is called "Storage Replication," which copies the data in real-time from one location to another over a Local Area Network (LAN), Wide Area Network (WAN), or a Storage Area Network (SAN). Synchronous replication is named to the fact that it occurs in real-time. Asynchronous replication, which produces data duplicates on a predetermined timetable, is also an option (Mazouz, 2021).

1.6.1.3 Warm site

Network connectivity and some equipment are deployed at the backup site. A setup is needed to get your secondary site up and running at total capacity. Synchronisation of the data is rare, which might lead to data loss.

Theoretically, a warm site has no work production until a disaster. Servers do not contain databases, but they are pre-configured. For logistical and performance reasons, the storage and servers at a warm site should be comparable to those at the core data centre. Internal or external DR sites are available, whereas a third party owns and operates an external site. Management and security control are two advantages of an internal site. The cost of construction and operation are both disadvantages. In most cases, an internal site will deliver a faster recovery time objective (RTO) than an external site. Management of an external site is left to the service provider. This might assist a company that lacks the personnel and resources to maintain a backup centre. The warm site must be far enough away from the primary data centre of a company to avoid being impacted by the same event, such as an earthquake or hurricane. As a result, it should not be connected to the primary data centre's power grid. However, a company must consider latency issues such as network connectivity and ensure that the site is not far away. When choosing a location, labour and pricing are important factors (Crocetti, 2018).

An example of a warm site is "Cloud-Based Recovery." You may connect, from anywhere, with a range of devices using this platform. You can regularly back up your data, and it can be cheaper than buying and maintaining

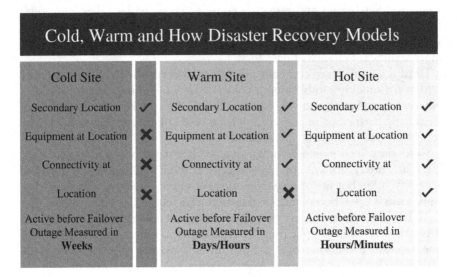

Cold, Warm and How Disaster Recovery Models		
Cold Site	**Warm Site**	**Hot Site**
Secondary Location ✓	Secondary Location ✓	Secondary Location ✓
Equipment at Location ✗	Equipment at Location ✓	Equipment at Location ✓
Connectivity at ✗	Connectivity at ✓	Connectivity at ✓
Location ✗	Location ✗	Location ✓
Active before Failover Outage Measured in **Weeks**	Active before Failover Outage Measured in **Days/Hours**	Active before Failover Outage Measured in **Hours/Minutes**

Figure 1.7 Comparison of cold, warm and hot disaster recovery models (Gardner, 2022).

an on-premise platform because you only pay for the capacity you use. Using the cloud can also help you save money by reducing or eliminating the requirement for a separate offshore backup site.

To sum up, while choosing a strategy for recovery, business objectives and security standards should be considered. A brief comparison of these three sites is shown in Figure 1.7.

1.6.1.4 Defining RPO and RTO

Two of the most critical components of a data protection or DR plan are the "Recovery Point Objective (RPO)" and "Recovery Time Objective (RTO)." These goals help businesses choose the best cloud backup and DR plan (Singh, 2021). The RTO is defined as the time it takes for a business to resume operations or for resources to become available after a disaster. If the RTO is 5 hours, you wish to restart product or service delivery or activity execution in 5 hours (Kosutic, 2015). The Recovery Point Objective (RPO) is the amount of time that can pass during a disruption before the amount of data loss exceeds the maximum permissible level for the business to continue operating (Business Continuity Plan – BCP), or "tolerance."

For example, if the RPO for this firm is 15 hours and the latest good copy available of data is from 12 hours ago, then we are still inside the BCP's RPO parameters. In other words, it responds to the query, "After what time of the incident might the business process be recovered tolerably given the volume of data lost during that interval?" (Singh, 2021). RPO and RTO, despite having commonalities, serve different functions, as illustrated in Figure 1.8. Applications and systems are the focus of RTO. Data recovery is

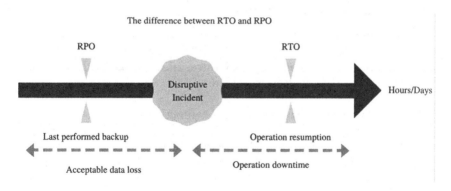

Figure 1.8 The difference between RTO and RPO (Kosutic, 2022).

included in the measurement, but the time limits on application downtime are the main focus. RPO refers to the amount of data that is lost as a result of a failure. It is one thing to have an irritated user. However, losing hundreds of thousands of dollars in client transactions is far more than a minor irritation that is catastrophic (Taylor, 2018).

To implement the DR plan, there should be a balance between costs, RTO, and RPO. The relationship between RTO, RPO, and expenses is depicted in the diagram below. RPO stands for maximum data loss, while RTO stands for the time it takes for a service to be restored after an incident, as shown in Figure 1.9. The cost of DR rises in direct proportion to the number of RTO/RPO requirements. That is, if the RTO/RPO is higher, i.e., in months, the investment or cost is lower.

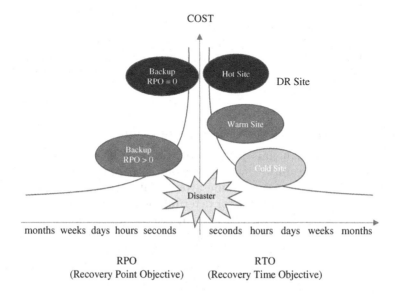

Figure 1.9 The relation between RPO, costs and RTO (Varghese, 2022).

1.6.2 Recovery plan creation

Once containment and eradication are complete, the plan for the recovery should include how to recover OT or/and IT Applications, systems, and networks (Australian Cyber Security Centre, 2021). Consider the following factors when creating the Recovery Plan:

- Restoration of the systems to regular functioning
- Methods for monitoring the systems, whether they are operating as desired or not compromised anymore
- Management of detected susceptibilities to avoid future occurrences

Data, software, hardware, and communication are all required for IT systems. The "system" may not function if one of its components is missing. As a result, recovery methods should be created to prepare for the loss of one or more of the system components listed below (Ready, 2021):

- The environment in a computer lab (secure computer room with climate control and conditioned and backup power supply)
- Apparatus (servers, networks, laptop/desktop computers, peripherals, and wireless devices)
- Connecting to a service provider
- Applicative software (electronic mail, electronic data interchange, office productivity, enterprise resource management)
- Data backup and recovery

To design an effective strategy, you must determine the organisation's essential applications, functions, and data. Personal data, proprietary assets, and financial records are all examples of crucial data. The systems that operate your core operations are critical applications and are essential to your company's success. In the event of an unforeseen outage, those systems must be recovered quickly to ensure the continuity of operations (Australian Cyber Security Centre, 2021).

1.6.2.1 Possible effective solutions for incidents

Ransomware is malicious software/malware that prevents access to a computer system until a fee (or ransom) is paid or another action is taken. While removing everything after a data breach is tempting, evidence preservation is essential for determining how the incident occurred and the people involved. After a breach, you should first figure out which servers have been compromised and isolate them as quickly as possible to avoid infecting additional servers or devices. You can do a few things right now to stop a data breach. Follow the procedures below to assist in removing and preventing cyber incidents, more specifically, ransomware (Moors, 2022):

1. **Disconnect the Device as Soon as Possible:** To prevent the ransomware from infecting additional linked devices, turn off your gadgets. Before encrypting the files, certain ransomware strains are made to lay dormant on a device and silently propagate to other network-connected devices. You might not be able to stop the ransomware's propagation in certain circumstances.

2. **Try to Remove the Malware:** To delete the malware from the devices, use the online decryption tool, which should unlock your data and make them accessible. If no tool is available online, wipe your device and securely reinstall the operating system.

3. **Restore from Backup:** Examine your data backups to be sure they are not infected with ransomware. To reduce the risk of malware spreading your backup files, keep them off the Internet. Recover your systems and gadgets from your safe backup once you are sure.

4. **Patch and Update:** Update your software, devices, and hardware, if any are available. Update your operating system and your firewall, antivirus, and anti-malware software.

5. **Passwords Should Be Changed:** Passcodes and other identifiers should be reset on all accounts, systems, and devices. Threat actors frequently save this information for future assaults. Consider utilising passcodes that are easier to remember and more secure on your gadgets. All these points above will help the owners to get the minimum harm from the data breach. Nevertheless, it should be more focused on long-term precautions to be taken.

1.6.2.2 Identify and evaluate

The diagnosis and assessment phase is the initial step in any effective DR plan. You will only be able to gauge the effectiveness of your DR plan if you know what it needs to accomplish regarding testing. When recognising and assessing, keep the following in mind:

- The first step is determining your company's primary business processes and assigning an RTO and RPO.
- Determine who, from individual employees to teams or entire departments, will be accountable for carrying out each aspect of the DR strategy in the case of an emergency. This is a critical phase since ownership and accountability are essential for a successful and effective DR plan.
- Assess the importance of each piece of software and hardware in your system. You may then order the most important hardware and software to retrieve them in the event of a disaster.

1.6.2.3 Create

You can begin working on the most important part of your DR strategy: how to recover in the event of a crisis, once you have determined which systems are essential, who is responsible for each element of the plan, and what your RPO/RTO is. Consider the following factors when you develop your plan:

- Determine which systems are necessary to achieve the RPO/RTO objective; these may be as simple as a daily data backup to the cloud or as complex as a system that is replicated live to another cloud provider or data centre. A virtual DR site is essential because it provides a backup data centre with replicated or backed-up data in a distant location.
- You must at the very least make sure that your business-critical data and systems are duplicated offshore and kept isolated from the production environment. Asking yourself if a crisis may impact both your production and backup systems at once is a useful exercise. If so, it's doubtful that they are fit for the job.

1.6.2.4 Training & development

There will be fewer vulnerabilities if you and your staff recognise the value of cloud computing security. It would be best if you thought about the following things to increase cloud computing security by improving your understanding:

- **Deliver Cloud Computing Training Sessions to Workers:** Providing cloud computing security training to employees ensures that everyone knows the importance of cloud computing security. Proper training will assist your personnel in understanding how to keep data safe, reduce risks, and what to do if risks become a problem.
- **Understand the Information Security Alternatives:** Simply being aware of your data security alternatives will allow you to improve cybersecurity as it will provide a good handle of the restrictions of cloud computing and possibilities for how your business may go around or work around them.
- **Off-Boarding Process:** We have already discussed the importance of a thorough off-boarding procedure for access management. However, it is critical to remember to teach your staff any off-boarding procedures you implement so that they are aware of the procedure. Avoiding avoidable and unintentional security breaches requires ensuring that all employees are on the same page.

1.6.2.5 Additional suggestions

Consider Cyber Insurance for Increased Recovery Capability: You may (and should) get cyber insurance for your facility, just like you can for fire or flood insurance. These services can help you recover more quickly and efficiently from an information security event, and they may pay the costs of Expertise in cybersecurity to aid in determining the scope of the harm.

Consultation to assist in the investigation and reporting of the occurrence to the proper authorities, income loss due to unavailability, expensed legal expenses, penalties, and fines. Choosing a cyber insurance provider with caution is crucial, just like any other partner would. It is also essential to look into the firm, its services, the events they cover, and its track record of sticking to its contracts (NIST, 2019).

Assess and Improve Your Procedures and Technologies: Examine your processes, procedures, and technological solutions and determine what changes you need to make to lower your risks. Try putting on a training session or some tabletop activities. Those case activities may be used to replicate a large event, allowing you to uncover possible flaws and levels of preparation. Then you may make any necessary changes (Hewitt, 2022).

1.6.3 Plan testing

After all this extensive work, the systems set up should be tested, and it is an essential part of the recover function. You may spot discrepancies and make changes when necessary. You minimise business interruptions, be sure to use a test environment. The following are some examples of test strategies:

- **Parallel Test:** Set up and test recovery systems to check if they can conduct operations to support critical processes in parallel. Your primary systems remain in full production mode.
- **Checklist:** Go over the phases of the recovery plan and explain them.
- **Walkthrough:** Go over the instructions without carrying them out.
- **Simulation:** Use a simulated event or disaster to acquaint the recovery team with their tasks and responsibilities.
- **Cutover Test:** You set up your recovery systems to take over all your business activities and turn off the primary systems. This sort of test disrupts operations and necessitates additional preparation.

The final phase in reacting to a cybersecurity incident is to return systems to regular operation, validate that they are working correctly, and address weaknesses to prevent future events. The following are the primary problems that organisations encounter while recovering from a cybersecurity event in a timely, effective, and consistent way, according to project research:

- Reconnecting networks, reconstructing systems, and restoring, recreating, or correcting information are all steps in the remediation process. As a result, having a proper recovery strategy in place is critical, which should include the following:
- Rebuilding affected systems (typically from known 'clean' sources)
- Replacing compromised data with clean ones
- Installing fixes, updating passwords, and increasing network perimeter security, such as firewall rulesets, to remove temporary limits imposed during the confinement phase

- Resetting passwords on compromised accounts
- Thoroughly testing systems, including security controls
- Verifying the integrity of business systems and controls

It is critical to confirm that systems are back up and running, which is frequently accomplished by conducting an independent penetration test of the impacted systems, followed by a security controls evaluation. Advanced cybersecurity attackers will frequently attempt to re-enter the network using all available techniques. They will also return knowing that they are being probed and that their current tactics and approaches are being scrutinised. It is critical to guarantee that all aspects of the assault have been eliminated and that the attackers cannot carry out subsequent attacks.

1.7 OTHER FRAMEWORKS

We have opted to use the NIST Framework as it is one of the most well-known cyber resilience frameworks, but apart from this, there are many more frameworks and standards created for cyber resilience. These frameworks are discussed in this section. The most frequently used existing guidelines and frameworks are explained briefly below. Explained frameworks can adapt to the constantly changing nature of the area (Kott & Linkov, 2022). Other frameworks used for different purposes are also mentioned, although not widely.

1.7.1 Center for Internet Security (CIS) Critical Security Controls

A publication released by the Center for Internet Security defines and describes CIS Controls (Gros, 2021). Each of the 18 CIS Controls is further broken down into sub-controls, totalling 153 sub-controls overall 18 controls. The 18 controls are broken down into the following categories: fundamental, foundational, and organisational (Carpenter et al., 2022). In version 8 of the CIS Controls, these 153 sub-controls are divided into three Implementation Groups (IGs). The IGs are a recommendation included in CIS Controls v8 to assist organisations in determining a starting point for CIS Controls implementation. Companies will occasionally have to use a higher IG to install CIS Controls. A business should thoroughly analyse and assess the potential risks and implications to data and assets while adopting new tech into an ecosystem, such as the cloud. Regardless of IG, this knowledge should guide the selection and implementation of suitable CIS Safeguards.

- **Implementation Guide (IG) 1:** This is the concept of basic cyber hygiene, and it reflects a minimal level of data protection for all businesses. IG helps businesses with less cybersecurity experience combat broad-based, non-targeted threats. It includes 56 safeguards, in other words, sub-controls.

Table 1.2 Controls for CIS

Access control management	Account management
Application software security	Audit log management
Continuous vulnerability management	Data protection
Data recovery	Email and web browser protections
Inventory and control of enterprise assets	Inventory and control of software assets
Incident response management	Malware defences
Network infrastructure management	Network monitoring and defence
Penetration testing	Secure configuration of enterprise assets and software
Security awareness and skills training	Service provider management

- **Implementation Guide (IG) 2:** It aids businesses in the management of IT infrastructure across many sectors with varying risk levels. IG2 attempts to assist businesses in dealing with rising operational complexities. It includes 74 safeguards.
- **Implementation Guide (IG) 3:** It provides IT, security professionals to help businesses safeguard critical and secret data. The goal of IG3 is to avoid and mitigate the effects of advanced assaults. It includes 23 safeguards of a total of 153 sub-controls.

According to the latest CIS report, which is version 8, there are 18 controls which are shown in Table 1.2 (Carpenter et al., 2022).

1.7.2 The Center on Local Government Research Framework

At the end of 2015, a report named "Managing Technology Risks through Technological Proficiency" was published by Rutgers University (Kott & Linkov, 2022). This study describes "risks" as the result of what humans do or when people miss something, technological systems failure, management system failure, or discontinuance caused by outside effects (Pfeiffer, 2015). Those dangers may be divided into six categories: legal, cybersecurity, financial, operational, social, and reputational hazards. The Rutgers research proposes a framework for firms to address these risks by enhancing their technical capabilities. This framework focuses on institutionalising and building four essential actions to achieve technical proficiency, which is as follows:

- **Governance:** The managing/governing body should be setting broad technology policy goals, giving direction, monitoring operations, and making risk management choices.
- **Planning:** To create the institution's short and long-term goals, construct a digital strategy, and suggest risk management techniques, government authorities, and technology administrators collaborate.

- **Cyber Hygiene:** To avoid technological compromise, staff are educated to comprehend and ensure the safe utilisation of the technology.
- **Technical Competence:** Sustaining the technical, financial, and human resources required to deploy strong technology practices properly. Developing technical competency is a continuous process that necessitates effectively utilising an institution's three primary resources: time, attention, and money.

1.7.3 ISO 27001 and ISO 27002 (International Organisation for Standardisation)

ISO27000, ISO 27001, and ISO 27002 standards, prepared for protecting information and information systems, are standards developed for companies or institutions to provide adequate information security. Companies or institutions that follow these standards achieve various control objectives, specific controls, directives, and requirements to ensure security thanks to this standard. While this information provides a guideline to companies and institutions, ISO 27001 also provides certification. Thanks to this certification, institutions and companies can prove that an internationally recognised institution provides that information security. In this way, these companies assure their customers and reduce the risk of paying compensation for companies and institutions with this certification in case of legal disputes (Pelnekar, 2011). ISO 27001 standards contain the Information Security Management System implementation requirements, and these specified applications are a summary of what needs to be done to achieve this. To meet these requirements, institutions or companies should (Irwin, 2021):

- A project team should be established to ensure these standards, and the project should be started.
- A gap analysis should be performed.
- The scope of the ISMS should be determined.
- In this context, it is necessary to work on the development of high-level policies.
- A risk assessment is required for the company and the institution.
- The controls to be made must be selected and applied after this selection.
- Risk documentation should be created after the controls.
- Personnel within the institution or company should be made aware of this issue. For this, training is organised.
- An internal audit should then be performed.
- After these stages, it is necessary to audit for certification.

ISO 27002, on the other hand, is a supplementary standard in Annex A of ISO 27001 that makes recommendations on implementing security measures (Disterer, 2013). This documentation contains detailed explanations of how each control works, its purpose, and how this control can be applied (Hsu et al., 2016).

1.7.4 Payment Card Industry Data Security Standard (PCI DSS)

Credit cards, debit cards, and prepaid cards are commonly called payment cards. Payment card usage continues to grow, and security is becoming a concern for such applications. Security vulnerabilities caused over one billion dollars annually. For the resilience of the system, the payment card network has developed a strategy by the Payment Card Industry Security Standards Council (PCI SSC), which is called the Payment Card Industry Data Security Standard (PCI DSS) (Lui et al., 2010).

PCI obedience is vital for numerous reasons; all of them have an essential mission that does not get ahead of one another. Each has two main targets: consumer confidence and effective business operations. From a consumer perspective, trust is the most critical parameter for the card company. Although the cardholder takes advantage of the efficiency of the electronic system, the card provider must provide expectations without reducing the security system. From the business perspective, they want to obtain their operations with a secured system for the confidence of their customers (Virtue, 1975). The PCI DCC categorises the requirements into 6 sections and 12 subsections. The six main groups are known as the control objectives (Lui et al., 2010).

1. Build and Maintain a Secure Network
   a. To secure cardholder data, focus on setting up a barrier setup.
   b. For network accounts and other security protocols, do not utilise provider defaults.
2. Protect Cardholder Data
   a. Safeguard information on cardholders that have been saved.
   b. Protect cardholder data and critical information transfer over public networks.
3. Maintain a Vulnerability Management Program
   a. Antivirus software should be used and updated regularly.
   b. Security services and applications should be developed and maintained.
4. Implement Strong Access Control Measures
   a. Accessibility to cardholder data should be limited to those who have a business need to know.
   b. Each individual with access to a computer should be given a unique ID.
   c. Physical access to cardholder data should be limited.
5. Regularly Monitor and Test Networks
   a. All network assets and cardholder data access are tracked and monitored.
   b. Check security systems and procedures regularly.

6. Maintain an Information Security Policy
   a. Establish an information security policy for both workers and contractors.

1.7.5 Less commonly used frameworks

As mentioned before, there are many frameworks for cyber resilience in the field. Those explained in the upcoming part are the ones that are not commonly used compared to the NIST and ISO 27001/27002 but are still popular.

1.7.5.1 Control Objectives for Information Technology (COBIT)

Control Objectives for Information and Related Technologies (COBIT) is a technology control framework. This control framework establishes IT alignment with businesses (Wulandari et al., 2019). The Information Technology Governance Institute (ITGI) is a division of the Information Systems Audit and Control Association (ISACA), and COBIT was established by the ITGI (Apriliana et al., 2018). COBIT 5 is divided into two areas: management and governance (Mallette, 2011). The activities carried out in the field of governance are an area where it is aimed at evaluating the needs, current conditions, and priorities for decision-making. Governance control consists of three processes. These processes consist of evaluation, directing and monitoring (EDM). After this process is completed, management control comes into play, and this stage includes alignment planning and organising steps (Awaludin Rizal et al., 2020). After these steps, the building, acquisition, and implementation processes are followed, and finally, the delivery, service, support, monitoring and evaluation processes are carried out (Andry & Aziza, 2020).

1.7.5.2 Health Information Trust Alliance Cybersecurity Framework (HITRUST CSF)

HITRUST CSF is a framework designed specifically for the healthcare industry in 2007 by a non-profit organisation in the USA. This framework aims to protect personal information and provides an efficient, flexible and comprehensive approach that ensures compliance with risk management and various compliance regulations (Garba & Bade, 2021). This framework is also a certified provider for the healthcare industry. Therefore, it is a widely accepted framework. This framework was also developed similarly to the widely used ISO27001. This framework has 845 requirements spread over each application level (Donaldson et al., 2015).

The essential components of the created framework are as follows:

- **Control Goal:** It describes the goal or situation to be achieved.
- **Control Specification:** It aims to meet the technical, managerial, administrative, or legal qualification control objective.

- **Implementation Requirement:** It provides support for achieving desired goals by applying control.
- **Control Audit Procedure:** The organisation needs control, and this phase describes the formal review activities required to examine whether the organisation has implemented the control requirement. This process includes a rigorous review of documents, interviewing personnel, and testing technical implementation.
- **Standard Mapping:** Several common standards are created for each application requirement level. The mapping performed here is benchmarking and cross-referencing.

1.7.5.3 Cybersecurity Maturity Model Certification (CMMC)

The US military first funded the development of maturity models for the software sector to establish a way for actual knowledge of software subcontractors' process capabilities and maturity. There is a need to objectively analyse the level of dependability, trust, and related hazards of software service quality in a unified manner due to diverse evolving technologies, standards, and provider quantities and capabilities. Maturity models also allow for a demonstrable transition between levels. They enable businesses to be compared based on their "maturity levels" and give an organised and prioritised approach to improvement strategies (Sharkov, 2020). The levels can be grouped into Progression Maturity Models, Capability Maturity Models (CMMs), and Hybrid Maturity Models.

1.7.5.4 Cloud Security Alliance (CSA) Cloud Controls Matrix (CCM)

The CCM created by CSA is a set of core security standards that cloud suppliers and potential clients may use to evaluate a cloud supplier's total risk in terms of security (Saxena, 2013). The Cloud Control Matrix is a controls framework that provides deep knowledge of security principles and ideas in 13 categories linked with CSA advice. This framework gives enterprises the structure, specificity, and clarity they need regarding IT security in the cloud. The CSA CCM improves current cybersecurity control systems by focusing on business information security control requirements and reducing and identifying consistent vulnerabilities and security risks in the cloud. The CSA CCM's foundations are built on a tailored interaction with other commonly used security regulations, control frameworks, and standards such as NIST, ISO27001/27002, PCI DDS, and CIS. In addition, many other frameworks in the fields are not as commonly used as the ones explained in the previous parts (Top 25 Cybersecurity Frameworks to Consider | SecurityScorecard, 2021).

- Australian Signals Directorate (ASD) Essential 8
- Cybersecurity and Infrastructure Security Agency (CISA) Transporation Systems Sector (TSS) Cybersecurity Framework

- European Telecommunications Standards Institute (ETSI)
- European Union Agency for Cybersecurity (ENISA) National Capabilities Assessment Framework
- Information Security Forum (ISF) Standard of Good Practice for Information Security (SOGP 2020)
- International Society of Automation (ISA/IEC 62443)
- IoT Cybersecurity Alliance (IOTCA)
- IoT Security Foundation (IoTSF) Security Compliance Framework
- MITRE ATT&CK
- National Cyber Security Centre (NCSC) Cyber Assessment Framework (CAF)
- New Zealand Protective Security Requirements (PSR)
- North American Electric Reliability Corporation (NERC)
- OASIS Security Assertion Markup Language (SAML)
- Saudi Arabian Monetary Authority (SAMA) Cybersecurity Framework
- Factor Analysis of Information Risk (FAIR) Cyber Risk Framework
- International Telecommunications Union (ITU) National Cybersecurity/Critical Information Infrastructure Protection (CIIP)

REFERENCES

Abomhara, M. & Køien, G. M., (2015). Cyber security and the Internet of Things: Vulnerabilities, threats, intruders and attacks. *Journal of Cyber Security and Mobility*, 4(1), 65–88.

Abraham, C., Chatterjee, D. & Simsa, R. R., (2019). Muddling through cybersecurity: Insights from the US healthcare industry. *Business Horizons*, 62(4), 539–548.

Alcaraz, C. & Zeadally, S., (2015). Critical infrastructure protection: Requirements and challenges for the 21st century. *International Journal of Critical Infrastructure Protection*, 8, 23–66. https://doi.org/10.1016/j.ijcip.2014.12.002.

American Public Power Association, (2019). *Public Power Cyber Incident Response Playbook*, s.l.: s.n.

Andry, J. & Aziza, C., (2020). Assessment IT governance of human resources information system using COBIT 5. *International Journal of Open Information Technologies*, 8(4), 59–63.

Annarelli, A., Nonino, F. & Palombi, G., (2020). Understanding the management of cyber resilient systems. *Computers & Industrial Engineering*, 149.

Apriliana, A., Sarno, R. & Effendi, Y., (2018). Risk analysis of IT applications using FMEA and AHP SAW method with COBIT 5. 2018 *International Conference on Information and Communications Technology* (ICOIACT), Yogyakarta, Indonesia.

Australian Cyber Security Centre, (2021). *Cyber Incident Response Plan*. Available at: https://www.cyber.gov.au/resources-business-and-government/essential-cyber-security/publications/cyber-incident-response-plan

Awaludin Rizal, R., Sarno, R. & Rossa Sungkono, K., (2020). COBIT 5 for analysing information technology governance maturity level on masterplan E-government. *2020 International Seminar on Application for Technology of Information and Communication (iSemantic)*, Semarang, Indonesia.

Awati, R. & Cole, B., (2021). *North American Electric Reliability Corporation Critical Infrastructure Protection (NERC CIP)*. Available at: https://searchcompliance.techtarget.com/definition/NERC-CIP-critical-infrastructure-protection [Accessed 20 March 2022].

Bank for International Settlements, (2016). *Guidance on Cyber Resilience for Financial Market Infrastructures*. Available at: https://www.bis.org/cpmi/publ/d146.pdf [Accessed 20 March 2022].

Bartock, M., Cichonski, J., Souppaya, M., Smith, M., Witte, G. & Scarfone, K., (2016). *Guide for Cybersecurity Event Recovery*. Available at: https://doi.org/10.6028/NIST.SP.800-184 [Accessed 20 March 2022].

BBC, (2014). *Sony Pictures Computer System Hacked in Online Attack*. Available at: https://www.bbc.com/news/technology-30189029 [Accessed 20 March 2022].

Belding, G., (2020). *NIST CSF Core Functions: Detect*. Available at: https://resources.infosecinstitute.com/topic/nist-csf-core-functions-detect/ [Accessed 20 March 2022].

Bossetta, M., (2018). The weaponisation of social media: Spear phishing and cyber-attacks on democracy. *Journal of International Affairs*, 71(15), 97–106.

Boyens, J., Paulsen, C., Moorthy, R., & Bartol, N., (2015). *Supply Chain Risk Management Practices for Federal Information Systems and Organizations*. National Institute of Standards and Technology (NIST) Special Publication 800-161. https://doi.org/10.6028/NIST.SP.800-161.

Canadian Centre for Cyber Security, (2021). *Developing Your IT Recovery Plan*. Available at: https://www.cyber.gc.ca/sites/default/files/publications/itsap40004-e_2.pdf [Accessed 20 March 2022].

Carías, J. F., Arrizabalaga, S., Labaka, L., & Hernantes, J., (2020). Cyber resilience progression model. *Applied Sciences*, 10, 7393. https://doi.org/10.3390/app10217393.

Carnegie Mellon Information Security Office, (2014). *Computer Security Incident Response Plan*. Available at: https://www.cmu.edu/iso/governance/procedures/incidentresponseplanv1.6.pdf [Accessed 20 March 2022].

Carpenter, G., Mowen, R. & Regnier, R., (2022). *CIS Controls Cloud Companion Guide*. CIS. [Online] Available at: https://www.cisecurity.org/insights/whitepapers/cis-controls-cloud-companion-guide [Accessed 2 June 2022].

Cashman, M. (2021). *HowTo: Protect Critical Infrastructure from Cyber-Criminals*. Available at: https://www.infosecurity-magazine.com/opinions/howto-protect-infrastructure/ [Accessed 20 March 2022].

Cichonski, P., Millar, T., Grance, T. & Scarfone, K., (2012). *Computer Security Incident Handling Guide*. s.l.: National Institute of Standards and Technology.

CISA, (2022). *Cybersecurity & Infrastructure Security Agency, Critical Infrastructure Sectors*.[Online]Availableat:https://www.cisa.gov/critical-infrastructure-sectors.

Conteh, N. Y. & Schmick, P. J., (2016). Cybersecurity: Risks, vulnerabilities and countermeasures to prevent social engineering attacks. *International Journal of Advanced Computer Research*, 6, 31–38.

CPNI, (2020). *Identify Your Most Valuable Assets*. [Online] Available at: https://www.cpni.gov.uk/content/identify-your-most-valuable-assets [Accessed 20 March 2022].

Creasey, J. & Glover, I., (2013). *Cybersecurity Incident Response Guide*. s.l.: CREST.

Crocetti, P., (2018). *Warm Site*. Available at: https://www.techtarget.com/searchdisasterrecovery/definition/warm-site [Accessed 20 March 2022].

Cybersecurity and Infrastructure Security Agency, (2021a). *Detection and Prevention.* Available at: https://www.cisa.gov/detection-and-prevention [Accessed 20 March 2022].

Cybersecurity and Infrastructure Security Agency, (2021b). *Enhanced Cybersecurity Services.* Available at: https://www.cisa.gov/enhanced-cybersecurity-services-ecs [Accessed 20 March 2022].

Dan, R., (2022). *What Is Encryption and How Does It Protect Your Data.* Available at: https://us.norton.com/internetsecurity-privacy-what-is-encryption.html [Accessed 20 March 2022].

DeSimone, A. & Horton, N., (2017). *Sony's Nightmare Before Christmas, The 2014 North Korean Cyber Attack on Sony and Lessons for US Government Actions in Cyberspace.* s.l.: Johns Hopkins Applied Physics Laboratory.

Digital Regulation Platform, (2021). *Enhancing the Protection and Cyber-Resilience of Critical Information Infrastructure.* Available at: https://digitalregulation. org/enhancing-the-protection-and-cyber-resilience-of-critical-information-infrastructure/#post-3004221-endnote-2 [Accessed 20 March 2022].

Disterer, G., (2013). ISO/IEC 27000, 27001 and 27002 for information security management. *Journal of Information Security*, 04(02), 92–100.

Donaldson, S., Siegel, S., Williams, C. & Aslam, A., (2015). Cybersecurity frameworks. *Enterprise Cybersecurity*, 01, 297–309.

EC, (2022). *European Commission, Critical Infrastructure.* [Online] Available at: https://home-affairs.ec.europa.eu/pages/page/critical-infrastructure_en.

Eytan, O. (2021). *Six Key Guidelines to Protect Critical Infrastructure from Cyber Threats.* Available at: https://www.forbes.com/sites/forbestechcouncil/2021/04/14/six-key-guidelines-to-protectcriticalinfrastructurefromcyber-threats/?sh=54339a8d7504 [Accessed 20 March 2022].

Farhat, V. et al., (2017). *Cyberattacks: Prevention and Proactive Responses.* s.l.: Practical Law.

Forescout Technology, (2021). *Gain Confidence in Protecting Critical Infrastructure from Cyber Attacks.* Available at: https://www.forescout.com/resources/critical-infrastructure-white-paper/?autosuggest-term=critical-infrastructure-white-paper [Accessed 20 March 2022].

Fuchsberger, A., (2005). Intrusion detection systems and intrusion prevention systems. *Information Security Technical Report*, 10(3), 134–139.

Galinec, D. & Steingartner, W., (2017). *Combining Cybersecurity and Cyber Defense to Achieve Cyber Resilience.* Poprad, Slovakia: IEEE.

Garba, A. & Bade, A. (2021). An investigation on recent cyber security frameworks as guidelines for organizations adoption. *International Journal of Innovative Science and Research Technology*, 6(2), 103–110. Available at: https://ijisrt. com/assets/upload/files/IJISRT21FEB114.pdf.

Gardner, K., (2022). *Disaster Recovery Models & Gauging Nine(s) | Maintaining Server Redundancy in a Highly Available Environment.* Available at: https://blog.vrad.com/disaster-recovery-models-gauging-nines [Accessed 20 March 2022].

Georgiadou, A., Mouzakitis, S. & Askounis, D., (2021). Designing a cyber-security culture assessment survey targeting critical infrastructures during COVID-19 crisis. *International Journal of Network Security & Its Applications (IJNSA)*, 13(1), 33–50. https://ssrn.com/abstract=3787197.

Gros, S. (2021). A critical view on CIS controls. *2021 16th International Conference on Telecommunications (ConTEL)*, Graz, Austria.

Gündüz, M. Z. & Das, R., (2018). Internet of Things (IoT): Evolution, components and applications fields, Pamukkale University. *Journal of Engineering Sciences*, 24(2), 327–335.

Gündüz, M. Z. & Das, R., (2019). *Analysis of Cyber-Attacks in IoT-Based Critical Infrastructures*. Available at: https://www.researchgate.net/publication/350374715_Analysis_of_cyber-attacks_in_IoT-based_critical_infrastructures [Accessed 7 March 2022].

Harrop, W. & Matteson, A., (2014). Cyber resilience: A review of critical national infrastructure and cyber security protection measures applied in the UK and USA. *Journal of Business Continuity & Emergency Planning*, 7(2), 149–162.

Haughey, C., (2020). *Cybersecurity Framework: How to Create a Resilience Strategy. Security Intelligence*. Available at: https://securityintelligence.com/articles/how-to-create-a-cybersecurity-framework/ [Accessed 20 March 2022].

Heinimann, H. R. & Hatfield, K., (2017). Infrastructure resilience assessment, management and governance - State and perspectives. In: *NATO Science for Peace and Security Series*. s.l.:Springer, pp. 147–187.

Hellström, T., (2007). Critical infrastructure and systemic vulnerability: Towards a planning framework. *Safety Science*, 45(3), 425–430.

Herrera, L.-C. & Maennel, O., (2019). A comprehensive instrument for identifying critical information infrastructure services. *International Journal of Critical Infrastructure Protection*, 25, 50–61. https://doi.org/10.1016/j.ijcip.2019.02.001.

Hewitt, N., (2022). *What to Include in a Cybersecurity Disaster Recovery Plan*. Available at: https://www.imperva.com/blog/what-to-include-in-a-cybersecurity-disaster-recovery-plan/ [Accessed 20 March 2022].

Homeland Security, Representing Chief Information Officers of the States, (2017). *State Cybersecurity Governance Case Studies*. Available at: https://www.cisa.gov/sites/default/files/publications/Cross_Site_Report_and_Case_Studies_508.pdf

Hopkin, P., (2018). *Fundamentals of Risk Management: Understanding, Evaluating and Implementing Effective Risk Management*. London: Kogan Page Publishers.

Hsu, C., Wang, T. & Lu, A., (2016). The impact of ISO 27001 certification on firm performance. *2016 49th Hawaii International Conference on System Sciences (HICSS)*, Hawaii, USA.

Infosec Institute, (n.d.). *NIST CSF Core Functions: Identify*. Available at: https://resources.infosecinstitute.com/topic/nist-csf-core-functions-identify/ [Accessed 20 March 2022].

International Business Machine (IBM), (2020). *Designing a Modern IAM Program for Your Business*. Available at: https://www.ibm.com/downloads/cas/9YBEK41O [Accessed 20 March 2022].

International Energy Agency (IEA), (2021). *Empowering Cities for a Net Zero Future: Unlocking Resilient, Smart, Sustainable Urban Energy Systems*. Paris, France: IEA.

Irwin, L., (2021). *ISO 27001 vs. ISO 27002: What's the difference?* IT Governance UK Blog. [Online] Available at: https://www.itgovernance.co.uk/blog/understanding-the-differences-between-iso-27001-and-iso-27002 [Accessed 2 June 2022].

ITGovernance (2020). *Penetration Testing.* Available at: https://www.itgovernance. co.uk/penetration-testing [Accessed 14 March 2022].

Johnson, A. & Morillo, C. (2020). *How to Implement Multi-Factor Authentication (MFA).* Available at: https://www.microsoft.com/security/blog/2020/01/15/ how-to-implement-multi-factor-authentication/ [Accessed 20 March 2022].

Jouini, M., Rabai, L. B. A. & Aissa, A. B., (2014). Classification of security threats in information systems. *Procedia Computer Science*, 32, 489–496. https://doi. org/10.1016/j.procs.2014.05.452.

Kosutic, D., (2015). *What Is the Difference Between Recovery Time Objective (RTO) and Recovery Point Objective (RPO)?* Available at: https://advisera. com/27001academy/knowledgebase/what-is-the-difference-between-recovery-time-objective-rto-and-recovery-point-objective-rpo/ [Accessed 20 March 2022].

Kosutic, D., (2022). *RTO vs RPO - What Is the Difference?* Available at: https:// advisera.com/27001academy/knowledgebase/what-is-the-difference-between-recovery-time-objective-rto-and-recovery-point-objective-rpo/ [Accessed 20 March 2022].

Kott, A. & Linkov, I., (2022). *Cyber Resilience of Systems and Networks.* 1st ed. Cham: Springer.

Kral, P. (2021). *Incident Handler's Handbook.* s.l.: SANS Institute.

Kure, H. I. & Islam, S., (2019). *Assets Focus Risk Management Framework for Critical Infrastructure Cybersecurity Risk Management.* s.l.: IET.

Lewis, J. A., (2016). *Advanced Experiences in Cybersecurity Policies and Practices.* s.l.: Inter-American Development Bank.

Lui, J., Xiao, Y., Chen, H., Ozdemir, S., Dodle, S. & Singh, V., (2010). A survey of payment card industry data security standard. *IEEE Communications Surveys & Tutorials*, 12, 287–290.

Mahn, A., Marron, J., Quinn, S. & Topper, D., (2021). *Getting Started with the NIST Cybersecurity Framework: A Quick Start Guide.* Available at: https://nvlpubs. nist.gov/nistpubs/SpecialPublications/NIST.SP.1271.pdf [Accessed 22 February 2022].

Mallette, D., (2011). *COBIT Mapping.* Rolling Meadows, IL: ISACA.

Maryann, F., (2021). *What Was Learned from the 2014 Sony Pictures Hack?* Available at: https://news.networktigers.com/opinion/what-was-learned-from-the-2014-sony-pictures-hack/#:~:text=The%20malware%20had%20been%20 siphoning,for%20the%20Sony%20management%20team [Accessed 20 March 2022].

Mazouz, A., (2021). *Inter-region Cold Site Disaster Recovery with Purity CloudSnap.* Available at: https://blog.purestorage.com/products/inter-region-cold-site-disaster-recovery-with-purity-cloudsnap [Accessed 20 March 2022].

McAfee Enterprise Security Solutions, (2021). *What Is Zero Trust Security?* Available at: https://www.mcafee.com/enterprise/en-us/security-awareness/cloud/what-is-zero-trust.html#overview [Accessed 20 March 2022].

Meer, S. V. D., (2015). *Foreign Policy Responses to International Cyber-attacks, Some Lessons Learned.* s.l.: Clingendael, Netherlands Institute of International Relations.

Moors, W., (2022). *How to Recover from a Cyberattack.* Available at: https://www. securiwiser.com/blog/how-to-recover-from-a-cyberattack/ [Accessed 20 March 2022].

Moteff, J. & Parfomak, P., (2004). *Critical Infrastructure and Key Assets.* Washington, DC: Library of Congress Washington DC Congressional Research Service.

Muray, G., Johnstone, M. N. & Valli, C., (2017). *The Convergence of IT and OT in Critical Infrastructure*, pp. 149–155. Available at: https://core.ac.uk/download/pdf/159235139.pdf [Accessed 20 March 2022].

Mylrea, M., Gourisetti, S. N. G. & Nicholls, A., (2017). *An Introduction to Buildings Cybersecurity Framework.* s.l.: IEEE.

National Cyber Security Center (NCSC), (2021). *10 Steps to Cyber Security.* Available at: https://www.ncsc.gov.uk/collection/10-steps [Accessed 20 March 2022].

National Institute of Standards and Technology, (2014). *Framework for Improving Critical Infrastructure Cybersecurity.* Available at: https://nvlpubs.nist.gov/nistpubs/CSWP/NIST.CSWP.04162018.pdf [Accessed 20 March 2022].

National Institute of Standards and Technology, (2018). *Framework for Improving Critical Infrastructure Cybersecurity.* Available at: https://nvlpubs.nist.gov/nistpubs/CSWP/NIST.CSWP.04162018.pdf [Accessed 22 February 2022].

NCSC, (2022). *National Cyber Security Centre, CNI Hub.* [Online] Available at: https://www.ncsc.gov.uk/section/private-sector-cni/cni

Neto, N. N., Madnic, S., Paula, A. M. G. D. & Borges, N. M., (2020). *A Case Study of the Capital One Data Breach.* s.l.: Massachusetts Institute of Technology.

NIST, (2018). *Framework for Improving Critical Infrastructure Cybersecurity, Version 1.1.* Available at: https://nvlpubs.nist.gov/nistpubs/CSWP/NIST.CSWP.04162018.pdf [Accessed 20 March 2022].

NIST, (2019). *How to Recover from a Cyber Attack.* Available at: https://www.nist.gov/blogs/manufacturing-innovation-blog/how-recover-cyber-attack [Accessed 20 March 2022].

Onwubiko, C., (2020). *Focusing on the Recovery Aspects of Cyber Resilience.* Available at: https://ieeexplore.ieee.org/document/9139685 [Accessed 20 March 2022].

Oracle, (n.d.). *What Is IoT?.* Available at: https://www.oracle.com/internet-of-things/what-is-iot/ [Accessed 5 March 2022].

Papastergiou, S., Polemi, N. & Kotzanikolaou, P., (2018). Design and validation of the Medusa supply chain risk assessment methodology and system. *International Journal of Critical Infrastructures*, 14, 1–39. Available at: https://www.inderscienceonline.com/doi/abs/10.1504/IJCIS.2018.090647.

Pelnekar, C., (2011). Planning for and implementing ISO 27001. *ISACA Journal*, 4(4), 1–8.

Petrenko, S. A. & Vorobieva, D., (2019). *Management of Cyber Resilience Is Critical, as It Is a Necessary Procedure for Stable Systems.* St. Petersburg, Russia: IEEE.

Pfeiffer, M., (2015). *Managing Technology Risk Through Technological Proficiency.* New Jersey: Bloustein Local Government Research Center.

Rapid7, (2017). *Detection and Analysis Phase of Incident Response Life Cycle of NIST SP 800-61.* Available at: https://www.rapid7.com/blog/post/2017/02/13/detection-and-analysis-phase-of-incident-response-life-cycle-of-nist-sp-800-61/ [Accessed 20 March 2022].

Ready, (2021). *IT Disaster Recovery Plan.* Available at: https://www.ready.gov/it-disaster-recovery-plan [Accessed 20 March 2022].

Rehacek, P., (2017). Risk management standards for project management. *International Journal of Advanced and Applied Sciences*, 4(6), 1–13. Available at: http://science-gate.com/IJAAS/Articles/2017-4-6/01%202017-4-6-pp.1-13.pdf

Reserve Bank of New Zealand, (2021). *Guidance on Cyber Resilience*. Available at: https://www.rbnz.govt.nz/-/media/ReserveBank/Files/Publications/Policy-development/Cyber%20resilience/Guidance-on-cyber-resilience.pdf [Accessed 20 March 2022].

Reuters, (2016). *Russian Central Bank and Private Banks Lose $31 mln in Cyber Attacks*. Available at: https://www.reuters.com/article/us-russia-cenbank-cyberattack-idUSKBN13R1TO [Accessed 23 February 2022].

Rinaldi, S. M., Peerenboom, J. P. & Kelly, T. K., (2001). Identifying, understanding, and analysing critical infrastructure interdependencies. *IEEE Control Systems*, 21(6), 11–25.

RSI Security, (2019). *Cyber Security Resilience Framework: How to Get Started*. RSI Security. [Online] Available at: https://blog.rsisecurity.com/cyber-security-resilience-framework-how-to-get [Accessed 20 March 2022].

Saxena, S., (2013). Ensuring cloud security using cloud control matrix. *International Journal of Information and Computation Technology*, 3(9), 933–938. Available at: https://mail.ripublication.com/irph/ijict_spl/11_ijictv3n9spl.pdf.

SecurityScorecard, (2021). *Top 25 Cybersecurity Frameworks to Consider*. SecurityScorecard. [Online] Available at: https://securityscorecard.com/blog/top-cybersecurity-frameworks-to-consider [Accessed 3 June 2022].

Sharkov, G., (2020). Assessing the maturity of national cybersecurity and resilience. *The Quarterly Journal*, 19, 4.

Shaw, R. S., Chen, C. C., Harris, A. L. & Huang, H.-J., (2009). The impact of information richness on information security awareness training effectiveness. *Computers & Education*, 52(1), 92–100.

Shoemaker, D., Kohnke, A. & Sigler, K. (2016). *A Guide to the National Initiative for Cybersecurity Education (NICE) Cybersecurity WorkforceFramework (2.0)*, Auerbach Publications, New York.

Singh, J., (2021). *Understanding RPO and RTO*. Available at: https://www.druva.com/blog/understanding-rpo-and-rto/ [Accessed 20 March 2022].

Skopik, F., Settanni, G. & Fiedler, R., (2016). A survey on the dimensions of collective cyber defense through security information sharing. *Computers & Security*, 60, 154–176.

Smart, W., (2018). *Lessons Learned Review of the WannaCry Ransomware Cyber Attack*. Available at: https://www.england.nhs.uk/wp-content/uploads/2018/02/lessons-learned-review-wannacry-ransomware-cyber-attack-cio-review.pdf [Accessed 20 March 2022].

Staves, A., Anderson, T., Balderstone, H., Green, B., Gouglidis, A. & Hutchison, D., (2022). A cyber incident response and recovery framework to support operators of industrial control systems. *International Journal of Critical Infrastructure Protection*, 37, 100505. https://doi.org/10.1016/j.ijcip.2021.100505.

Sullivan, E. & Betan, H., (2018). *What's the Difference between a Hot Site and Cold Site for DR?* Available at: https://www.techtarget.com/searchdisasterrecovery/answer/Whats-the-difference-between-a-hot-site-and-cold-site-for-disaster-recovery [Accessed 20 March 2022].

Sutcliffe & Co., (2020). *Cyber-continuity and Incident Response Plan Toolkit*. s.l.: s.n.

Symantec, (2014). *The Cyber Resilience Blueprint: A New Perspective on Security.* Available at: https://www.ten-inc.com/presentations/Symantec-The-Cyber-Resilience-Blueprint.pdf [Accessed 26 February 2022].

Symantec, (2015). *The Cyber Resilience Blueprint: A New Perspective on Security.* Available at: https://www.ten-inc.com/presentations/Symantec-The-Cyber-Resilience-Blueprint.pdf [Accessed 20 March 2022].

Taylor, C., (2018). *RPO and RTO: Understanding the Differences.* Available at: https://www.enterprisestorageforum.com/management/rpo-and-rto-under-standing-the-differences/ [Accessed 20 March 2022].

Ten, C.-W., Manimaran, G. & Liu, C.-C., (2010). Cybersecurity for critical infra-structures: Attack and defense modeling. *IEEE Transactions on Systems, Man, and Cybernetics - Part A: Systems and Humans,* 40(4), 1–3.

The Washington Post, (2019). *An Indian Nuclear Power Plant Suffered a Cyberattack. Here's What You Need to Know.* Available at: https://www.washingtonpost.com/politics/2019/11/04/an-indian-nuclearpower-plant-suffered-cyberattack-heres-what-you-need-know/ [Accessed 23 February 2022].

Tkachenko, L., (2011). *When to Use Mirroring as a Data Recovery Solution.* Available at: https://info.focustsi.com/IT-Services-Boston/bid/77545/When-to-Use-Mirroring-as-a-Data-Recovery-Solution [Accessed 20 March 2022].

Trautman, L., (2018). *Wannacry, Ransomware, and the Emerging Threat to Corporations.* s.l.: SSRN Electronic Journal.

Tunggal, A. T. (2021). *What is Continuous Security Monitoring?* UpGuard. [Online]. Available at: https://www.upguard.com/blog/continuous-secu-rity-monitoring#:~:text=Continuous%20security%20monitoring%20(CSM)%20is [Accessed 20 March 2022].

Under Defense, (2020). *Incident Response Lifecycle.* Available at: https://underde-fense.com/blog/incident-response-life-cycle-underdefense/ [Accessed 17 March 2022].

Uppal, D., Sinha, R., Mehra, V. & Jain, V., (2014). *Malware Detection and Classification Based on Extraction of API Sequences.* s.l.: IEEE.

Varghese, G., (2022). *Disaster Recovery Sites - Delving into ITDR.* Available at: https://www.theresilience.ml/disaster-recovery-sites-delving-into-itdr [Accessed 20 March 2022].

Virginia Tech, (2016). *Virginia Tech Guide for Cybersecurity Incident Response.* s.l.: s.n.

Virtue, T. M. (1975). *Payment Card Industry Data Security Standard Handbook.* Hoboken, NJ: John Wiley, Sons, Inc.

Vmware Inc., (2021). *What Is a Network Sandboxing?* Available at: https://www.vmware.com/topics/glossary/content/network-sandbox.html [Accessed 20 March 2022].

Vukalovic, J. & Delija, D., (2015). *Advanced Persistent Threats - Detection and Defense.* Opatija, Croatia: IEEE.

Webb, J. & Hume, D., (2018). *Campus IoT Collaboration and Governance Using the NIST Cybersecurity Framework.* s.l.: IET.

Wiese, M. & Aanenson, A., (2020). *The Cyber Incident Response Lifecycle.* AXA XL Insurance Reinsurance. Available at: https://axaxl.com/fast-fast-forward/articles/the-cyber-incident-response-lifecycle [Accessed 17 March 2022].

World Economic Forum, (2021). *Global Risks Report, 2021.* Available at: https://www.weforum.org/reports/the-global-risks-report-2021/

Wulandari, S., Dewi, A., Pohan, M., Sensuse, D., Mishbah, M. & Syamsudin, (2019). Risk assessment and recommendation strategy based on COBIT 5 for risk: Case study SIKN JIKN helpdesk service. *Procedia Computer Science*, 161, 168–177.

Zaballos, A. G. & Jeun, I., (2016). *Best Practices for Critical Information Infrastructure Protection (CIIP)*. Available at: https://publications.iadb.org/publications/english/document/Best-Practices-for-Critical-Information-Infrastructure-Protection-(CIIP)-Experiences-from-Latin-America-and-the-Caribbean-and-Selected-Countries.pdf [Accessed 20 March 2022].

Zografopoulos, I., Ospina, J. & Konstantinou, C., (2021). Cyber-physical energy systems security: Threat modeling, risk assessment, resources, metrics, and case studies. *IEEE Access*, 9, 29775–29818. https://doi.org/10.1109/ACCESS.2021.3058403.

Chapter 2

Emergency services sector

The Emergency Services Sector (ESS) is an industry that provides various prevention, preparedness, response, and recovery services in day-to-day operations. ESS is one of the most critical infrastructure sectors and has primary responsibility for protecting other assets and infrastructure. Because of its importance, the ESS is the first line of defence against technological, artificial, and natural hazards that may threaten infrastructure. This vital sector carries out prevention, protection, response, improvement, and mitigation activities against dangers and threats. As a result of the technologically developing world, this sector has also become electronic, which has revealed the necessity of including physical and cyber assets to ensure this sector's continuity. Worldwide, ESS generally consists of both voluntary and paid forces. This sector is organised at the government, state, regional, and local levels. This sector, therefore, includes primary first responders at the government level. There are also private sector personnel serving in this sector. Examples include personal security or fire/emergency medical services. This industry faces several challenges securing ESS assets, such as communications and data networks, as it protects other sectors. The interruption of these services can pose significant risks to public safety.

2.1 WHAT IS EMERGENCY SERVICES AS AN INFRASTRUCTURE?

The ESS has elements related to the cyber, human, and physical components (Simpkins, 2019). Volunteer individuals paid staff in the related fields and disciplines of the primary response form the "human" part. The "physical" section is made up of two types of facilities. While the first type of facility helps the administration of everyday operations, the second type assists the storage and training. In addition to these assets, there are also "vehicles" that are focused on particular capabilities and areas, such as fire engines/trucks and ambulances; "equipment" such as surveillance and communication equipment, and personal protective equipment (PPE).

DOI: 10.1201/9781003449522-2

Table 2.1 Human, Physical, and Cyber Components of Emergency Services Sector (ESS)

Human Component	Physical Component	Cyber Component
Paid staff	Operation facilities	Operational communications
Volunteer individuals	Training and storage facilities	Databases
	Equipment	Management
	Vehicles	Security systems
		Information networks

The cyber" section contains criminal record databases and security systems. In Table 2.1, all three components of ESS can be found:

According to the Emergency Services Sector-Specific Plan (ES SSP), which is designed to integrate and guide the collaborative, voluntary endeavour to enhance the resilience and security of the sector by US Department of Homeland Security, the "Emergency Services Sector" is divided into five main sections as mentioned in a detailed way before which are as follows (CISA, 2022a):

- Law Enforcement
- Fire and Rescue Services
- Emergency Medical Services
- Emergency Management
- Public Works

2.2 WHY ARE EMERGENCY SERVICES IMPORTANT?

The continuity of emergency services and emergency risk management is critical for events recognised as potentially disastrous by emergency risk managers during critical infrastructure risk assessments. Catastrophic repercussions vary depending on context; what is disastrous for a tiny regional town differs considerably from what is disastrous for a metropolitan metropolis. The essential idea is that an institution or society must function in a way that is substantially different from regular; there is a requirement for non-routine activities (Emergency Management Australia, 2003). The potential effect disastrous emergencies may create are as follows:

- Long-term incapacity to supply vital infrastructure services or facilities
- The shift from ordinary to emergency procedures
- A multi-agency/jurisdiction (state/federal/international) reaction would be required
- Heavy reliance on outside resources
- A high number of fatalities/deaths or serious injuries necessitating prolonged hospitalisation

- A large-scale and widespread relocation of people over long periods
- A large amount of property harm
- Environmental severe consequences, including long-term or irreversible harm and massive financial loss.

When assessing the strategic significance of these occasions, it is not advisable to overlook the possible impact of being unprepared on stakeholders or communities. While the continuity of emergency services is critical, workplaces must have a strategy for crises that might have a significant impact. The situation can be improved, and the effects can be reduced, with a quick and effective response. In an emergency, people are more likely to react trustworthily if they:

- Are knowledgeable and skilled
- Practice on a regular and practical basis
- Intentions, actions, and duties have been explicitly agreed upon, recorded, and practised.

A corporation should develop an emergency plan if a crisis requires employee rescue, public safety, or the coordination of emergency services. Emergency service or management training is provided to prepare facility inhabitants for crises. The preparation is critical to ensure that the actions that must be taken during an emergency and the time management for the emergency are not causing further company interruption. The employees may feel concerned if they are not adequately trained, but if they are appropriately trained, they will respond correctly in an emergency. To learn the protective procedure for safety and life safety, all personnel in a corporation should take emergency preparation training. Each sector has a significant risk of emergencies. Thus emergency procedures should be evaluated in collaboration with all emergency services. The following are reasons why emergency procedures should be practised continuously:

- There is little time to plan in a disaster and much less time to learn. The accuracy and efficiency of an emergency procedure are only as strong as the employees who carry it out. Individuals may reduce the uncertainty and fear around an event by rehearsing a response to a potential or actual threat, able to respond more quickly in an emergency. Regular practice also reveals any faults in the approach, which may be addressed before it is employed in the real world.
- Emergency management simulations are essential, so everyone is ready for the worst-case situation. In an emergency, being able to react quickly is crucial.
- All employees in the company must follow the emergency procedures taught to them. As employers, we have to do all necessary to ensure

the safety of our employees in our immediate vicinity. To lessen the incidence of workplace accidents, we must develop safe working environments and protocols.

- This training offers the respondent more confidence when confronted with a potentially dangerous situation. When a member of staff receives sufficient crisis response instruction, they gain confidence in their abilities, which can lead to feelings of self-assurance.
- All participants will receive critical training due to these protocols, enabling a more proactive and successful reaction to a workplace accident or incident.
- This assists in the detection of occupational hazards and risks. This will help the company design a strategy that takes into account available resources, skilled workers, and industry-best practices, as well as safety, the environment, properties, as well as company continuity.
- Routine equipment inspections and emergency drills are essential for preparing for any eventuality at work.
- Workers can quickly learn emergency protocols and dial 911. They can immediately locate the relevant emergency contact information and call the appropriate assistance provider.
- In an emergency, multiple decisions must be made quickly. Emergency personnel are well-equipped to handle any situation as quickly as feasible.
- It is vital to practice emergency procedures periodically to detect any vulnerabilities in the current emergency system. This technique can reveal problems such as a lack of equipment, resources, or adequately skilled staff and enhance company morale in an emergency. This increases staff confidence in their ability to respond quickly in any situation.
- Emergency procedures increase safety awareness and reflect the company's commitment to employee safety. In an emergency, this will help the company personnel.

2.3 KEY PLAYERS AND STAKEHOLDERS

The main system elements in ESS may vary from country to country. For example, looking at the ESS overview for the US, there are five prominent sector members. These are Law Enforcement, Fire and Rescue Services, Emergency Medical Services, Emergency Management, and Public Works. Apart from these prominent sector members, specialised staff such as Tactical Teams or Private Security Guard Forces also exist (Emergency Services Sector – Cisa, 2022a).

- **Law Enforcement:** This sub-sector consists of the police department, sheriff's offices, correctional institutions, private security agencies, and courts. Furthermore, it encompasses the enforcement of existing laws, the conduct of criminal investigations, and the collection of evidence for those investigations. Accordingly, they ensure that suspects are caught and that the judicial system is secured (Simpkins, 2019).
- **Fire and Rescue Services:** This sub-sector comprises volunteer and paid personnel. It is responsible for responding to fire situations, performing extinguishing and prevention operations, ensuring the control of dangerous substances, and ensuring the safety of life and property. In addition, it provides services such as implementing building regulations and delivering fire safety training.
- **Emergency Medical Services:** This sub-sector is responsible for providing services such as triage, treatment, and transport in cases of injury or illness. They are also responsible for protecting staff, patients, institutional facilities and the environment, and providing patients with the necessary comprehensive medical care (Simpkins, 2019).
- **Emergency Management:** This unit provides incident management and coordination between interdisciplinary and non-emergency service organisations. This coordination includes pre- and post-event activities. The emergency operation centres (EOC) in this unit, by activating and running planned or unannounced events, provide services to the personnel working in the emergency to manage the incident. Thus, multi-institutional coordination is realised. In addition, EOCs can support response and rescue efforts between neighbouring regions and at all levels of government when necessary (Simpkins, 2019).
- **Public Works:** This sub-sector provides services such as assessing damage to buildings, roads, or bridges and their repair after damage assessment. In addition, responsibilities such as cleaning, removing, and disposing of the debris formed in public spaces are also carried out by this sector. It also has responsibilities in strengthening security systems for critical facilities and monitoring the safety of public water resources, which is another crucial issue (US Department of Homeland Security, 2015).

The ESS can be defined differently within the borders of each country. The sub-sector mentioned above is defined for the US. This sector is divided into four different sub-sectors in the UK. These are classified as police, ambulance, fire and rescue, and Maritime & Coastguard Agency (Emergency services in the UK, 2022).

- **Police:** While protecting the public from crime, the police department provides reassurance to the local community by supporting victims and witnesses of crimes. The primary goal of a police officer working in the police department is to improve society's quality of life. This increase in quality of life can only be achieved by maintaining law and order, protecting the people and their property, preventing crime and criminals, and reducing fear of crime. In addition, the police department collaborates with groups working in many different areas, such as the criminal justice system, schools, local businesses, health organisations, social workers, urban planners, and community groups, to reduce crime rates or provide advice, education, and assistance to those affected by crime (Prospects.ac.uk, 2022).
- **Ambulance:** This sub-sector is responsible for providing treatment and transportation to hospitals in injury and illness cases. In addition, this sub-sector is responsible for providing comprehensive medical care to patients.
- **Fire and Rescue:** The Fire and Rescue unit has four primary responsibilities (Local.gov.uk, 2022). This department is responsible for extinguishing the fires in the region of this department. Second, in the event of a fire in their region, ensuring the safety of life and property of the people around is also among the job descriptions of this department. Moreover, it is the responsibility of this department to save people and ensure property safety when situations such as traffic accidents occur. Lastly, this department is also required to assess the risks involved in its area and gather information to protect the health and safety of its employees.
- **Maritime and Coastguard Agency:** This sub-sector is engaged in 24-hour maritime and coastal search and rescue operations. This unit provides coordination and response in emergencies. Apart from this, this unit produces various legislations and guides. This sub-sector provides certificates to ships and seafarers. In addition, it sets out flags to ship safety, prevents marine pollution, protects seafarer health, and ensures the safety and well-being of seafarers through survey and inspection regimes (GOV.UK, 2022).

2.4 CYBER RESILIENCE IN EMERGENCY SERVICES INFRASTRUCTURE

As in many sectors, cyberattacks are common in the ESS sector and pose a threat to this sector. The risks of cyberattacks are increasing because the number of systems connected to information networks is increasing. This is also true for the ESS industry, and like many industries, it is vulnerable to various attacks (US Government Accountability Office 2008,

2014; Green, 2016; Cisa, 2022b). Cyberattacks pose a significant threat to sectors that depend on cyberinfrastructure and work with data-driven infrastructure. In addition, ready-made products are used in many sectors, and these products are vulnerable to attack. According to the United States Department of Defense, the number of foreign organisations or individuals trying to exploit cybersecurity vulnerabilities will increase. Since ESS is one of the sectors that have the potential to be affected by this increase, providing cyber resilience in this sector becomes even more critical (Cisa, 2022c).

It is vital for organisations that the Emergency Services ecosystem provides reliable, safe, and efficient communication solutions. In this ecosystem, information about any city or country-wide organisations, public officials working in these institutions and important buildings for these institutions are included in the infrastructure systems created for this ecosystem. In addition, many sensitive details are also included in the systems owned by these institutions. For this reason, these systems become targets for malicious users. Here, malicious users may aim to access sensitive data or disrupt emergency services. With the integration of innovative technologies into ESS systems, more opportunities arise, especially for malicious computer users. Devices and systems with 5G, AI, and IoT technologies enable the performance of ESS systems to be improved. However, before switching to these systems, the integrity of ESS services should be protected, and various measures should be taken against security vulnerabilities that may occur (McElroy, 2021).

Although the mechanism of each type of attack mentioned above is different, it causes Emergency Services to be adversely affected. As a result of the prevalent attacks stated in Figure 2.1, system infrastructure can be damaged, information can be stolen, and communication can be prevented.

In case of this service disruption, many devastating effects may occur, and citizens may be put at risk. Disruption of services can cause many people to put their lives in danger. Therefore, it is crucial to continue these services. Interruptions that may occur here can result in many disaster scenarios. For this reason, it becomes even more essential to provide cyber resilience so that these services are not disrupted. These threats are becoming increasingly complex, and it takes time and resources to counter them. For this, the units responsible for these services must take the necessary steps to provide cyber resilience (McElroy, 2021).

Cyber resilience is becoming increasingly important in emergency services as these organisations rely on technology to support their operations, communication, and decision-making. Emergency services are responsible for providing critical services that are essential to public safety, and any disruption to their services can have severe consequences.

The importance of cyber resilience in emergency services can be summarised as follows:

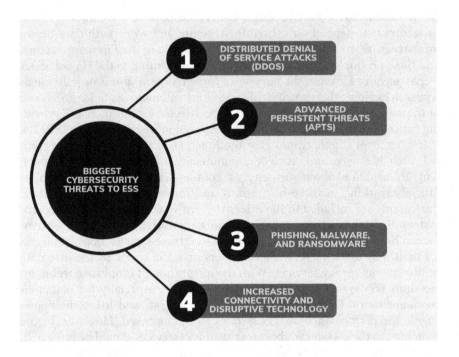

Figure 2.1 Summary of cases with the biggest cybersecurity threats to emergency services sector.

- **Continuity of Operations**: Emergency services rely on technology to support their operations, and any disruption to these systems can have a significant impact on their ability to provide critical services. Cyber resilience measures help to ensure that emergency services can continue to operate even in the face of a cyberattack, by enabling them to detect and respond to incidents quickly, and recover from them effectively.
- **Protection of Sensitive Information**: Emergency services collect and process sensitive information, including personal information, medical records, and sensitive operational data. This information needs to be protected from cyber threats, such as unauthorised access, theft, or manipulation. Cyber resilience measures, such as access controls, encryption, and network segmentation, can help to protect sensitive information from cyber threats.
- **Maintaining Public Trust**: The public expects emergency services to be reliable and trustworthy. Any disruption to services, or breach of sensitive information, can erode public trust and confidence in these organisations. Cyber resilience measures help to maintain public trust by ensuring that emergency services can provide critical services in a

timely and effective manner, while protecting sensitive information from cyber threats.

- **Compliance with Regulations**: Emergency services are subject to various regulations and standards, such as the Health Insurance Portability and Accountability Act (HIPAA) and the National Institute of Standards and Technology (NIST) Cybersecurity Framework. Cyber resilience measures help emergency services to comply with these regulations by providing a structured approach to managing cyber risks and ensuring the confidentiality, integrity, and availability of sensitive information.

In summary, cyber resilience is critical for emergency services as these organisations rely on technology to provide critical services. Cyber resilience measures help to ensure the continuity of operations, protect sensitive information, maintain public trust, and comply with regulations. Emergency services should prioritise the development and implementation of cyber resilience measures to ensure they can effectively respond to cyber threats and protect their critical services.

2.5 CASE STUDIES

2.5.1 Case 1: BlueLeaks

On 19 June 2020, a significant breach of law enforcement websites' data sparked outrage by an activist organisation named Distributed Denial of Secrets, abbreviated as DDoSecrets, claiming to have released 269 GB of material from various institutions (Brewster, 2020). This massive amount of data breach is called BlueLeaks. It includes the FBI and police reports. Moreover, Emails, names, bank info, phone numbers, images, videos, ZIP, and CSV files are also included in the list. In addition to these, breached data includes guides which deal with two of the most acute crises in the US: protests of the community right after the death of George Floyd, who died under the surveillance of the Police Department of Minneapolis and Covid-19. The breach data was released on the anniversary, also known as Juneteenth, marking the end of slavery in the United States.

DDoSecrets is a group of hacktivists whose members are still unknown. It is known that the group was launched in December 2018 (Silverman, 2021). They led to critical leaks, a massive amount of messages and emails from Russian officials in 2017. Their only member who is not anonymous, Journalist Emma Best, said that they want to make all this info accessible and inhibit it from vanishing. This breach led the police department of the US to more transparent processes. The National Fusion Center Association (NFCA) has validated the legitimacy of the stolen data in a warning from 1996 to 2020 (Krebs, 2020).

Identify: The strategies employed during the Identify phase were not made public.

Protect: NIST Framework says that implementing and developing appropriate protections ensures vital service delivery (Barrett, 2018). Nevertheless, when the incident is analysed, it can be observed that safeguards were insufficient to prevent the cyber incident. Furthermore, NFCA and Kerbs mentioned that the breach occurred on Netsential, the third-party web-development firm used by the police department.

Detect: According to NIST Framework, this function is summarised as implementing and developing the relevant actions to detect the existence of a cyber incident. In other words, it allows cybersecurity incidents to be discovered quickly. This section of the framework needs to be covered by the police departments. In other words, they could not take the necessary actions during the cyber incident.

Respond: Right after the incident, Twitter restricted spreading of URLs that could harm the affected people (Ikeda, 2020). Moreover, German authorities found a network server where the BlueLeaks data from DDoSecrets were hosted and restricted the operation of the server. In addition, nearly one year after the leakage, the FBI created a document of 354 pages called "Digital Exhaust Opt Out Guide," which focuses on how the staff can protect themselves from possible vulnerabilities (Stone, 2020).

Recover: According to Mike Reimer, global chief security architect at Pulse Secure, as federal institutions grow their usage of third-party suppliers, they must improve their surveillance of these firms (Olenick, 2020). In addition, Austin Police Department (APD) created an online tool that helps people check whether their private information was breached to increase their resilience against such attacks.

Lessons Learned: One of the essential lessons from this significant incident is monitoring and controlling the companies cooperating for cyber resilience. Moreover, to not be damaged too much by the incident, it is essential to concentrate on the cyber resilience of the staff.

2.5.2 Case 2: Baltimore's emergency system

In March 2018, the Baltimore, Maryland, U.S. authorities reported that their Computer-Aided Dispatch (CAD) system was under a cyberattack. CAD is used to provide emergency help in the most effective and timely way. It is used to redirect calls to the nearest emergency personnel in a computerised way (Osborne, 2018). Otherwise, doing all this manually leads to a slower response in emergencies. The CAD system of the city included calls from 911 and 311. The hacker(s) were not identified. The network's communications operations within the CAD system were purportedly affected.

Identify: Authorities from Baltimore said that this attack was allowed as a result of the inattention of the IT team. While the team was regularly troubleshooting, they changed the network's firewall. However, one port was missing, which stayed connected to the internet for 24 hours. The hackers found this vulnerability and easily accessed the network of Baltimore.

Protect: The city collaborated with a security software company called Tritech to ensure that communications on their critical infrastructure work normally. In this way, it is thought that the necessary protection step to ensure cyber resilience is provided. However, according to the statement made by the Tritech company after the incident, the company's software did not cause the incident.

Detect: Frank Johnson, the CIO of Baltimore, said they could detect this "limited breach" and isolate it quickly (Beavers, 2018).

Respond: Right after the incident was detected, the officials decided to isolate the emergency system. They shut down the network systems so that there was no internet connection. After shutting down, they continued operating manually, which was the slower but most efficient option to keep the system operating.

Recover: The communication system started operating normally 17 hours after the cyber incident. Moreover, city officials planned to invest $20 million in cybersecurity to increase their resilience against such incidents. This investment is planned to cover all the networks of the city. In addition, the spokesperson of the FBI, Dave Fitz, said they supported Baltimore with technical assistance.

Lessons Learned: As can be understood from the information shared in this corpse, various studies have been carried out to protect the Baltimore Emergency System from cyberattacks. These studies have taken steps regarding the necessary steps to ensure cyber resilience, and studies have been carried out in this direction. Thanks to these steps, possible losses were reduced as much as possible, and the system was made operational again within 17 hours. Although these steps have been taken, it has been understood that such situations may occur due to personnel error. In this case, to minimise the errors that may be experienced due to the personnel, it is necessary to train the personnel on this subject and to carry out studies to ensure that the work done is controllable among the personnel. In addition, city officials have planned to invest an additional $20 million in cyber resilience to increase these services' security against such cyber security attacks.

2.5.3 Case 3: DC Metropolitan Police Department

On 6 April 2021, the DC Metropolitan Department (DCMPD) announced that it had suffered a massive ransomware attack. The responsible for this attack is a foreign group called Babuk. As a result of this attack, 250 gigabytes of data belonging to the police department fell into the hands of this group. Thanks to the phishing software, they reported this situation to the police department and forced them to contact them to access the data. Babuk requested US$4 million to regain access to the files, but the police department said it would pay $100,000 to get this data back. In this case, there was no agreement, and the Babuk group posted the entire 250 gigabytes of personal and federal data online on 13 May 2021 (Suderman, 2022).

This attack took place as follows. Initial access to DCMPD's systems is required as the first stage of the attack. This means that attackers must complete their reconnaissance and find as much information as possible about DCMPD. After this information is collected, attackers must scan for security vulnerabilities from where they can enter the system. Here are three possibilities for the first access to the system:

- The first of these may be to exploit a vulnerability found during the scan. Various tools are available to achieve this, and the attacker Babuk has used publicly available applications.
- Another way to gain access to the system is by emailing the fishing rod. The first access to the system is provided as soon as this email is clicked or downloaded.
- The third possibility is that the attacker Babuk finds a vulnerable password and can be accessed remotely due to guessing this password.

Babuk's ransomware was written in the open-source language Golang, and according to McAfee's technical analysis, it is compatible with both Windows and Mac (Sere & Keijzer, 2022). Babuk terminated databases, office programs, and anti-malware services after gaining access to the system so that their background activities wouldn't be noticed. Sql.exe, Firefox. exe, Outlook.exe, OneNote.exe, and PowerPnt.exe are a few examples of the common services that Babuk terminates. Additionally, the following list includes instances of malware services that have ceased to function: DefWatch, GxVss, GxBlr, and GxFWD. Attackers spread their access covertly by using command-line activities that offer flexibility and using shell functions. Additionally, they employ a number of methods, including QueryServiceStatusEx, OpenServiceA, EnumDependentServicesA, CloseServiceHandle, and GetLastError, to cease services when they are discovered. CreateToolhelp32Snapshot, lstrcmpw, OpenProcess, TerminateProcess, and CloseHandle are the functions used to end the operations. The malware used in this process traverses and encrypts the files using recursive methods. These files cannot be accessed after this encryption process without the private key. While encrypting the files in this attack, the attackers, Babuk, also left some specific files and folders, like Windows and Firefox, to stop the victim's computer from crashing (Caroscio et al., 2022).

After Babuk carried out the attack and leaked the ransomware into the system, the final step was to demand ransom from the victims. For this, the attackers left a ransom note titled "How to Restore Your Files.txt."

In this attack, until Babuk shared this file, they could not detect that a system security breach had occurred. After this attack, Babuk claimed that 250 gigabytes of data were stolen from DCMPD. The data stolen due to this attack compromised both sensitive information about individuals and federal documents. Among these documents is sensitive information about the police (financial information, social security numbers, and employment history). In the leaked information about DCMPD, information such as psychiatric records and drug use details were in the attackers' hands.

Identify: The reason for entering the system is evident that the institution has various problems in the identification step. Even if the access is provided via an email or from a user in the system, it has been observed that risk management needs to be done better and access to the files within the organisation is easy. Because of this shortcoming, the attackers caught the vulnerabilities in the system and used these vulnerabilities.

Protect: There are also various areas for improvement in the Protect part. Since adequate protection activities were not carried out in the system, the information of many personnel and federal sources could be easily accessed after entering the system. This reveals that the resources are not adequately protected paving the way for data theft.

Detect: The attacker group remained undetected throughout the attacks, and it was understood that this infiltration occurred when the ransom was demanded. This situation reveals the inadequacies in the detect section under the title of cyber resilience. Due to the deficiency, the attackers worked comfortably within the system after entering and collecting data.

Respond: In this attack, the problems experienced in the Detect section also affected the Response section. Thanks to the software, the system continued to work thanks to the software, but the files were stolen. In this case, since the attack could not be understood during the attack, it was not possible to give any response against the attack.

Recovery: As a result of this attack, the system operation was not affected because of this attack. Recovery of the files was impossible due to the software used, and the files could not be seized because the requested ransom was not paid. In this case, recovery could not be performed because the lost resources are files.

Lessons Learned: The biggest lesson from these attacks is that every step must be carried out in detail to ensure cyber resilience. It will be understood from the above explanations that the institution does not follow the necessary steps to provide cyber resilience. If these steps are not followed, it becomes difficult to identify and detect the attack and ensure the system's protection. As a result, cyberattackers can easily access the data they want by navigating the system. Identify, protect and detect steps should be performed first to prevent this. After these steps have been taken, studies should be carried out in this area by emphasising the response step to determine how to respond to the attack. Although there were no significant problems in this situation regarding the rapid recovery of the system, in case of a different type of attack, the recovery step should also be emphasised to ensure the system's rapid recovery.

2.5.4 Case 4: AAA Ambulance Service

A Mississippi ambulance service reported a data breach with a ransomware attack. AAA Ambulance Service said the attack was on 1 July 2020, and the investigation started on 26 August. The breach involved some personal information being accessed or taken from the systems of AAA (French, 2020).

Identify: The strategies employed during the Identify phase were not made public.

Protect: There needs to be a clear explanation or statement about the protection part of the system. This leakage shows that there is no durable protection and that the attackers have reached the personal data of individuals and the system.

Detect: The AAA Ambulance Service discovered a cyber security problem in their system. They were unaware of the attack and that any data was displayed or misused. The data leakage involved several pieces of information like last and first names, social security numbers, financial account numbers, health insurance information, date of birth, medical history and treatment information, medical record numbers, and more personal data.

Respond: The business said that once the attempted ransomware assault was discovered in July, swift action was taken, including steps to stop data from being encrypted and rendered unavailable to AAA.

Recover: The firm added that they took steps to strengthen the security of AAA's data storage systems and started an investigation that included consulting outside forensic specialists.

Lessons Learned: AAA took the above procedures to address the occurrence as soon as they became aware of the breach. They provided free credit monitoring services as part of the direct notice to affected people. In addition, the warnings provide information on how individuals may monitor and protect their personal information. AAA has taken extra security precautions to avoid a repeat of the incident.

REFERENCES

Barrett, M., (2018). *Framework for Improving Critical Infrastructure Cybersecurity Version 1.1*. NIST. [Online] Available at: https://www.nist.gov/publications/framework-improving-critical-infrastructure-cybersecurity-version-11 [Accessed 21 May 2022].

Beavers, O., (2018). *Baltimore's Emergency Call System Was Struck by a Cyberattack*. The Hill. [Online] Available at: https://thehill.com/policy/cybersecurity/380727-baltimores-emergency-call-system-struck-by-cyberattack/ [Accessed 21 May 2022].

Brewster, T., (2020). *BlueLeaks: Huge Leak of Police Department Data Follows George Floyd Protests*. Forbes. [Online] Available at: https://www.forbes.com/sites/thomasbrewster/2020/06/22/blueleaks-huge-leak-of-police-department-data-follows-george-floyd-protests/?sh=65e077cb509b [Accessed 21 May 2022].

Caroscio, E., Paul, J., Murray, J. & Bhunia, S., (2022). Analysing the ransomware attack on DC metropolitan police department by Babuk. *IEEE International Systems Conference (SysCon), 2022*, Virtual Location, pp. 1–8. https://doi.org/10.1109/SysCon53536.2022.9773935.

Cisa.gov., (2022a). *Emergency Services Sector*. CISA. [Online] Available at: https://www.cisa.gov/emergency-services-sector [Accessed 22 May 2022].

Cisa.gov., (2022b). [Online] Available at: https://www.cisa.gov/sites/default/files/publications/Emergency_Services_Sector_Cybersecurity_Framework_Implementation_Guidance_FINAL_508.pdf [Accessed 22 May 2022].

Cisa.gov., (2022c). [Online] Available at: https://www.cisa.gov/sites/default/files/publications/emergency-services-sector-specific-plan-112015-508_0.pdf [Accessed 22 May 2022].

Emergency Management Australia, (2003). Critical infrastructure emergency risk management and assurance, *Cyber Resilience in the Emergency Services Sector*. Available at: https://www.files.ethz.ch/isn/10231/doc_10261_290_en.pdf

French, L., (2020). *Miss. Ambulance Service Reports Ransomware Data Breach*. [Online] Available at: https://www.ems1.com/cybersecurity/articles/miss-ambulance-service-reports-ransomware-data-breach-sIoioSsCzjrLFJy0/ (Accessed May 2022).

GOV.UK., (2022). *About Us*. [Online] Available at: https://www.gov.uk/government/organisations/maritime-and-coastguard-agency/about#:~:text=Our%20core%20responsibilities%20are%3A&text=preventing%20maritime%20pollution%20and%20responding,administering%20the%20UK%20Ship%20-%20Register [Accessed 22 May 2022].

Green, J., (2016). *DHS: Hackers Increasingly Target Emergency Systems*. WTOP. Retrieved from: https://wtop.com/j-j-green-national/2016/02/dhshackers-increasingly-targeting-emergency-systems/

Ikeda, S., (2020). *"BlueLeaks" Data Dump Contains Police Files of Hundreds of Law Enforcement Agencies, Tied Back to a Third-Party Services Provider*. CPO Magazine. [Online] Available at: https://www.cpomagazine.com/cyber-security/blueleaks-data-dump-contains-police-files-of-hundreds-of-law-enforcement-agencies-tied-back-to-a-third-party-services-provider/ [Accessed 21 May 2022].

Krebs, B., (2020). *'BlueLeaks' Exposes Files from Hundreds of Police Departments - Krebs on Security*. Krebsonsecurity.com. [Online] Available at: https://krebsonsecurity.com/2020/06/blueleaks-exposes-files-from-hundreds-of-police-departments/ [Accessed 21 May 2022].

Local.gov.uk., (2022). *Roles and Responsibilities of Fire & Rescue Authorities*. [Online] Available at: https://www.local.gov.uk/topics/fire-and-rescue/fire-role-models/roles-and-responsibilities-fire-rescue-authorities [Accessed 22 May 2022].

McElroy, T., (2021). *Mission Critical Magazine*. Missioncriticalmagazine.com. [Online] Available at: https://www.missioncriticalmagazine.com/articles/93822-mitigating-ess-cybersecurity-challenges? [Accessed 30 August 2022].

Olenick, D., (2020). *Police Data Leaked: A Sign of the Times?*. Bankinfosecurity.com. [Online] Available at: https://www.bankinfosecurity.com/police-data-leaked-sign-times-a-14488 [Accessed 21 May 2022].

Osborne, C., (2018). *A Cyberattack Disrupted Baltimore Emergency Responders*. ZDNet. [Online] Available at: https://www.zdnet.com/article/cyberattack-disrupted-baltimore-emergency-responders/ [Accessed 21 May 2022].

Prospects.ac.uk., (2022). *Police Officer Job Profile*. Prospects.ac.uk. [Online] Available at: https://www.prospects.ac.uk/job-profiles/police-officer [Accessed 22 May 2022].

Sere, N. & Keijzer, N., (2022). Mcafee.com. [Online] Available at: https://www.mcafee.com/enterprise/en-us/assets/reports/rp-babuk-moving-to-vm-nix-systems.pdf [Accessed 22 May 2022].

Silverman, J., (2021). *The New WikiLeaks*. The New Republic. [Online] Available at: https://newrepublic.com/article/163106/ddossecrets-new-wikileaks-julian-assange [Accessed 21 May 2022].

Simpkins, B.K., (2019). Critical infrastructure: Emergency services sector. In: Shapiro, L., Maras, M.H. (eds) *Encyclopedia of Security and Emergency Management*. Cham: Springer, pp. 1–10. https://doi.org/10.1007/978-3-319-69891-5_62-1.

Stone, J., (2020). *The FBI's Digital Security Guide for Local Police Has Good OPSEC Advice*. CYBERSCOOP. [Online] Available at: https://www.cyberscoop.com/fbi-digital-security-guide-blueleaks-opsec/ [Accessed 21 May 2022].

Suderman, A., (2022). *DC Police Victim of Massive Data Leak by Ransomware Gang*. AP NEWS. [Online] Available at: https://apnews.com/article/police-technology-government-and-politics-1aedfcf42a8dc2b004ef610d0b57edb9 [Accessed 22 May 2022].

US Government Accountability Office, (2008). *Critical Infrastructure Protection: Further Efforts Are Needed to Integrate Planning for and Response to Disruptions on Converged Voice and Data Networks (GAO-08-607)*. Washington, DC: US Government Accountability Office.

US Government Accountability Office, (2014). *Critical Infrastructure Protection: More Comprehensive Planning Would Enhance the Cybersecurity of Public Safety Entities' Emerging Technology (GAO-14-125)*. Washington, DC: US Government Accountability Office.

Chapter 3

Energy sector

Energy is crucial for sustaining businesses and society by providing for basic needs. It is necessary for all routine tasks like heating and cooling our homes, lighting our surroundings, producing commodities, and operating machinery. Our society and economy are built on the foundations the energy sector provides. We can provide the planet's inhabitants with food, water, energy, or gas with power plants.

The energy sector refers to a network of businesses directly and indirectly engaged in producing and distributing the energy necessary to power a nation's economy and support its means of production and transportation. Since the energy sector is continually evolving, energy providers must create ever-newer technologies to produce and store energy and deliver energy to homes and businesses. In other words, an energy sector is a group of stakeholders involved in producing or distributing power. Companies engaged in drilling for oil and gas, developing oil and gas reserves, and processing oil and gas make up a significant part of the energy sector or industry. The energy sector is divided into two distinct segments: renewable energy, which offers green solutions and conventional energy, which also provides other effective solutions but is generally attributed as harmful to the environment.

3.1 WHAT IS ENERGY AS AN INFRASTRUCTURE?

As energy is an indispensable input to production and consumption, the energy infrastructure is becoming more significant and evolving with energy demand. Energy infrastructure refers to the comprehensive framework that connects the old and innovative flow of energy between consumption and production centres. Large-scale energy transmission from production to delivery and the directing and controlling of the flow of energy are all mainly owing to the energy infrastructure (Spellman & Bieber, 2010). Conventional services such as oil and gas pipes, power lines, and train lines are examples of energy infrastructures. Recent infrastructure expansion and modernisation developments accelerate investment in existing and new energy infrastructures such as progressive electrical metering and delivery systems, power plant automation systems, and intelligent building mechanisms (IEF, 2022). Among these extensive developments, energy infrastructure contains complex systems that fuel the global economy.

As the global world rapidly changes with sustainable economic growth models, the importance of energising securely has significantly increased. The global energy infrastructure consists of pipelines for natural gas and oil, storage facilities, and transmission lines. It has expanded tremendously to provide all sectors of the global economy with an immense delivery system between supply and demand affordably and reliably.

Historically, the energy sector in developed countries has been funded privately. Until the early 20th century, private firms mostly harvested and delivered wood, oil and gas, electricity and coal. Public participation grew as network energy services became increasingly popular. The increasing necessity for integrated energy systems has started to be supplied from nuclear and renewable energy sources. Moreover, the request to increase efficiency and performance in energy and develop green energy technologies on the verge of environmental concerns leads to progress in energy infrastructure using various emerging technology systems.

Energy infrastructures have many components, from manufacturing to distribution. Some parts are electricity generation, transmission, and distribution; natural gas and oil pipe systems; oil wells; and modes of transportation, including sea and railway transport, which are all examples of physical networks. We can divide the energy infrastructure into subheadings: production, distribution, and management.

Production: The power generation transfer to power plants is an integral part of the energy infrastructure. Elements of production are classified as renewable, non-renewable, and nuclear. Energy is produced from various sources. These include coal, oil, natural gas, hydropower, wind, geothermal, tidal, solar, and nuclear power. The fundamental production unit is electricity. The electricity segment could contain several energy sources for power plants with nonutility power producers and conventional electric services. According to IEA statistics, approximately 48% of electricity is generated by the direct combustion of coal, delivered mainly by rail, nuclear power stations generate 20%, and the combustion of natural gas generates 22%. The remaining generation is provided by hydroelectricity (6%), oil (1%), and renewable energy sources such as solar, wind, and geothermal (3%) (CISA, 2021).

Distribution: The foundation of the energy infrastructure is distribution/transmission, which enables the transfer of electricity from producing facilities to final consumers. Energy distribution technology is essential for the transmission of energy, including primary energy sources like coal or crude oil, as well as energy currency for end users like gasoline or electricity. They are essential for the energy industry because they enable the global transportation of goods that fuel the global economy. Energy must be carried to a location where it may be used, whether in electricity, fuel, liquefied natural gas, or any other form. To minimise energy loss while travelling through transmission lines, the generated energy is also prepared for transfer using transformers with low voltage levels. Energy transportation systems come in a wide variety depending on what is being delivered. Large-scale infrastructure is required for these systems, including a train, a water shipping network, a pipeline grid, and an energy grid.

Management: Management practices in energy infrastructure are crucial in coordinating and progressing medium to long-term programmes aimed at upgrading the energy performance of various missions, such as managing energy flow. In the face of this phase, the control for remote monitoring of assets and equipment is entailed to ensure the accuracy and continuity of operation. The management of energy infrastructure takes responsibility for maintaining secured energy and administration of energy consumption and efficiency.

3.2 WHY IS ENERGY INFRASTRUCTURE IMPORTANT?

The fundamental importance of energy infrastructure is that it directly affects the economy and the related socioeconomic situation of the public. The energy sector is uniquely critical because it provides an "enabling function" across all critical infrastructure sectors. Health and welfare are jeopardised without a reliable energy supply, and the economy cannot function. Furthermore, energy infrastructure is a crucial driver of economic growth, job creation and competitiveness.

The vice president of public affairs for Kinder Morgan, Inc. is one of North America's sea-level energy infrastructure companies. He underlines the importance of energy infrastructure by stating, "It is imperative to the industry, all of us, to better communicate about the vital and significant role the energy infrastructure plays in our economy because many people just do not understand it" (Christensen, 2017). The infrastructure, which includes everything from oil and gas pipelines to railroads and roads, transports vital energy resources to homes and businesses.

Besides the increasing demand for energy supply, the concerns about climate change and extreme weather events increasingly affect all aspects of the energy infrastructures (EEA, 2019). These dramatic changes could have an impact on traditional energy sources, particularly non-renewable energy sources. These impacts could be enlarged in the energy transformation, transmission, distribution, and storage functions through those non-renewable energy sources. According to an assessment of the European Energy Agency, impacts of climate change include reduced cooling water availability for thermal power plants and reduced water availability for hydropower production, as well as increased risks for energy infrastructure from extreme weather events and sea-level rise (EEA, 2019). The developments in the energy infrastructure are essential since these will enable producers and consumers to achieve their common goals of sustainable development and climate change.

Globally, innovation is transforming energy infrastructure. In more dynamic energy markets, nations benefit from efficiency gains and new production flows, digitalisation, smart grids, and other modern and contemporary transportation techniques (IEF, 2022). Energy infrastructure investment and technological advancements may provide more flexible options to meet the world's growing and diverse needs for long-term economic growth and climate necessities.

3.3 KEY PLAYERS AND STAKEHOLDERS

To evaluate the cyber security risks of the energy sector, it is essential to identify some stakeholders and key players in the sector. Energy suppliers refer to entities that sell energy to the final consumer. These entities are not necessarily a part of energy production but can form an intermediate stage between the producer and the final consumer. Nevertheless, energy suppliers and producers have historically been in a vertical monopoly. In other words, due to the economics of scale and high transaction costs, energy production and supply are carried out by the same companies/entities (Roberts, 2022).

Producers are responsible for the production of energy supplied to consumers. Many different sources provide energy production. To give an example, as of 2021, 61% of electricity generation in the USA is provided by fossil fuels such as coal, natural gas, and petroleum, 20% by renewable energy sources and 19% by nuclear energy (US Energy Information Administration (EIA), 2022). Transmission System Operators (TSO), defined by the European Commission, refer to institutions that are nationally or regionally responsible for the transport of energy, in the form of natural gas or electricity, to another distribution network or directly to the consumer itself (EUR-Lex, 2017). Distribution System Operators (DSO) are part of the energy distribution network. The differences between TSOs and DSOs and the way of coordination may differ from country to country. For example, in some coordination models, TSOs deal with traditional energy distribution on a large scale and have a structure that adjusts generation depending on the energy demand periodically. At the same time, DSOs continue production by increasing the number of grids without making adjustments (NODES, 2022).

The regulatory institutions act as supervisors and rule makers in various fields, such as ensuring efficiency and security in the energy sector, determining the rules of competition between companies, managing national strategic reserves against disaster situations such as war, and protecting the interests of consumers. According to a report published by United States Homeland Security, the energy sector was recorded as the infrastructure that suffered the most cyberattacks among critical infrastructures, with 79 cyberattacks in 2015 (Reuters, 2015). Attackers frequently target the energy infrastructure as this sector provides the necessary inputs for the survival of all other critical infrastructure. It is, therefore, essential to understanding this sector, its infrastructure and the critical players and stakeholders in depth.

Infrastructure security and resilience in the energy sector rely on public and private partnerships. For this purpose, two leading Subsector Coordinating Councils (SCCs) and Government Coordinating Councils (GCC) have been established under Cybersecurity & Infrastructure Security Agency (CISA) within the United States. Electricity and Oil & Natural Gas SCC include the representatives of the relevant industries. These institutions, whose organisational structure and dynamics are determined autonomously, aim to enable the interaction of stakeholders in the public and private sectors (Energy Sector-Specific Plan, 2015). On the other hand, Energy GCC, together with the Department of Energy (DOE) and Department of Homeland Security (DHS), represents the government on a federal, state, local, tribal, and territorial basis. Since Energy GCC works within the framework of SCCs and the GCC Critical Infrastructure Partnership Advisory Council, it is exempt from the Federal Advisory Committee Act, which allows the public-private critical infrastructure community to engage in open dialogue to help mitigate critical infrastructure vulnerabilities and mitigate the impact of threats (CISA, 2021).

The energy sector is divided into two pillars, namely Electricity and Oil & Natural Gas, and SCCs have been established based on this distinction. Notably, the Electricity Subsector Coordinating Council (ESCC) is an institution that puts the vulnerabilities of electricity infrastructure on its agenda and aims to solve these vulnerabilities with the cooperation of the public and private sectors. To achieve this goal, ESCC works in coordination with the Energy GCC and provides information and technology transfer among critical stakeholders in the sector, such as Utilities, Trade Associations, Information Sharing and Analysis Centres, state agencies, critical sectors, and media and vendor councils.

In addition to the ESCC, the Oil and Natural Gas Subsector Coordinating Council (ONG SCC) is an institution that aims to ensure the infrastructure security of oil and natural gas subsectors and achieve this goal. It ensures the interaction of critical stakeholders in the oil and natural gas sector with each other and the public. ONG SCC is an institution that places extra emphasis on intersectoral work. For example, it works with the transportation industry through the Pipeline Working Group. It collaborates with the Chemical industry to conduct cross-industry analysis and implement the Chemical Facility Anti-Terrorism Standards and the Maritime Transportation Security Act. In addition, ONG GCC assists participation in the National Petroleum Council from both the public and private sectors. To facilitate all these goals, ONG SCC's key stakeholders include the American Gas Association, the American Petroleum Institute, the Interstate Natural Gas Association of America, the International Liquid Terminals Association, and the American Fuel and Petrochemical Manufacturers Association.

The counterpart of the SCC is the Energy Government Coordinating Council (EGCC) on the public side, co-chaired by the DOE and DHS, with both federal and international partners. EGCC is an advisory group that does not regulate the legal responsibilities of participants, established as a government sector partner and counterpart to the industry-led ESCC and the ONG SCC (CISA, 2021). EGCC strives to serve as a single point of contact to facilitate communication between the government and the private sector as they prepare for and respond to the problems and threats arising from potential incidents in natural disasters, cybersecurity and related matters. As with the private sector pillar, the EGCC protects energy and other critical infrastructure sectors. EGCC meets at least twice yearly for these purposes and holds additional meetings when necessary.

3.4 CYBER RESILIENCE IN ENERGY INFRASTRUCTURE

Energy infrastructure technologies are becoming more digitalised, making the energy system smarter and allowing customers to benefit more from improved energy services. Cyber resilience and cybersecurity in critical infrastructure, particularly in this industry, are becoming increasingly vital for the protection and well-being of power generation, distribution, transfer, and storage, as well as the energy market's reliability (Blueprint Energy Solutions GmbH, 2019). The energy sector's importance and potentially enormous impact on the economy and society in the event of widespread damage caused by cyber events and threats are widely acknowledged among stakeholders (Energy Expert Cyber Security Platform, 2017).

According to a study issued by the Energy Expert Cyber Security Platform (EECSP), two significant goals for the energy sector's cyber security have been established. One is securing energy systems that provide vital services to Europe's community. The other is protecting data in the energy sector and European consumers' privacy (Energy Expert Cyber Security Platform, 2017). The European Commission states that digitalisation, on the other hand, raises serious problems, such as increased vulnerability to cyberattacks and cybersecurity incidents, which might jeopardise energy supply security and data privacy (European Commission, 2022). Detection and control of a significant outage in the energy business have traditionally addressed concerns like mechanical fault or stormy weather through sophisticated mitigation and recovery procedures. Furthermore, cyberattackers have been known to target information technology (IT) systems. However, this pattern is beginning to shift. Cyberattackers are actively pursuing industrial control systems (ICS), according to a report published by Deloitte, with the potential to cause physical harm to the grid (Livingston et al., 2019). The report also states that the decade-long targeting of ICS is failing to distinguish between cyber and physical attacks, raising security and resilience problems at the national level in many countries (Livingston et al., 2019).

Additionally, the European Commission emphasises the unique characteristics of energy to pay special attention. Grids of electricity and gas pipes are highly integrated across the country, and a power cut in one state might cause blackouts and supply shortages in other states. Moreover, fast response in the energy infrastructure is crucial, but the delay is caused by typical security procedures such as command authentication or digital signature verification. The Office of Cybersecurity, Energy Security, and Emergency Response (CESER) prioritises increasing the energy sector's daily operational capacity, conducting cyber incident response and recovery, and strengthening institutional and procedural cyber security strategies to assist in making US energy infrastructure more resilient and secure. Table 3.1 demonstrates the main five cybersecurity priorities determined by CESER. These priorities help provide cyber resilience at the national level and indicate the steps companies could benefit from implementing.

Table 3.1 CESER's Cybersecurity Priorities (US Department of Energy, 2022)

CESER's Cybersecurity Priorities	
Priority 1	Developing technologies that increase cyber visibility. Therefore, organisations can respond and mitigate cyberattacks before they impact.
Priority 2	Adding appropriate cybersecurity protections into the growing system. Working to ensure that renewable energy technologies can produce a large amount of electricity while also addressing security vulnerabilities.
Priority 3	Finding dispensable digital components in the nation's critical energy systems, executing specialist testing, and sharing information on digital supply chain flaws.
Priority 4	Training to prepare a highly qualified cybersecurity workforce to improve the states' and corporates' preparation for cyber threats and coordination in the case of a cyber threat.
Priority 5	Establish the policies, processes, and skills required to increase the energy sector's cyber resilience, respond to emerging threats more efficiently and effectively, and reduce power outages.

Building ecosystem resilience is a problem for all corporations. Still, it is crucial for critical infrastructures like the electricity industry (World Economic Forum, 2022). According to The World Economic Forum, cyber threat actors actively target the energy industry for at least three reasons (Kariger & Moura, 2020):

- The first reason for this targeting is that organised crime groups seeking monetary profit have targeted power IT networks through ransomware assaults.
- The second is cyber espionage, which various groups have carried out.
- The third one is the operations of deception.

Besides the causes for being the target of cyber threats, the energy industry is susceptible to cyberattacks due to three critical features (Bowcut, 2021).

- Energy companies are seen as an attractive target by enemies of the nation and for-profit cybercriminals.
- There is an increase in cyberattacks since they can be carried out due to complex third-party supply chain links.
- Electricity, energy, and gas companies have specific physical and cyber infrastructure dependencies making OTOT systems and IT networks vulnerable to damage.

Utilities are required to manage a physically spread-out structure over several locations by their very nature, therefore bringing difficulties in giving the necessary visibility between the systems in this circumstance (Bailey et al., 2020). In addition, aside from utility-controlled locations, utilities have regional weaknesses in consumer-facing equipment that might have cybersecurity risks that endanger a company's income or the grid's general stability. The amount of differentiation within different elements constituting the organisation and geographical dispersion also makes firms vulnerable to cyberattacks.

Cyber resilience is crucial in the energy sector, as the industry is increasingly reliant on technology to support its operations, control systems, and infrastructure. The energy sector is responsible for providing critical services, including electricity, gas, and oil, and any disruption to these services can have severe consequences for public safety, economic stability, and national security.

The importance of cyber resilience in the energy sector can be summarised as follows:

- **Protection of Critical Infrastructure**: The energy sector's infrastructure, including power plants, oil and gas pipelines, and refineries, is a critical component of national infrastructure. Cyber resilience measures help to protect this infrastructure from cyber threats, such as cyberattacks or ransomware, which can cause physical damage, disrupt operations, and compromise the safety of workers and the public.

- **Continuity of Operations**: The energy sector's operations are increasingly reliant on technology, such as supervisory control and data acquisition (SCADA) systems, distributed control systems (DCS), and programmable logic controllers (PLCs). Any disruption to these systems can have a significant impact on the energy sector's ability to provide critical services. Cyber resilience measures help to ensure continuity of operations by enabling organisations to detect and respond to cyber incidents quickly, and recover from them effectively.
- **Protection of Sensitive Information**: The energy sector collects and processes sensitive information, including intellectual property, trade secrets, and financial data. This information needs to be protected from cyber threats, such as theft, espionage, or manipulation. Cyber resilience measures, such as access controls, encryption, and network segmentation, can help to protect sensitive information from cyber threats.
- **Compliance with Regulations**: The energy sector is subject to various regulations and standards, such as the North American Electric Reliability Corporation (NERC), Critical Infrastructure Protection (CIP) standards, and the European Union Agency for Cybersecurity (ENISA) Cybersecurity Act. Cyber resilience measures help energy organisations to comply with these regulations by providing a structured approach to managing cyber risks and ensuring the confidentiality, integrity, and availability of sensitive information.

In summary, cyber resilience is critical for the energy sector as these organisations rely on technology to provide critical services. Cyber resilience measures help to protect critical infrastructure, ensure continuity of operations, protect sensitive information, and comply with regulations. The energy sector should prioritise the development and implementation of cyber resilience measures to ensure they can effectively respond to cyber threats and protect their critical services.

3.5 CASE STUDIES

3.5.1 Case 1: Stuxnet attack

Iran's efforts to develop nuclear weapons are subjected to intense criticism by the USA, especially during increased tension between the United States and Iran. Although there was industrial sabotage of Iran's facilities, the Stuxnet worm was a powerful malware that targeted Iran's nuclear program and changed the perspective on cyberattacks. It is estimated that Stuxnet has affected approximately 100,000 hosts since its invention (Masood et al., 2021).

Stuxnet worm, discovered in 2010, is malicious computer software used to attack Iran's nuclear facilities, most prominently the Bushehr Natanz nuclear power plant. It is estimated that the worm was placed in 2010, at least six months before the attack occurred, due to research on nuclear facilities and uranium enrichment facilities by programmers (Baezner & Robin, 2017). Experts of the security company, Symantec, believe that the malware may have infected a motivated or uninformed third party, such as a contractor or insider, with access to the system (Falliere et al., 2010). The link file and rootkit modules within Stuxnet respectively spread copies of the malware throughout the system, making it difficult to detect malware by changing the code in PLC and Siemens Step 7 and giving commands to the PLC, presenting the users with the normal system values in operation. Consequently, hackers took control of the system, and the virus spread to various hosts thanks to the four zero-day vulnerabilities they discovered (Plėta et al., 2020).

According to security companies such as Symantec and Kaspersky, four zero-day vulnerabilities used by Stuxnet were a Windows rootkit, a PLC rootkit, antivirus evasion techniques and stolen certificates from trusted Certificate Authorities (Wolf, 2022). Antivirus software had a hard time discovering this malware because of zero-day vulnerabilities. It was more difficult for antiviruses to detect low-volume threats such as Stuxnet then.

Identify: Since the necessary frameworks for cyber resilience were not present at the site, the identify function was not practised, and the necessary actions could not be taken during the incident.

Protect: The protection function could not be fulfilled because the security of the system infrastructure needed to be adequately monitored. In other words, the simulations about detecting possible zero-day vulnerabilities in the system and what action plan should be taken against these vulnerabilities needed to be implemented sufficiently. Also, Siemens controller and PLC protocols were not public. Thus, security experts could not detect the hard-coded passcode used in their software as a specific security flaw (Wolf, 2022).

Detect: The attack was discovered on 17 June 2010 by Sergey Ulasen and Oleg Kupreev, analysts at Minsk-based anti-malware company VirusBlokAda (Shakarian, 2011). Analysts sensed a problem when a client in Iran reported random Blue Screen of Deaths (BSoDs) and computer resets (Kaspersky, 2011). They recognised that the problem could be caused by malware when they saw similar problems on many different computers, not just on a single computer.

Respond: Iran did not immediately publicise the impact of the attacks, as uranium enrichment facilities were targeted, and the attack itself was likely politically motivated. After Iranian authorities revealed that some personal computers were compromised with a virus infection, Iran suspended enrichment uranium production for no reason (Baezner & Robin, 2017).

Subsequently, Iranian engineers are said to have eliminated the malware. Still, as far as we know, there needs to be a clear explanation of the methodology they followed and the exact timing of neutralisation. Still, it is known that once discovered, Stuxnet was not a problematic malware to neutralise by reverse engineering (Hosenball, 2022).

Recover: According to US Ambassador Glyn Davie, Iran resolved its technical problems at an astonishing speed and cleaned the adverse effects of malware from its systems (Warrick, 2022). However, the experts were still determining if the malware was wiped entirely from their equipment and, if so, when.

Lessons Learned: It can be seen from this significant incident that Iran has experienced that it is essential to organise a team that will regularly test the security procedures and SCADA systems. Also, it is critical to use vital encryption techniques, have at least two-way verification procedures, and tighten the rules on using private keys. Apart from the organisational and technical deficiencies Iran experienced regarding the system's security, another shortcoming was that they needed clear and open communication with the public. This is a big problem because, in attacks such as zero-day vulnerabilities, vulnerabilities in the system were not detected beforehand due to the nature of the attack. This makes it less likely that conventional defences against malware work. In this case, it is essential to cooperate with competent institutions and authorities from the outside to get rid of the attack with minor damage (Plèta et al., 2020). Stuxnet also demonstrates how the protection provided by opacity can increase harm. If Siemens controller and PLC protocols were public, security experts could point out that the problematic passcode used in their software is an obvious security issue (Wolf, 2022).

3.5.2 Case 2: The Shamoon malware

On 15 August 2022, an organisation calling itself the "Cutting Sword of Justice" carried out a cyberattack with severe effects on Saudi Aramco. The hack wiped out 75% of the data on Aramco's business network, replacing it with pictures of a burning American flag (Perlroth, 2012). This attack was the most severe cyberattack in the company's history.

The attack was carried out with a virus called W32.DistTrack, possibly by an insider who had access to the user information and domain controller. The incident in question is an Advanced Persistent Threat (APT), which means that hackers have discovered password hashes for authenticated users and have gained access to higher tiers of the system (NHS Digital, 2018). The virus has three essential components. The dropper element is in charge of producing the essential system files and activating a service. It is called "TrkSvr," and it boots Windows by itself. It also tries to copy itself to accessible network shares, and if successfully copied, it will execute itself remotely. The wiper function is enabled only when a hard-coded setting period has expired. The module then drops into a legitimate and digitally signed device driver, collects the filenames and starts writing JPEG images or 192 KB data blocks onto it. The reporter component transfers data to the attacker's computer (Wuuest, 2014).

Identify: It is observed that this function was weak, as the company had to pre-identify and prepare the key users and the critical data accordingly that these users can access, especially when remote working is present among employees. On the contrary, their knowledge of the attack was limited, so the virus spread widely, wiping out production and drill data (Plèta et al., 2020).

Protect: Unfortunately, the protect function was poorly executed. First, the system was not backed up because the attack occurred during Ramadan, when most employees took holiday time off (Cohen, 2021). However, in the security of critical infrastructures, the phenomenon called "redundancy" has particular importance. This concept means that various backup points will ensure the system's sustainability against natural or artificial disasters that may happen to critical infrastructures (Smith, 2022). After the attack on Saudi Aramco, the fact that the data could be deleted quickly and cannot be restored indicates that, unfortunately, the systems did not have redundancy.

Detect: As far as we know, although there is no chronological and transparent information on how the attack was detected, the attack was not difficult to spot, as three-quarters of the company's files were deleted, and images of the burning American flag were replaced. For this reason, according to news sources, the company was able to detect the attack immediately after the incident (Perlroth, 2012).

Respond: To prevent the virus from spreading, Saudi Aramco had to quickly shut down the company's internal connection and limit workers' email and Internet usage (Perlroth, 2012). The company then publicised the incident on its Facebook account and claimed that even though many of its critical data were deleted and there were no backups, the data was restored, there was no physical problem, and everything was fine and remained silent until a further statement was released on 25 August 2012. However, the photos were leaked after several days showing many gasoline trucks that cannot be loaded due to operational problems resulting from the cyberattack.

Recover: To recover and retain business processes, Saudi Aramco used its hefty funding and large fleets of aircraft to purchase hard drives (Kubecka, 2022). The purchases were so heavy and fast that the demand caused the market price of the hard disks to increase rapidly.

Lessons Learned: The most critical lesson to be learned after this attack is that, in any case, critical data for institutions should be determined beforehand, and this data should be regularly backed up. In terms of cyber resilience, it is evident that the concept of "redundancy," which indicates that the critical system infrastructures should be regularly backed up in order to provide cyber resilience against cyberattacks and that the operation of the system should not be dependent on a single hub, should be adequately examined and implemented by institutions. In addition, institutions should be transparent in communication and not give false information to their stakeholders after a cyberattack. Thus, a more effective response to the cyberattack can be provided, stakeholders can be prepared for possible losses, and the stakeholders' trust will not be lost in the long run.

3.5.3 Case 3: Colonial Pipeline

On 7 May 2021, a cyberattack occurred against the Colonial Pipeline in the US. The Colonial Pipeline carries gasoline, diesel and jet fuel from the Gulf Coast of the United States to the East Coast of the United States. It is one of the primary pipelines. The Colonial Pipeline comprises four significant lines and several branch lines. During the cyber assaults, Colonial shut down the main lines for five days, interrupting roughly half of the gasoline supply (Isenberg et al., 2021). DarkSide, a cybercriminal hacking group's ransomware software, was used to attack the company. A lot of sensitive corporate data was stolen.

Moreover, the Colonial Pipeline company was not the only party affected by this incident. Nervous car owners depleted stocks in Southeast petrol stations, airlines rescheduled flights to airports with accessible gasoline, traders were shaken by unexpected price fluctuations, and logistics businesses hurried to find new fuel sources. A Colonial Pipeline employee discovered an electronic ransom letter demanding millions of dollars (Reeder & Hall, 2021). Blount, the CEO of Colonial Pipeline, agreed to pay the approximately $5 million ransom to the DarkSide hackers.

Identify: Since the appropriate cyber resilience frameworks were not applied, the identify function did not operate, and the necessary actions could not be executed during the event.

Protect: Even though it does not seem that the operational network was impacted, as a measure, Colonial Pipeline shut down its system to protect against penetration. Moreover, Colonial Pipeline was not using multi or two-factor authentication. Therefore, it caused a lack of safeguards against hacker penetration that could have been otherwise prevented (Reeder & Hall, 2021).

Detect: The application of this phase seems weak. Given that the attack must be detected before an employee notices the ransom note, it is reasonable to conclude that there is a significant concern. It is critical to detect it in advance via monitoring in such instances.

Respond: Colonial Pipeline officials contacted federal authorities within hours and reported the problem during the response phase. They were able to prevent more damage in this manner. They also worked promptly and securely to restore and safeguard their activities.

Recover: After Blount paid the $5 million ransom, US government authorities revealed they could retrieve $2.3 million in bitcoin from the hacking gang (Wilkie, 2021). Therefore, Colonial Pipeline mitigated the financial impact of the cyberattack.

Lessons Learned: One of the critical lessons to be learned from this case to ensure cyber resilience is that using multi-factor authentication is required. DarkSide hackers exploited the lack of this fundamental multi-factor authentication cybersecurity requirement by employing a single password stolen from the deep web to connect a VPN service to Colonial Pipeline's network (Reeder & Hall, 2021). Blount confirmed that the account was not secured using multi-factor authentication (Isenberg et al., 2021). Although Blount claimed that the password was complex, single-factor authentication was insufficient to protect it (Wilkie, 2021).

3.5.4 Case 4: Oiltanking Deutschland attack

The hack affected one of the world's leading independent operators of tank terminals for oils, chemicals, and gases in early 2022 by disrupting its operations in Germany (Sababa Security, 2022). The firm affected by the hack, Oiltanking Deutschland, is responsible for storing and transporting oil, motor fuels, and other petroleum goods for corporations. The Federal Office for Information Security (BSI) investigation report states that the BlackCat ransomware gang was behind the attacks on Oiltanking Deutschland (Grelg, 2022). Oiltanking announced "force majeure" for most of its interior supply business in Germany following the disclosure of the cyber assault (Tidy, 2022). According to Sababa Security, Oiltanking provides fuel to more than 20 firms in Germany, including Shell, which runs 1,955 gas stations on its own. In the aftermath of the event, the decades-old oil and gas behemoth shifted operations to other suppliers to avoid further interruption (Sababa Security, 2022).

Identify: The strategies employed during the Identify phase were not made public.

Protect: Although the specifics of how the system is protected are kept under wraps, the fact that the attack effect did not bring the system to a halt suggests that the Protect phase was not as severe as first anticipated.

Detect: Although not all details are known, according to a statement from the company, the attempt was detected early, averting severe harm. This circumstance once again demonstrated the significance of the Detect phase.

Respond: Although this is recent, more information needs to be released. Given the severity of the cyber assault, it is fair to claim that the Respond phase was not adequately implemented in this circumstance.

Recover: Arne Schoenbohm, the head of Germany's information security service, stated at a seminar that the event was significant but not fatal (SecurityWeek, 2022). Following the incident, the affected firms added that they attempted to restore regular operations to their terminals as quickly as possible. Despite the lack of technical specifics, it is evident that recovery measures are in place.

Lessons Learned: Any business might be the target of a supply chain attack. However, they significantly impact industrial enterprises, as their priority concerns people and the environment's safety (Sababa Security, 2022). For this reason, institutions operating on this subject must exercise much greater caution. The efficacy of the attacks can be increased if any of the phases mentioned above need to be carried out correctly or at all. The absence of the response phase is particularly noticeable in this case. The attack's impact may have been significantly mitigated if this step had been successfully implemented.

3.5.5 Case 5: Ukrainian power grid hack

In December 2015, three regional energy distribution providers, Kyivoblenergo, Prykarpattyaoblenerho, and Chernivtsioblenerho, located in Ukraine, reported service interruptions to customers. The outages resulted in the loss of electricity for 225,000 consumers and the disconnection of 7 110 kV and 23 35 kV power stations (Shehod, 2016). The attack was planned and started in March 2015 via spear-phishing emails containing malware Microsoft Office attachments (Lee et al., 2016). With this malicious file, a popup emerged asking if the macros in the document should be enabled. BlackEnergy 3 virus was installed when the user enabled it. The BlackEnergy 3 virus was utilised to open a channel of communication to the command and control mechanism of the attacker. The attacker obtained information from the compromised system via this communication route. As a consequence, the attackers gained access to the energy providers' IT networks, the ICS network-connected infrastructure, and the ICSs' operation via supervisory control systems such as Uninterruptible Power Supplies (UPSs) and Human Machine Interface (HMI) (Lee et al., 2016).

Identify: The strategies employed during the Identify phase were not made public such as risk and asset management or strategies.

Protect: In this case, the protection function was inadequate. Access control, protective technology, data security, etc., should have been provided in this step. For example, there are no multi-factor authentication or protective mechanisms.

Detect: Detect function was weak in this case. For detection, monitoring is a requirement, but the companies were not monitoring possible breaches.

Respond: Although there was an effort to regain control of the system, it was unsuccessful because employees were logged out of the system, and their passwords were changed during the attacks. When the cyber assault was discovered, the incident was promptly reported to the emergency response team. Computers were isolated from the network to mitigate the impacts of the last-minute incident. This phase is designed to prevent intruders from progressing further into the system. To respond, utility staff had to switch to manual mode due to an infection in SCADA systems. They manually recovered the system, re-closed the breaker, and re-energised it (Miková, 2018).

Recover: This function seems weak because providers were still not fully recovered more than a month after the attack, and SCADA systems were working limited. To recover, companies should strengthen their security measures, reconfigure software and firewalls and try to find as much data as possible to conduct an investigation. At the beginning of January 2016, an energy provider said that workstations (PCsPCs), local networks and software were restored, but Internet access was still limited (Miková, 2018).

Lessons Learned: Companies in Ukraine lack a multi-factor authentication technique, allowing attackers to obtain access to systems quickly. Furthermore, Ukraine enterprises lack firmware driver signing and application whitelisting (AWL) (Shehod, 2016). Firmware Driver signing protects against malicious drives and firmware overwrites. AWL provides detection and protection malware execution such as BlackEnergy 3. This shortcoming disrupts the protection function. Moreover, Ukraine utilities were not using credential monitoring. Shehod (2016) stated that Ukraine lacked credential monitoring and network monitoring to identify stolen credentials being used by unauthorised attackers, and credential monitoring should be implemented to detect unauthorised attackers' actions and presence in the network.

3.5.6 Case 6: COPEL and eletrobras cyberattack

Two large Brazilian electric companies, Centrais Elétricas Brasileiras (Eletrobras) and Companhia Paranaense de Energia (Copel), suffered ransomware attacks in 2021. Both are state-controlled and essential participants in the country's economy (Ilascu, 2021). Copel is the largest corporation in Paraná, whereas Eletrobras is Latin America's largest power company and controls Eletronuclear, a branch that builds and operates nuclear power reactors. Both electrical companies were forced to disengage from the National Interconnected System, causing widespread inconvenience (Prospero Events Group, 2022). According to ThreatPost's research, the hackers gained access to Copel's CyberArk cloud security solution for limited access management and unencrypted credentials across the company's local and Internet networks (Seals, 2021).

Identify: Although no specific details concerning the Identify phase have been released, it is safe to assume that it was a success based on the low harm sustained during the attack.

Protect: In the face of the attack, the Protect phase was done quite successfully. In this way, the effects of the attack were significantly reduced, preventing extensive damage. Implementing first-line security measures that reduce the impact of any potential threat and, to the extent possible, safeguard the organisation's infrastructure and data against ransomware attacks was successful.

Detect: Even though the technical specifics of the Detect phase are unknown, its successful execution stopped the assault from succeeding as planned.

Respond: Eletronuclear halted several systems after detecting the cyber-attack to safeguard the network's functionality (Ilascu, 2021). Ilascu also states that the organisation isolated the virus and limited the impact of the incident with the help of the managed security services team (Ilascu, 2021).

Recover: The firm does not specify which procedures were employed during the Recovery phase. What seems to be definite is that the core systems were unharmed, and the electrical supply and telecommunications services were undisturbed. COPEL stated that the examination of what transpired was done, and the company took the required actions to restore stability.

Lessons Learned: An essential lesson from this case is how the Protect phase, executed by putting first-line security protocols, and the Respond phase, implemented effectively, helped to avert even more destruction. Meanwhile, an attempt was made to fix the system as quickly as possible by advancing to the Recovery phase as soon as practicable, and a significant step in cyber resilience was taken.

REFERENCES

Baezner, M. & Robin, P., (2017). *Hotspot Analysis: Cyber-conflict between the United States of America and Russia*, ETH Zürich: Center for Security Studies (CSS).

Bailey, T., Maruyama, A. & Wallance, D., (2020). *The Energy-Sector Threat: How to Address Cybersecurity Vulnerabilities.* [Online] Available at: https://www.mckinsey.com/business-functions/risk-and-resilience/our-insights/the-energy-sector-threat-how-to-address-cybersecurity-vulnerabilities [Accessed 3 November 2020].

Blueprint Energy Solutions Gmb H, (2019). *Final Report - Study on Cyber Security in the Energy Sector of the Energy Community.* s.l.: s.n.

Bowcut, S., (2021). *Cybersecurity in the Energy Industry.* [Online] Available at: https://cybersecurityguide.org/industries/energy/ [Accessed 19 April 2022].

Christensen, L., (2017). *Energy Infrastructure is Critical to Economic Growth.* [Online] Available at: https://www.utahbusiness.com/energy-infrastructure-critical-economic-growth/

CISA., (2021). *Critical Infrastructure Partnership Advisory Council.* CISA. [Online] Available at: https://www.dhs.gov/critical-infrastructure-partnership-advisory-council [Accessed 24 April 2022].

Cohen, G., (2021). *Throwback Attack: Hackers Take Advantage of the Holidays to Hit Oil Giant Saudi Aramco*. [Online] Available at: https://www.industrialcybersecuritypulse.com/throwback-attack-hackers-take-advantage-of-the-holidays-to-hit-oil-giant-saudi-aramco/ [Accessed 20 May 2022].

EIA, (2022). *Frequently Asked Questions (FAQs) - US Energy Information Administration (EIA)*. [Online] Available at: https://www.eia.gov/tools/faqs/faq.php?id=427&t=3 [Accessed 23 May 2022].

Energy Expert Cyber Security Platform, (2017). *Cyber Security in the Energy Sector*. s.l.: s.n.

Energy Sector-Specific Plan, (2015). *US Department of Homeland Security*. Available at: https://www.energy.gov/sites/default/files/2016/02/f29/2015%20Energy%20Sector%20Specific%20Plan.pdf [Accessed 24 April 2022].

EUR-Lex, (2017). Guideline on Electricity Transmission System Operation [Online] Available at: https://eur-lex.europa.eu/EN/legal-content/summary/guideline-on-electricity-transmission-system-operation.html.

European Commission, (2022). *Critical Infrastructure and Cybersecurity*. [Online] Available at: https://energy.ec.europa.eu/topics/energy-security/critical-infrastructure-and-cybersecurity_en [Accessed 19 April 2022].

European Energy Agency, (2019). *Climate Change Puts Pressure on Europe's Energy System*. European Environment Agency (europa.eu).

Falliere, N., Murchu, L. & Chien, E., (2010). *W32.Stuxnet Dossier Version 1.3*. [Online] Available at: https://www.wired.com/images_blogs/threat-level/2010/11/w32_stuxnet_dossier.pdf [Accessed 26 April 2022].

Grelg, J., (2022). *BlackCat Ransomware Implicated in Attack on German Oil Companies*. [Online] Available at: https://www.zdnet.com/article/blackcat-ransomware-implicated-in-attack-on-german-oil-companies/ [Accessed 20 May 2022].

Hosenball, M., (2022). *Experts Say Iran has "Neutralised" Stuxnet Virus*. Reuters. [Online] Available at: https://www.reuters.com/article/us-iran-usa-stuxnet-idUSTRE81D24Q20120214 [Accessed 26 April 2022].

Ilascu, I., (2021). *Eletrobras, Copel Energy Companies Hit by Ransomware Attacks*. [Online] Available at: https://www.bleepingcomputer.com/news/security/eletrobras-copel-energy-companies-hit-by-ransomware-attacks/ [Accessed 3 May 2022].

Isenberg, R., Kristensen, I., Mysore, M. & Weinstein, D., (2021). *Building Cyber Resilience in Critical National Infrastructure*. [Online] Available at: https://www.mckinsey.com/business-functions/risk-and-resilience/our-insights/building-cyber-resilience-in-national-critical-infrastructure [Accessed 30 April 2022].

Kariger, R. & Moura, G. D., (2020). *Building a Cyber-Resilient Electricity Sector is an Important Priority for the Post-COVID Era*. [Online] Available at: https://www.weforum.org/agenda/2020/11/cyber-resilient-electricity-sector-priority-post-covid/ [Accessed 5 May 2022].

Kaspersky, E., (2011). *The Man Who Found Stuxnet - Sergey Ulasen in the Spotlight*. [Online] Available at: https://eugene.kaspersky.com/2011/11/02/the-man-who-found-stuxnet-sergey-ulasen-in-the-spotlight/ [Accessed 26 April 2022].

Kubecka, C., (2022). Youtube.com. [Online] Available at: https://www.youtube.com/watch?v=WyMobr_TDSI [Accessed 1 May 2022].

Lee, R. M., Assante, M. J. & Conway, T., (2016). *Analysis of the Cyber Attack on the Ukrainian Power Grid.* [Online] Available at: https://media. kasperskycontenthub.com/wp-content/uploads/sites/43/2016/05/20081514/E-ISAC_SANS_Ukraine_DUC_5.pdf [Accessed 1 March 2022].

Livingston, S., Sanborn, S., Slaughter, A. & Zonneveld, P. (2019). *Managing Cyber Risk in the Electric Power Sector.* s.l.: Deloitte.

Masood, Z., Raja, M., Chaudhary, N., Cheema, K. & Milyani, A. (2021). Fractional dynamics of stuxnet virus propagation in industrial control systems. *Mathematics,* 9(17), 2160.

Miková, T., (2018). *Cyber Attack on Ukrainian Power Grid.* [Online] Available at: https://is.muni.cz/th/uok5b/BP_Mikova_final.pdf [Accessed 1 March 2022].

NHS Digital, (2018). *Shamoon Wiper Trojan.* [Online] Available at: https://digital. nhs.uk/cyber-alerts/2018/cc-2844#:~:text=First%20observed%20in%20 2012%2C%20Shamoon,against%20governments%20in%20the%20region [Accessed 29 April 2022].

NODES, (2022). *Hallstein Hagen: Market-Based TSO/DSO Coordination - NODES.* [Online] Available at: https://nodesmarket.com/blog/hallstein-hagen-market-based-tso-dso-coordination/ [Accessed 23 May 2022].

Perlroth, N., (2012). *In Cyberattack on Saudi Firm, US Sees Iran Firing Back (Published 2012).* Nytimes.com. [Online] Available at: https://www.nytimes. com/2012/10/24/business/global/cyberattack-on-saudi-oil-firm-disquiets-us. html [Accessed 29 April 2022].

Pléta, T., Tvaronavičienė, M., Casa, S. & Agafonov, K., (2020). Cyber-attacks to critical energy infrastructure and management issues: An overview of selected cases. *Insights into Regional Development,* 2(3), 703–715. Available at: https:// jssidoi.org/ird/uploads/articles/7/Pleta_Cyberattacks_to_critical_energy_ infrastructure_and_management_issues_overview_of_selected_cases.pdf [Accessed 26 April 2022].

Prospero Events Group, (2022). *Some of the Most Significant Cyberattacks on Energy Infrastructure in Recent Years.* [Online] Available at: https://www.prospero-events.com/biggest-cyberattacks-energy-infrastructure/ [Accessed 3 May 2022].

Reeder, J. R. & Hall, T., (2021). *Cybersecurity's Pearl Harbor Moment: Lessons Learned from the Colonial Pipeline Ransomware Attack.* [Online] Available at: https://cyberdefensereview.army.mil/Portals/6/Documents/2021_summer_ cdr/02_ReederHall_CDR_V6N3_2021.pdf?ver=6qlw1l02DXt1A_1n5KrL4g %3D%3D [Accessed 30 April 2022].

Reuters, (2015). *Cyber Attack on US Power Grid Could Cost the Economy $1 Trillion.* Available at: https://www.reuters.com/article/us-cyberattack-power-survey-idUSKCN0PI0XS20150708 [Accessed 23 April 2022].

Roberts, D., (2022). *Power Utilities Are Built in the 20th century. That Is Why They Are Flailing in the 21st.* Vox. [Online]. Available at: https://www.vox. com/2015/9/9/9287719/utilities-monopoly [Accessed 23 May 2022].

Sababa Security, (2022). *Cyber Attack Strikes German Oil Storage Firm.* [Online] Available at: https://www.sababasecurity.com/cyber-attack-strikes-german-oil-storage-firm/ [Accessed 2 May 2022].

Seals, T., (2021). *Ransomware Attacks Hit Major Utilities.* [Online] Available at: https://threatpost.com/ransomware-attacks-major-utilities/163687/ [Accessed 3 May 2022].

SecurityWeek, (2022). *Germany: 2 Oil Storage and Supply Firms Hit by Cyberattack.* [Online] Available at: https://www.securityweek.com/germany-2-oil-storage-and-supply-firms-hit-cyberattack [Accessed 2 May 2022].

Shakarian, P., (2011). *Stuxnet: Cyberwar Revolution in Military Affairs.* [ebook] Available at: https://citeseerx.ist.psu.edu/viewdoc/download?doi=10.1.1.702.944&rep=rep1&type=pdf [Accessed 26 April 2022].

Shehod, A., (2016). *Ukraine Power Grid Cyberattack and US Susceptibility: Cybersecurity Implications of Smart Grid Advancements in the US.* [Online] Available at: https://web.mit.edu/smadnick/www/wp/2016-22.pdf [Accessed 1 March 2022].

Smith, C., (2022). *What is Redundancy? - Cybersecurity & Data Management.* Cybersecurity & Data Management. [Online] Available at: https://www.fiber.net/blog/what-is-redundancy/ [Accessed 30 April 2022].

Spellman, F. R. & Bieber, R. M. (2010) *Energy Infrastructure Protection and Homeland Security*, Government Institutes Press, Volume 1.

Tidy, J., (2022). *Cyber-attack Strikes German Fuel Supplies.* [Online] Available at: https://www.bbc.com/news/technology-60215252 [Accessed 2 May 2022].

US Department of Energy, (2022). *CESER's Cybersecurity Priorities.* [Online] Available at: https://www.energy.gov/sites/default/files/2021-10/DOE_CESER_Cyber_Overview%20%28Updated%2010.28.21%29.pdf [Accessed 3 May 2022].

Warrick, J., (2022). *Iran's Natanz Nuclear Facility Recovered Quickly from the Stuxnet Cyberattack.* Reuters. [Online] Available at: https://www.washingtonpost.com/world/irans-natanz-nuclear-facility-recovered-quickly-from-stuxnet-cyber-attack/2011/02/15/ABUIkoQ_story.html [Accessed 29 April 2022].

Wilkie, C., (2021). *Colonial Pipeline Paid $5 Million Ransom One Day After a Cyberattack, CEO Tells Senate.* Updated 9 June 2021. [Online] Available at: https://www.cnbc.com/2021/06/08/colonial-pipeline-ceo-testifies-on-first-hours-of-ransomware-attack.html [Accessed 30 April 2022]

Wolf, M., (2022). *Cyber-Physical Systems.* ScienceDirect. [Online] Available at: https://www.sciencedirect.com/topics/computer-science/stuxnet [Accessed 26 April 2022].

World Economic Forum, (2022). *Cyber Resilience in the Electricity Industry.* [Online] Available at: https://www.weforum.org/projects/systems-of-cyber-resilience-electricity [Accessed 5 May 2022].

Wuuest, C., (2014). *Targeted Attacks Against the Energy Sector.* Symantec. [Online] Available at: https://docs.broadcom.com/doc/targeted-attacks-against-engery-sector-14-en [Accessed 29 April 2022].

Chapter 4

Finance sector

The financial sector is the collection of organisations, products, services, and legislative and regulatory structures that enable operations to be carried out using credit. Long-term growth rates are often higher in nations with more advanced financial systems, and a vast body of research demonstrates that this impact is significant: Financial growth does not only follow economic success; it also contributes to it (The World Bank, 2016). The finance system also encompasses a diverse range of activities in industries, including property investment, consumer finance, banking, and insurance. Additionally, a wide range of investment funds is covered (Asmundson, 2011). Furthermore, there are particular indicators that each sub-sector of finance should monitor. The success of the sub-sectors and, subsequently, the success of the financial sector can be paved by paying attention to these indicators. Table 4.1 lists several financial system sub-sectors and offers meaningful measures of their volume and progress. Analysis of the financial system's broadness could also consider the scope of the current financial establishments (IBRD et al., 2005).

Before the industrial revolution, most people kept livestock and farmed their food, making it possible for them to exist for many days without money. Additionally, they often resided in houses handed down through generations. As communities expanded, most residents were compensated with money to purchase housing and food. In today's capitalist society, customers have access to an overwhelming selection of both needed and non-essential commodities. Payment methods encompass actual currency, digital currency, and legally enforceable agreements, such as mortgages. Payment and financial systems have developed over many thousand years, despite the common perception that they are contemporary developments. How transactions are conducted has evolved drastically throughout time, but the primary goals have remained constant. For example, the economic functions of the first modern banks in Renaissance Italy are still relevant today.

Table 4.1 Sectoral Indicators of Financial Development (IBRD et al., 2005)

Sub-sector	Indicator
Banking	• Total number of banks • Number of branches and outlets • Number of branches/thousand population • Bank deposits/GDP (%) • Bank assets/total financial asset (%) • Bank assets/GDP (%)
Insurance	• Number of insurance companies • Gross premiums/GDP (%) • Gross life premiums/GDP • Gross non-life premiums/GDP (%)
Pensions	• Types of pension plans • Percentage of labour force covered by pensions • Pension fund assets/GDP (%) • Pension fund assets/total financial assets (%)
Mortgage	• Mortgage assets/total financial assets • Mortgage dept stock GDP
Leasing	• Leased assets/total domestic investment
Money markets	• Types and value of money market instruments • New issues and growth in outstanding value • Number and value of daily (weekly) transactions in the instruments
Foreign exchange markets	• Volume and value of daily foreign exchange transactions • Adequacy of foreign exchange
Capital markets	• Number of listed securities (bonds and equities) • Share of households, corporations and financial institutions in the holdings of securities • Number and value of new issues (bonds and equities) • Market capitalisation/GDP (%) • Value traded/market capitalisation (%) • Size of derivative markets
Collective investment funds	• Types and number of schemes (unique and mixed funds) • Total assets and growth rates (nominal and as percentage of GDP) • Total number of investors and average balance per investor • Share of households, corporations, and financial institutions in total mutual funds assets

4.1 WHAT IS FINANCE AS AN INFRASTRUCTURE?

We must be able to depend on the most cost-effective transmission of our payments. The financial infrastructure enables individual households, businesses, and government agencies to send and receive payments securely and effectively. It also enables financial markets, shares, bonds, and other financial products may be purchased and delivered.

Financial market infrastructure (FMI) is a coordinating mechanism bringing together a network of counterparties to facilitate trading liquidity, netting of exposures, and settlement requirements. In addition, they develop secure arrangements for the prompt clearing and settlement of obligations between counterparties, support institutions in managing counterparty credit risks, and assist in coordinating actions in the case of a default by a market player. As an example, the Reserve Bank of Australia states that it is principally interested in regulating three categories of FMIs (Reserve Bank of Australia, 2022):

- **Significantly Systemic Payment Systems:** This FMI facilitates the settlement of interbank payments at the wholesale level.
- **Central Counterparties (CCPs):** A CCP operates as both the seller and the buyer in a particular market. Typically, it does this by substituting itself as the legal counterparty to all purchases and transactions, a practice known as novation.
- **Securities Settlement Facilities (SSFs):** SSFs facilitate the settlement of securities transactions at their conclusion. Settlement entails the transfer of the security's ownership and cash. These tasks are related to incorporating delivery versus payment (DvP) agreements into the settlement process.

A vital aspect of financial infrastructure is the market. A financial market is any place or mechanism that supports purchasing and selling capital instruments, including bonds, foreign currencies, shares, and derivatives. The connection between people with capital to invest and those who need capital is facilitated by financial markets. Financial markets enable participants to transfer risk, often through derivatives and advanced trade, making it feasible to raise funds (Office of the Comptroller of the Currency, 2022). FMI's operations could be classified into four titles:

- **Payment Systems:** A payment service is a collection of devices, methods, and regulations for transferring payments between many players; participants and the company executing the arrangement are included in the system. Generally, payment systems are founded on an agreement between many players and the operator of the arrangement, and monies are transferred through an agreed-upon operational infrastructure. Payment systems are often classified as large value payment systems (LVPS) or retail payment systems. A retail payment system is a money transfer system that often processes a large volume of relatively low cheques, credit transference, and direct deposit payments. Private or governmental entities may run retail payment systems using multilateral real-time gross settlement (RTGS) or deferred net settlement (DNS) methods. In the financial industry, LVPS is a system that processes high-priority, high-value transactions. Many LVPSs, unlike commercial systems, are managed by central banks utilising an RTGS system or a similar approach (Bank for International Settlements, 2016).

- **Central Securities Depositories (CSDs):** A CSD offers securities portfolios, central safety services, and property services, such as the administration of company practices and refunds, and plays a vital role in ensuring the security of securities issuance (that is, ensuring that securities are not produced, destroyed, or have their information changed inadvertently or fraudulently). A CSD may retain securities in either dematerialised or physically immobilised shape. The particular functions of a CSD vary by jurisdiction and industry customs. For instance, a CSD's operations may differ depending on whether it functions in a country with a direct holding arrangement, an indirect holding arrangement, or both. A CSD may keep the final record of legal possession for security, but in other instances, a distinct securities registrar will perform this notarial duty. A CSD manages a securities settlement system in various nations (Bank for International Settlements, 2016).
- **Securities Settlement System (SSS):** A securities settlement system permits the transfer and settlement of securities by book entry per a set of specified multilateral norms. These methods facilitate the transfer of securities for a charge or at no cost. Several methods provide DvP where a transfer is dependent on payment, in which the security is given if and only if payment is made. A SSS may be structured to perform additional securities settling and clearing tasks, including confirming transaction and settlement orders. This report's description of an SSS is more strict than that of the RSSS, which defined an SSS broadly to encompass all institutions for verification, clearing, and resolution of securities transactions, as well as custody of securities throughout the entire trading of securities. For instance, the RSSS definition of SSSs comprised CSDs, CCPs, and commercial bank services, including securities transfers. CSDs and CCPs are regarded as distinct FMI categories in this analysis. As stated above, in many nations, CSDs also run an SSS (Bank for International Settlements, 2016).
- **Central Counterparties:** A CCP mediates between the counterparties traded on one or more financial markets, serving as the buyer to each seller and the seller to each purchaser to ensure the fulfilment of model offers. A CCP may become the counterparty to deals with market players through novation, an access mechanism, or a comparable legally enforceable arrangement. Through multilateral netting of transactions and the imposition of more appropriate risk management controls on all participants, CCPs can drastically minimise participant risks. CCPs often demand members to task support (in the type of original amount and other finances) to cover present and future potential risks. CCPs can also mutualise some risks with each other through tools like default financing. CCPs may minimise vulnerability in the marketplaces they service due to their capability to lower

participant risk. The efficacy of a CCP's preventive actions and the sufficiency of its financial resources are essential for obtaining these risk-reduction advantages (Bank for International Settlements, 2016).

- **Trade Repositories:** A trade repository is an institution that keeps a centralised electronic archive (database) of transactional information. Trade transparency reports have arisen as a novel sort of FMI and gained prominence in recent years, especially in the over-the-counter derivatives market. By centralising the picking, storage, and spreading of information, a well-designed TR that operates with efficient risk checks may play a crucial act in enhancing the clearness of operation records to relevant authorities and the general public, promoting financial steadiness, and facilitating the detection and mitigation of market misuse. A crucial role of a Technical Report is to give knowledge that helps reduce risk, operational effectiveness and efficiency, and cut costs for both individualistic organisations and the market in general. These entities can include the parties of a transaction, their agencies, CCPs, and other service providers providing supplementary services, such as the central settlement of payments, electronic novation, confirmation, portfolio compressing, compromise, and collateral management. Because several parties may use a TR's data, its accessibility, reliability, and accuracy are vital (Bank for International Settlements, 2016).

4.2 WHY IS FINANCE INFRASTRUCTURE IMPORTANT?

The finance industry is one of the most crucial economic stability and growth sectors. FMIs must operate safely and effectively to sustain and foster financial stability and economic progress. FMIs have the potential to either develop into essential conduits for the transmission of financial shocks across domestic and international financial markets, or they can develop into causes of financial impacts, such as credit losses and liquidity disruptions if improperly managed (European Central Bank, 2018).

Banks should be allowed to lend money to individuals and companies regardless of the economic climate. Additionally, payments for products and services must be completed quickly, securely, and cheaply. If banks fail to execute their responsibilities, the repercussions for the economy as a whole might swiftly become so severe that even the financial sector would be vulnerable to big shocks. Banks must have the ability to withstand losses and satisfy their present payment commitments. To do this, banks must adhere to stringent regulatory restrictions. Among them are the capital and liquidity (capital that can be paid quickly) criteria that banks must fulfil in order to meet their present payment commitments (Norges Bank, 2019).

Confidentiality and non-compliance concerns are highly relevant to the banking industry, which manages many customers' financial information. There is a need for financial sector participants to build resilience in order to respond to and recover from a catastrophic data breach or other cyber disasters.

Furthermore, any organisation that collects or retains personally identifiable data must now protect the confidentiality of sensitive consumer information. Names and addresses are examples of sensitive general data, while card and bank numbers are examples of sensitive financial data. Such high-profile corporate breaches demonstrate the problems that even the largest global businesses have in ensuring the continuous security of their digital assets. Even with advanced data privacy rules and security safeguards, companies are vulnerable to fraud owing to data protection systems and procedures gaps.

In light of data privacy regulations and the reputational repercussions of data breaches, it is even more crucial to design a thorough data privacy policy. Protecting data privacy is a crucial responsibility for companies and governments worldwide. Most countries have privacy laws and regulations protecting private and sensitive consumer data. These standards govern how organisations use, store, and utilise such data. Countries such as the United States have enacted laws demanding quick reporting of data breaches to consumers. In most of the world's leading countries, data privacy regulations exist. These constraints include data security, accountability, access, integrity, authorisation, disclosure, and notification.

In today's business world, data breaches are all too common and often make headlines. In recent years, the cost of a data breach to an organisation has skyrocketed. In 2010, the median price of a data breach grew globally, with US breaches costing approximately US$214 per exposed record and the worldwide average being US$156. Expenses associated with breach discovery and escalation, alerting impacted customers, and establishing a communication system to assist breach sufferers are direct costs that may be quantified by the time and money spent on these operations. In addition, companies found guilty of data breaches owing to non-compliance with current privacy regulations and inadequate data security practices may pay additional expenses in court penalties. Major General Data Protection Regulation (GDPR) infractions in the banking industry will likely result in hefty penalties. Given the scale of any data protection authority's annual revenue, it is highly prudent for big financial institutions to impose a 4% annual revenue fee.

In finance, activity logs, financial reports, and earnings reports are considerably important information. Critical to the performance of a financial institution is the administration and analysis of this data. In order to unleash the value of this data, the IT departments of financial firms must manage data using optimal storage alternatives. This enables them to predict client behaviour and develop tactics that return more value to the organisation. However, transferring data appropriately is a complex operation. There is danger whenever unstructured data is transported from one storage platform to another, whether on-premises or in the cloud. There is a possibility for error if the team relocating the data needs to take the necessary safeguards. During data transmission, human or machine faults or malicious assaults may compromise the data's integrity. This might result in significant fines for non-compliance and prolonged downtime.

Financial institutions are susceptible to availability attacks because of the sensitive nature of the data they store and the high value of their assets. This risk increases as financial institutions become more reliant on digital channels and third-party service providers. Access to the institution's website, networks, and online financial platforms, as well as its internal systems and procedures that enable it to operate and service its customers, are all susceptible to availability attacks. In addition to its IT systems, a typical financial institution's attack surface typically comprises customer accounts and a more extensive payment network. The repercussions extend beyond the company's everyday operations when customers cannot access their financial data and cash. Given the lucrative nature of this industry, it is not surprising that hackers would want to target a financial institution. The average cost of a distributed denial-of-service attack (DDoS) on a financial services company is estimated to be $1.8 million. Banks and other financial institutions are examining their security posture in light of the rising digitalisation trend, which compels them to shift data and apps to the cloud.

The finance industry is a very interconnected sector. Asset and liability management (ALM) policies of their governments, financial corporations, and institutions connect nations economically. This has both benefits and drawbacks. During the last three decades, an increase in financial interconnection has accompanied the growth of financial globalisation – as evidenced by the sixfold increase in the proportion of external liabilities and assets to gross domestic product (GDP). Since the mid-1990s, governments, financial institutions, and enterprises' ALM policies have taken on a more global character.

A bank failure is considered a crisis that severely affects its services. This vital economic sector will eventually decline if banks fail to fulfil their responsibilities. For example, the 2008 Great Recession was a financial disaster. This recession was directly caused by the inability of individuals with bad credit to repay mortgage loans, leaving banks without adequate capital. Given that a bank failure reduces a country's GDP, it is logical to assume that it will have repercussions in several other economic sectors. The bank collapse has repercussions on the economy.

It has been widely acknowledged for a very long time that the financial system is essential for encouraging economic growth. Banks and other financial institutions play a crucial role in efficiently allocating resources, promoting fast economic development, and assessing credit risk. Credit distribution in all areas (primary, manufacturing, and services) got increasingly sophisticated as economies grew. In this regard, banks and other financial institutions have a responsibility. As economic complexity increases, the financial industry must adapt and expand in breadth and depth. During the 1997–1998 Asian financial crisis, the banking industry's resilience became evident.

4.3 KEY PLAYERS AND STAKEHOLDERS

Defining key players in the finance industry and understanding their characteristics is crucial for comprehending the cybersecurity capabilities of this sector. This enables us to evaluate cyber resilience more accurately. Even though these key players may vary from country to country, key players are expressed in a general way here. In Figure 4.1, key players are demonstrated.

- **Investors:** These can be divided into two main groups: individual and institutional investors. A retail (individual) investor makes investments through a bank, stockbroker, or mutual fund. These types of investors make investments to achieve their unique objectives, such as saving for retirement, a child's education, or increasing their overall wealth. These investors differ from institutional investors in the volume of investment, knowledge, and research.
- **Regulators:** Central Banks are one of the finance industry's primary regulators since they are required to set the central interest rates for the market as part of their obligation to carry out monetary policy.

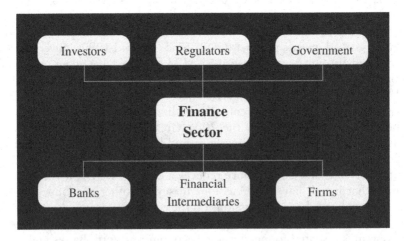

Figure 4.1 Key players and stakeholders in finance sector.

Moreover, to avoid any liquidity problems, the central bank can bring in new regulations to the commercial banks (Rolland, 2011).

- **Government:** These institutions control and have a variety of influences on all forms of finance. They include not only activities of the central bank but also taxation and regulations for accounting procedures. Tax policies implemented by the government impact financial transactions as a whole.
- **Banks:** This category can be divided into two main parts: commercial banks and investment banks. Although investment and commercial banks are critical fiscal entities in the contemporary economy, their roles and hiring needs differ. Commercial banks serve a wide range of clients, including the general public and businesses, by accepting deposits, disbursing loans, protecting assets, and working with them. However, investment banks' services towards big businesses and institutional investors can be categorised as large scale (Saunders et al., 2022). A merger and acquisition (M&A) advisor, a securities issuer, or a source of financing for significant business initiatives are all examples of what an investment bank can do.
- **Firms:** These are also one of the main actors in the finance industry, a profit-focused institution such as a corporation, partnership, proprietorship, etc.
- **Financial Intermediaries:** These are the companies such as insurance companies, mutual funds, and banks that enable the exchange of money between borrowers and lenders (Hubbard & O'Brien, 2022).

4.4 CYBER RESILIENCE IN FINANCE INFRASTRUCTURE

The financial infrastructure consists of increasingly linked IT systems. This has generated new opportunities, such as quicker and more effective payment mediation, but it also makes it easier for an assault on a participant's IT system to spread to other systems. For instance, a cyberattack might result in the cessation of a bank's activities or the deactivation or loss of dependability of payment systems due to the manipulation of data.

Cyber resilience is crucial for the financial sector, as even the best technology and security firms are responsive to disastrous cybersecurity breaches. Even for firms with the highest operational security requirements and perhaps the most advanced cybersecurity procedures, it is not easy to ensure the integrity of computer systems. In addition, the financial sector is a prime target for cybercriminals since it entails hacks and theft. Cybercriminals can launch attacks on banking credentials, financial apps, and settlement systems. Faced with the sad realisation that no system may guarantee impregnability in the face of continual attacks, companies are accepting the necessity to build procedures and technology that offer assistance following catastrophic attacks. The inevitability and destructiveness of cyberattacks have become a digital danger for even the most prepared financial institutions. This shows us that cyber resilience is an obligation in the finance sector. When we look at some devastating events targeting financial institutions, we understand that cyber resilience has become an absolute need. The financial sector requires a cyber-resilience approach to multi-form risks that menace the critical systems it owns and operates and the data that flows through them. No matter how much money financial institutions spend on the most advanced security technologies, cyberattacks have become an unavoidable digital risk that they will never be able to eliminate (Conference Board of Canada, 2018). Consequently, the cyber-resilience framework becomes a vital implementation to do. While the finance industry has historically had more robust cyber defences than other industries, the many third parties involved in its extensive supply chain – such as legal firms, auditing, and information technology firms – have contributed to the problem. These entities, including software vendors, are potential weak points (BitSight, 2019).

With those third parties involved, the finance sector infrastructure becomes highly complex. Financial institutions are responsible for a diverse set of infrastructure. Financial services firms had an average of 9.9k end-user devices per company in 2017, demonstrating this. Of course, to protect the business from cyber threats, all of these devices must be managed and adequately protected. With an average of 12.2k end-user devices per bank in 2017, banks have the most to manage in any industry. By comparison, only defence, telecommunications, professional services, and government come close to these figures. The complexity of financial services companies' infrastructure and the use of a hybrid cloud add to the challenge of protecting them from cyber criminals. Only a quarter (24%) of non-financial institutions use a mix of on-premise and cloud-hosted virtual desktop infrastructure, compared to around a third (31%) of financial institutions (Kaspersky Labs, 2017).

Fraud is also a costly and concerningly common threat to banks. Financial fraud has affected as many as seven out of ten banks, and it is costly when it occurs. The average financial fraud loss per incident for a consumer customer is $1,446, rising to $10,312 for business customers. It does not end there, either. Overall, 59% of banks anticipate an increase in financial fraud losses over the next three years, highlighting the need for more robust and effective security solutions (Kaspersky Labs, 2017).

An FMI needs a framework that specifies cyber resilience and risk tolerance to analyse, minimise, and control its cyber risks effectively to achieve its goals and continue functioning successfully. In order to make sure that the business is adhering to its declared cyber-resilience plan, the FMI should support this structure. The architecture for cyber resilience should achieve objectives for financial stability while maintaining the profitability, efficacy, and sustainability of its customer-facing services. The FMI's cyber-resilience framework must be periodically checked and revised to remain relevant.

Regulators anticipate that banks' specific cybersecurity policies and frameworks for risk management and information security will address cyber risk. It also involves routinely checking and monitoring information security, business continuity, incident response, and recovery planning policies. The latter implies taking ownership of and responsibility for risk (Bank for International Settlements, 2019).

Centralised financial services might become unavailable in the event of an all-out assault. Cyberattacks are defined by the fact that the perpetrator, a hacker, intends to do damage, steal data, or engage in extortion. The perpetrator is often relentless and erratic, making it more difficult for the assaulted to protect themselves. Authorities and other players in the financial system are paying a growing amount of attention to cyber dangers since financial institutions have been subjected to severe cyberattacks in recent years (Roszbach, 2017).

Regardless of the threats caused by infrastructure, banks acknowledge that their customers may be the weakest link in their IT security (63% of banks believe this). Banks recognise the importance of customer communication in preventing online fraud. Customers will be encouraged to use security software on their devices by 35% of banks, and customers will be risk-assessed by a third (32%) of banks (Kaspersky Labs, 2017). The following are nine prevalent methods used for cybercrime within the financial infrastructure:

1. **DDoS:** Distributed denial of Services, an attempt to deplete finite resources, take advantage of flaws in software design or implementation, or take advantage of a lack of infrastructure capacity. In the financial services sector, DDoS assaults increased by 30% between 2019 and 2020 (Kost, 2022). DDoS attacks primarily target stock markets and the settlement system. DNS tunnelling, rebinding attacks, Phantom domain attacks, Cache poisoning, DNS hijacking, and Domain lock-up are among the most common DNS assaults.

2. **Local File Inclusion–SQL Injections–Cross-Site Scripting–OGNL Java Injections:** According to Akamai's findings, 94% of financial services attacks used one of four techniques: Local File Inclusion (LFI), SQL Injection (SQLi), Cross-Site Scripting (XSS), and OGNL Java Injection (which accounted for more than 8 million attempts during this reporting period). Years after remedies were provided for OGNL Java Injection, which acquired prominence due to the Apache Struts vulnerability, it is still being utilised by attackers (Akamai, 2019).

3. **Ransomware:** During a ransomware attack, cybercriminals encrypt victims' computers with malware, locking them out. Only by paying a ransom can the damage be undone. Ransomware criminals use a

variety of tactics to persuade victims to pay a ransom. Until a ransom is paid, the most prevalent tactic is to publish larger quantities of confiscated critical material on criminal forums. Unfortunately, these extortion tactics are very successful against financial institutions, whose tight laws need a more robust defence against cyberattacks and data breaches. As ransomware assaults approach the area of data breaches, a successful attack might have significant repercussions for regulatory compliance (Kost, 2022).

4. **Phishing:** Phishing is a kind of social engineering that deceives individuals into divulging their login credentials to access an internal system. Email phishing is the most prevalent kind of phishing, in which victims receive an email posing as legitimate communication. Any interaction with the infected links or files in a phishing email may result in installing malware or activating a phoney website that gathers user credentials. These scam emails appear very convincing to the unsuspecting recipient, mainly when delivered with a feeling of urgency (Kost, 2022).

5. **Supply Chain Attacks:** A compromised third-party vendor compromises the target's supply chain during a supply chain assault. Cyberattackers can bypass security safeguards by gaining access to a target's sensitive resources via a third-party vendor, which allows them to circumvent security controls. Because vendors, on average, take cybersecurity less seriously than their customers, it is far simpler to compromise them; and because third-party vendors keep sensitive data for all of their clients, a single breach might impact hundreds of firms. Financial institutions should implement a Zero Trust Architecture with specific Privileged Access Management policies to protect against supply chain risks (Kost, 2022).

6. **State-Sponsored Attacks:** Nation-state assaults carried out by foreign governments, state-sponsored attacks carried out by connected cybercriminal gangs, and Advanced Persistent Threats (APTs) conducted by competent APT groups are three significant threats to the financial sector. Many of the same attack vectors used by less capable threat actors, such as phishing and ransomware, are used by these threat actors but with higher technical capacity and financing (Özarslan, 2022).

7. **Cloud Providers:** To save money on data storage, many banks store information in the cloud. If these servers are not secure, the banks may lose crucial data if destructive malware is installed and erases data. Unsecured cloud providers may also source a massive data leak, putting users at risk of identity theft and other privacy issues (Cisomag, 2020).

8. **Data Theft and Manipulation:** Criminals may make minor changes to data that are not immediately detected in some cyberattacks.

Employees may not recognise the attack because nothing is stolen at the time. Once criminals access this information, they can alter the system's algorithms for financial gain (Cisomag, 2020).

9. **Insider Threats:** Many security issues are attributable to insider threats provided by existing or recently departed employees, as well as unwitting staff blunders, regardless of the sophisticated means malevolent actors use to access an organisation's network (Özarslan, 2022).

Cyber resilience is critical in the finance sector as the industry is heavily reliant on technology to support its operations, transactions, and data management. Financial institutions are responsible for managing and safeguarding vast amounts of sensitive data, including personal and financial information of their customers. Any disruption to their services, or breach of sensitive data, can have severe consequences for public trust, economic stability, and the financial system as a whole.

The importance of cyber resilience in the finance sector can be summarised as follows:

Protection of sensitive data: Financial institutions are responsible for managing and safeguarding sensitive data, including personal and financial information of their customers. Cyber-resilience measures help to protect this data from cyber threats, such as theft, fraud, or manipulation. Financial institutions should implement robust security measures, such as access controls, encryption, and multi-factor authentication, to ensure the confidentiality, integrity, and availability of sensitive data.

Continuity of operations: Financial institutions are heavily reliant on technology to support their operations, transactions, and data management. Any disruption to these systems can have a significant impact on their ability to provide critical services. Cyber-resilience measures help to ensure continuity of operations by enabling organisations to detect and respond to cyber incidents quickly, and recover from them effectively.

Maintaining public trust: The public expects financial institutions to be reliable and trustworthy. Any disruption to services, or breach of sensitive data, can erode public trust and confidence in these institutions. Cyber-resilience measures help to maintain public trust by ensuring that financial institutions can provide critical services in a timely and effective manner, while protecting sensitive data from cyber threats.

Compliance with regulations: The finance sector is subject to various regulations and standards, such as the Payment Card Industry Data Security Standard (PCI DSS) and the GDPR. Cyber-resilience measures help financial institutions to comply with these regulations by providing a structured approach to managing cyber risks and ensuring the confidentiality, integrity, and availability of sensitive data.

In summary, cyber resilience is critical for the finance sector as financial institutions rely on technology to provide critical services and manage sensitive data. Cyber-resilience measures help to protect sensitive data, ensure continuity of operations, maintain public trust, and comply with regulations. Financial institutions should prioritise the development and implementation of cyber-resilience measures to ensure they can effectively respond to cyber threats and protect their critical services.

4.5 CASE STUDIES

4.5.1 Case 1: Bitmart

On 4 December 2021, a severe security vulnerability at crypto trading firm BitMart gave hackers access to $200 million in assets. Two of its well-known Ethereum (ETH) wallets and the Binance smart chain (BSC) were impacted by the security lapse caused by a stolen private key. By compensating victims, BitMart promised to compensate for any losses (Carnegie, 2022). The $200 million worth of cryptocurrency was stolen by thieves using just one private key. It is a piece of cake for a malicious adversary. The cryptocurrency exchange claims that two of its hot wallets were penetrated by hackers who obtained a private key on the ETH blockchain and the BSC (Stealth Labs, 2021). While all of BitMart's other wallets are secure and untouched, a small percentage of their assets were kept in the ETH hot wallet and the compromised BSC hot wallet. BitMart has identified the impacted assets and conducted preliminary security checks to address this problem. The main reason for this security event was a stolen private key that compromised two of their hot wallets. The rest of BitMart's assets were safe and undamaged (Bitmart, 2021).

According to the company, the incident amounted to a substantial security breach, and the attackers stole bitcoin assets worth roughly USD 150 million. Hackers gained access to assets worth $150 million. According to blockchain security company PeckShield, the first to disclose the crime, the actual value of the heist is closer to USD 200 million. The hackers used a decentralised exchange aggregator of 1inch to convert the money they had stolen into ETH. After that, Tornado Cash coins were added to an ETH privacy mixer. The Tornado is a gadget that breaks the on-chain connection between the source and destination addresses, rendering it impossible to track payments (Stealth Labs, 2021).

Identify: The BitMart Risk Control Team discovered a series of strange transactions on 4 December at around 6:30 PM EST. As soon as the Security Team became aware that they had been the target of a significant attack, they took security measures to protect their users and their assets. They started a thorough internal and external investigation in collaboration with security specialists and other experts in the field of digital asset security and investigations. Internal investigations sought to determine the root causes of vulnerabilities to address them quickly. The investigation's preliminary findings showed that the attacker had successfully stolen important private keys from two "hot wallets," or bitcoin wallets that can be accessed online. While the investigation into the event was ongoing, law enforcement officials, partners, and BitMart's security staff were all striving to identify and apprehend those involved (BitMartExchange, 2021).

Protect: The exchange temporarily stopped all deposits and withdrawals after the hack was discovered to limit future damage and address potential system weaknesses. BitMart modified all token deposit addresses, including those for BTC, ETH, and SOL, to close any potential hot wallet vulnerabilities that might still exist. Before beginning any new deposits to BitMart, users were encouraged to log into their accounts and validate their new deposit addresses. BitMart made an effort to communicate openly and honestly throughout this problem without endangering security (BitMartExchange, 2021).

Detect: An improved risk management and security solution were introduced by BitMart. Because big data and machine learning had been used to spot any suspicious activity quickly, user accounts and assets were assumed to be secure. BitMart set up the network security infrastructure for banking and finance. BitMart improved key management procedures and safeguarded the execution of code connected to transactions to increase blockchain security. They improved blockchain security in several additional ways as well. They worked with three top cybersecurity firms to create and enforce stricter legislation. The BitMart Security Team was reorganised to work more closely with external cybersecurity companies like Peckshield and SlowMist to exchange security intelligence and professional guidance on their new security infrastructure and communications. A brand new BitMart Security Response Center is also planned to be built and is expected to be responsible for detecting any strange behaviour and ensuring any potential hazards are responded to quickly and efficiently (BitMartExchange, 2021).

Respond: BitMart disabled any unneeded public endpoints. They also used new policy control runs with parameter integrity checks in a reliable environment. Now available online is BitMart's cutting-edge Single-Sign-On (SSO) authentication integration with the Google Identity system. BitMart also mandated stringent packet filtering down to the Micro-service level and mutual TLS between all API connection routes (BitMartExchange, 2021). Additionally, on 6 December at 8 PM EST, their CEO, Sheldon Xia, hosted an AMA on Telegram to review the security breach, compensation, and how they plan to resume operations. They tried to be approachable (Bitmart, 2021).

Recover: Client data and financial security were always of the highest significance to BitMart. On Tuesday, 7 December, BitMart started accepting ETH deposits and withdrawals after concluding it was secure to do so. On this date, a small quantity of ERC-20 tokens was also returned. The process of carefully assessing and validating the security of each function is currently ongoing. Avalanche, Binance Chain, Bitcoin, Casper Network,

Chia, ETH, Harmony, HecoFi, IoTeX, Internet Computer, Kusama, NEAR Protocol, Platon Network, Polkadot, Polygon, Solana, Stellar, Tether, Tron, VeChain, Filecoin, Litecoin, Apollo, and Dash are some of the mainnet tokens for which BitMart has since enabled deposit and withdrawal. After the event, BitMart promised to cover all asset losses caused by the security breach. All services were currently being worked on to make it possible for it to process any user withdrawal requests safely. The BitMart staff continued to work around the clock to strengthen their security protocols, restore services, and provide dedicated customer support (BitMartExchange, 2021). BitMart paid the victims back with their own money to fix the issue. They also interviewed other project teams to guarantee acceptable solutions, like token swaps. They have committed to safeguarding all user assets (Bitmart, 2021).

Lessons Learned: Since MtGox, centralised bitcoin exchanges have advanced significantly, yet they are still prone to hacking. After suffering a security breach that cost them $196 million in bitcoins, BitMart had to learn this hard. It is required to disable any superfluous public endpoints first. Up to the level of Microservices, each route for an API connection should demand reciprocal TLS and stringent packet filtering. Your identity should be verified using two-factor authentication since it adds a layer of security and a step to the process.

4.5.2 Case 2: Coinbase

Coinbase is among the most significant cryptocurrency exchanges. Coinbase provides its consumers with a platform for online cryptocurrency trading. Coinbase provides comprehensive services, ranging from statistics and analytical data on the values of supported cryptocurrencies to the ability to purchase and sell all cryptocurrencies. Its price feeds are also inputs for oracles, establishing reliable token prices for applications like decentralised finance (DeFi) protocols. It enables more than 73 million registered users and quarterly transactions of over $300 billion.

A white-hat hacker using the alias "Tree of Alpha" on Twitter attracted the attention of Coinbase's leadership after stating that they had discovered a "possibly market-nuking" flaw and were recommending a HackerOne report. HackerOne is a platform that manages bug bounty programmes for businesses such as Coinbase. Tree of Alpha discovered "a weakness in the new Advanced Trading feature that would have permitted a malevolent user to sell BTC or any other cryptocurrency without actually possessing them." This new Coinbase functionality allows users to place orders to trade one cryptocurrency and use the funds to purchase another. After the initial statement sparked alarm in the cryptocurrency world, Tree of Alpha sent a second Twitter stating, "No actual Coinbase systems (cold or otherwise) are affected." After two hours after the initial tweet from Tree of

Alpha, the Coinbase Support Twitter account said that the new Advanced Trading platform would be disabled for technical reasons. Users can only cancel orders that have already been placed, though the service will remain accessible. The Advanced Trading service is restricted to a select clientele (Salt Labs, 2022).

Two hours after the initial tweet from Tree of Alpha, the Coinbase Twitter account said that, for technical reasons, "Trading on Coinbase's new Advanced Trading functionality was suspended." Users will only be able to terminate orders that have already been placed, though the service will remain accessible. The Advanced Trading service is restricted to a select clientele. Coinbase avoided a "potential disaster" as a result of the hacker's prompt actions and the "overwhelming community response." Due to the crucial importance of the transactions on the Coinbase platform, even a minor security concern might have devastating consequences. As a result, Coinbase invests significant work and resources in safeguarding its platform from end to end.

Identify: Coinbase goes through an extensive review process to meet security and compliance requirements. They are the only major crypto exchange to have never been hacked since 2022. They welcome future submissions from researchers via the HackerOne bug bounty program.

Protect: Cryptocurrencies like Bitcoin and ETH are open source, meaning anyone can look at the blockchains they run on. This makes sure that every transaction is correct. Coinbase contains automated price protection circuit breakers, and its trade surveillance staff regularly checks markets for healthy and unusual trading activity. However, this can also make security vulnerabilities noticed by malicious people in some circumstances. Thus, organisations must develop their security teams and communities in this direction.

Detect: White-hat hacker decided to poke around the new Advanced Trading platform to find out how orders are sent and what a successful one looks like. The white-hat hacker conducted a few basic tests and learned they lack proper essential validation checks while those parameters exist in every request. More specifically, he could change the 'product' parameter by hand, but Coinbase's back-end system did not check if the user had the wallets listed in the product. Thus, anyone might initiate a fund transfer from a nonexistent wallet.

Respond: On 11 February 2022, Coinbase learned about a vulnerability in the trading interface through a tip from a third-party researcher. They quickly mobilised their security incident response team to find and fix the flaw. Using HackerOne, Coinbase's bug bounty site, the cryptocurrency researcher reports a vulnerability that pertains to a particular Retail Advanced Trading API. The other user interfaces and Coinbase Exchange APIs are also examined by Coinbase engineers, who conclude that they are unaffected.

Recover: When Coinbase developers reproduce the error, the Retail Advanced Trading interface is switched to a cancel-only mode, which stops new deals. The situation is resolved when a patch is approved and made available. Because of this discovery, Coinbase paid the biggest-ever bug bounty: $250,000.

Lessons Learned: This API security hole if exploited maliciously, may throw millions of users and possibly the entire bitcoin ecosystem in grave danger. Moreover, it might have easily pushed Coinbase out of operation. The cause is partially attributable to short development lifecycles. In the modern era of cloud computing and innovative CI/CD practices, it is simpler than ever for any online business to publish new, highly reliable, and scalable elements within minutes or hours. Sometimes, the pressure to innovate rapidly occurs at the cost of security. As the history of computing – and human behaviour – teaches us, new functionality and capabilities will always be more profitable and indispensable to any business (Salt Labs, 2022). At the same time, rewarding prevention of this flaw has also been an incentive for other white-hat hackers. The ideal course of action for businesses would be to promote independent security research heavily, and when those researchers find significant problems, they would like to make sure that they are compensated appropriately. The Coinbase incident is simply the latest red caution flag for online services and users to ensure they make API security a top priority in protecting their online services.

4.5.3 Case 3: DAO hack

The DAO (distributed autonomous organisation) was a decentralised autonomous organisation that utilised various blockchains to do duties typically handled by a corporation. The system was built to accept directions from its members, who were awarded voting privileges proportional to their ownership stake – roughly equivalent to one share equals one vote. At least US$150 million worth of ether tokens were drained from this system in June 2016 due to a hack, as it was an ambitious project with much potential.

DAO was launched on the ETH blockchain in 2016. Due to code vulnerabilities, after earning $150 million during a token sale, the DAO was compromised. Eventually, the ETH blockchain was hardforked to restore the stolen cash, but not all network participants agreed with this course of action, causing the network to split into two separate blockchains: ETH and ETH Classic. There was a timeline for the token sale, which would run for 28 days. The tokens were to be "locked up" during this time, and after the token sale, the DAO would operate. Three weeks after the token sale began, more than 11,000 people contributed $150 million to the DAO, making it one of the greatest crowdsourcing projects ever. However, numerous observers raised doubts about the DAO's code prior to the conclusion of the token sale. A flaw in the smart contracts of the DAO's wallet might allow a user to empty it. Specifically, computer scientists were concerned about the wallet being depleted by smart contracts. While developers attempted to address the issue, an attacker exploited it and began taking DAO funds.

Several members of the ETH community examined the DAO's code to see how it worked. They found that the DAO's smart contracts contained code that they believed could be exploited to steal funds. Hackers exploited their bug on Thursday morning, 30 May 2016, and drained approximately 13% of ETH's ether supply. At the end of that evening, the ETH developers had fixed their bug, and the ICO process had resumed. The ETH community debated how to react to the attack throughout this time. Not only would the failure of the DAO result in economic losses for participants, but it would also have far-reaching consequences for ETH's young network. Roughly 14% of all ETH in use at the time was in DAO contracts, as it had become such a massively invested initiative. A year after its inception, ETH's innovative technology encountered an existential dilemma. A soft fork was created that returned the stolen funds to the original owners after retrieving the funds from the attacker's DAO. Transactions or contracts already made on ETH would not be affected, but the attacker would not be able to withdraw funds. This was a very novel move in the blockchain world. Through a hard fork, they could undo the DAO hack entirely by changing the underlying code base of ETH.

Identify: Computer scientists feared a flaw in DAO's smart contracts could enable their depletion. While engineers worked to address the issue, an attacker discovered the vulnerability and started syphoning DAO's assets.

Protect: It is essential to realise that this flaw did not originate from ETH itself but rather from a specific ETH-based application. The DAO code contained numerous vulnerabilities, including the recursive call vulnerability.

Detect: DAO.sol contract was being analysed by the attacker when the attacker discovered that the 'splitDAO' function could be exploited via the recursive send pattern. We can use the infinite recursion to move as many funds as we want by getting any function call before this happens to call splitDAO again.

Respond: Vitalik Buterin, the creator of ETH, called for a soft fork of the ETH network, including a single line of code that would effectively denylist the attacker and prevent them from moving the stolen funds. Initially, it was uncertain whether the fork would be executed. Even though ETH developers recommended the change, they lacked the authority to implement it unilaterally.

Recover: Two competing ETH blockchains were created due to the hard fork. Conservatives of the hard split that altered the blockchain's history supported ETH Classic, the prefork version of ETH (ETC). This blockchain, formerly known as ETH, participated in the hard fork, which altered its history and blockchains' general history. Although the DAO's stolen funds were returned to its investors, the criminals were not penalised. In the months after the breach, the stolen tokens remained in their owners' possession on the ETH Classic chain and were worth around $8.3 million in ETC. The ETH hard fork was implemented on block 192,000 on 20 July 2016 as a result of heated debates in public forums.

Lessons Learned: In 2016, smart contracts were a fascinating field. In many cases, communities had only scratched the surface. Clearly, composing a solid and safe smart contract demands tremendous diligence. In reality, developing a secure smart contract is more comparable to writing code for a nuclear power plant than writing standard web code. All DAO users could see its code online (as is customary with smart contracts and blockchain applications), and days before the attack, the DAO creators themselves pointed out that they had found the problem and would fix it. The attack was already underway before they could do this. The attack illustrates some of the dangers of using such new technologies, where minor coding errors can have disastrous effects. These risks are often discussed because it is nearly impossible to create an error-free application, so smart contracts have inherent vulnerabilities. Even though regulation would counteract the decentralised nature of blockchains and their applications, questions arise regarding how the following hack will be handled and who will make that decision. Despite the technology's infancy, regulators are also working hard to determine how blockchain fits within the existing legal framework. As a result, regulators are unlikely to create and impose regulations until a complete understanding of the technology can be arrived at.

4.5.4 Case 4: Wormhole token hack

A Wormhole is a decentralised, cross-chain message-passing protocol (Chainalysis, 2022). It allows applications to send messages from one chain to another (Extropy, 2022). The network is run by a decentralised group of nineteen Guardians who sign each transmitted message to testify its authenticity. The protocol uses a multi-party signature system where a message is treated as authentic if ⅔+ of the Guardians have signed it (Yakovenko, 2017). The Portal is a token bridge built on top of the Wormhole network. The Portal allows participants to deposit funds into a contract on a source chain and then mint a Wormhole-wrapped version of the token on a destination chain. The minting process needs a Wormhole-authenticated message from the source chain contract. This check guarantees that Wormhole-wrapped tokens are backed 1:1 by tokens in the source chain contract (Wormhole, 2022).

The Guardians are also liable for governing the Wormhole network. Upgrades to the protocol and contracts require a ⅔+ supermajority vote of Guardians (Wormhole, 2022). A blockchain bridge, also known as a cross-chain bridge, joins two blockchains and enables the transfer of bitcoin between them. If it owns bitcoin and wishes to spend it similarly to ETH, we can facilitate this through the bridge. These blockchains mint various coins and perform on different rules; the bridge acts as a neutral zone so users can smoothly swap between one and the other. Access to multiple blockchains through the same network improves the crypto experience for most of us (Liquid, 2021). Wormhole node operators temporarily stopped relaying messages from on-chain contracts to prevent further exploits, then upgraded the contract to fix the vulnerability. Jump Crypto has recapitalised the contract to ensure that all Wormhole-wrapped Ether on every chain is fully backed. At 13:29 UTC, 3 February 2022, the Wormhole network was restored to entire operations. The incident lasted approximately 16 hours.

Identify: Wormhole is a decentralised, cross-chain message-passing protocol. It allows applications to send messages from one chain to another. The network is run by a decentralised group of 19 Guardians who sign each transmitted message to testify its authenticity. The transaction submitted by the attacker was shown to contain the guardians' valid signatures.

Protect: The contributors set up a "war room" conference call. Wormhole contributors from Jump Crypto, an auditor from Neodyme, and other trusted external researchers participated in the call. The Wormhole Guardians running the network were in contact. Multiple third-party auditing companies and internal peer reviews confirmed the bug conclusively. A contract upgrade governance proposal was circulated to Guardians for their approval. Simulations and testing of the fix were conducted in parallel to expedite the process. The Guardian had approved a plan to safely bring the node back online and vote for governance.

Detect: An undetected attacker exploited a vulnerability in the Solana-side Wormhole contract and fooled it into minting 120,000 uncollateralised Wormhole-wrapped ETH (weETH) (Rekt, 2022). During a routine review, Wormhole contributors noticed the anomaly in outstanding funds and quickly investigated.

Respond: To communicate with the attacker, a $10 million deal was offered in exchange for returning the stolen funds. Neodyme built and tested a prototype to use the exploit as a fallback upgrade plan. Due to the possibility of the fastest possible fix, the contributors decided to apply this plan.

Recover: The vulnerability has been fixed. A new fraudulent Wormhole message could not be created at this point. Although the attacker had already prepared several other Wormhole messages as part of the original exploit, they had been able to steal additional funds. The team continued addressing this problem and maintained frequent communications with Wormhole network community members. In addition to addressing this problem, the team frequently communicated with community members of the Wormhole network. 120k ETH has been supplied by Jump Crypto, restoring total collateral. A portal bridge and the Wormhole network were reconnected. Wormhole's official account sent out a tweet informing the community that the network had been restored.

Lessons Learned: The Wormhole contract's signature verification code contained a bug that facilitated the exploit. Through this bug, the attacker could mint Wormhole-wrapped Ether using a message forged by the Guardians (Kudelski Security, 2022). The vulnerability has been fixed by adding the following check. Wormhole's roadmap must contain several components enhancing cross-chain messaging and bridging security. These components follow:

- Risk-isolating accounting technique for individual chains
- Dynamic risk management
- Continuous monitoring and early event detection.

Also, selected audit firms must schedule comprehensive and ongoing audits of the Wormhole code base before the incident. The community must take the necessary steps to launch a formal bug bounty program. No matter the future of DeFi, the road there will be difficult and dangerous, regardless of whether it will be cross-chain or multi-chain. Despite all the damage, every exploit teaches us how to secure a rapidly evolving ecosystem.

4.5.5 Case 5: EnergoBank

In just 14 minutes, Russian hackers drastically altered a currency exchange rate. Bloomberg reports that a group of Russian hackers manipulated the ruble's value against the dollar using the Corkow Trojan software, citing an interview with Group IB, the firm that examined the issue. According to the study, the virus that infiltrated Energobank in February 2015 led hackers to purchase over $500 million "at non-market rates." The move caused the ruble's exchange rate to rise from 55 to 66 rubles per dollar before settling back down. Surprisingly, the hackers were not thought to have benefitted from the attack since they did not sell any currency while rates changed. However, according to Bloomberg, Group IB believes it was a proof-of-concept in preparation for a future hack. Nevertheless, Energobank is said to have attempted to declare losses of 244 million rubles ($3.2 million) due to the deals. According to Group IB, the Corkow Trojan is one of the more advanced tools hackers can employ to investigate high-profile cybercrimes and cyber-theft. It may even potentially attack PCs that are not connected to the Internet. To accomplish this, the Trojan detects that it is connected to a local enterprise network and infects it by worming its way through internal connections between those machines. In the long run, this gives the attacker access to offline computers (Reisinger, 2016).

Identify: After examining the day's currency trading, Russia's central bank and the Moscow Exchange identified the attack. According to Bloomberg, while the Moscow Exchange confirmed that it had not been hacked, the central bank asserts that it has found no proof of market manipulation. Instead, the central bank believes erroneous trades caused the giant swings. In any case, Group IB believes the hack was significant enough to alter the ruble-dollar exchange rate (Reisinger, 2016). As part of the case investigation, the security firm Group IB determined that the Metel Hacking group penetrated Kazan-based Energobank, using the Corkow Trojan to place over $500 million in non-market orders. The threat actors employed spear-phishing messages with malicious links to hacking the victims' accounts. The attack's economic damage has been assessed at 244 million rubles ($3.2 million). According to Kaspersky, the organisation used the malware Metel (aka Corkow) to target a Russian bank and infect bank networks using spear-phishing emails (Paganini, 2016). Corkow is a backdoor that has infiltrated 250,000 systems in over 100 financial institutions worldwide. Criminals utilise a drive-by downloads approach to propagate the Corkow virus, infecting victims when accessing compromised websites. Hackers employ the "Nitris Exploit Kit" (formerly known as CottonCastle) exploit, which is not open source and is only offered to trusted customers. Criminals exploited a variety of sites to distribute the Trojan, including mail tracking services, news portals, electronic books, computer graphics resources, and music portals. Criminals aim their attacks for maximum publicity, not just corporate websites, as seen by the wide range of websites exploited during the campaign (Group IB, 2019).

Protect: The attack was conducted with the Corkow malware, also known as Metel, which has modules specific to Russian trading sites. These trading platforms can be accessed remotely through 153 Corkow. On 18 September 2014, 154 fraudsters exploited a vulnerability in the system and installed the Trojan, which was continually updated to prevent detection by the bank's antivirus software, which was otherwise operational. According to Group IB, no antivirus software could detect Corkow version v.7.118.1.1 in March 2015. After that, the data collection phase began, and keyloggers were turned on in December 2014. Remote access was eventually acquired on 27 February 2015, and trade orders were sent. Finally, 14 minutes after the first order was placed, the fraudsters attempted to remove Corkow from the trading system and erase all evidence of its previous activity (Neyret, 2020). Banks did not have a chance to intercept the malware. The intruders erased it. Also, banks could not detect malware in the system after the attack by IB Group and Kaspersky. They look at the anomaly in the financial market and investigate it.

Detect: Metel (also known as Corkow) is a banking Trojan identified in 2011 and used to attack online banking system customers. The Metel gang began aggressively targeting banks and financial institutions in 2015

(Kaspersky, 2016). The malware is modular, so its capabilities can be altered depending on the attack's goal. Remote access and password stealing are two capabilities that appear to fit the attack on Energobank's strategy (Muncaster, 2016). Following infection, thieves use legitimate and pentesting tools to migrate laterally, obtaining passwords from their initial victims (entry points) to acquire access to computers within the firm that has access to money transactions. The gang was able to pull off a brilliant trick by automating the rollback of ATM transactions with this level of access. This means that money can be taken from ATMs using debit cards while the cards' balances remain unchanged, allowing for many transactions at different ATMs (Kaspersky, 2016). Organisations should employ System Watcher, which contains the BSS (Behavior Stream Signatures) module, to increase their level of protection (Kaspersky, 2016).

Respond: First, institutions act transparently and accept the attack to respond. In this case, hackers cannot obtain any profit from that attack. Institutions were lucky that hackers only tested the malware. Experts from Group IB stated, "You cannot just withdraw and grab money from a bank or broker; you must learn how to transfer dollars to your account. This is a difficult operation, and you are more likely to be caught if you proceed in this manner: you cannot create a stock account without presenting identification, and money must still be transmitted to the bank." All of this results in the conclusion that hacking attacks on the financial markets are a serious but modest concern. Insiders who utilise their position to provide data that offers them a trading edge are far more difficult to dismiss than outsiders who are "outside the system" (SudoNull, 2016). Financial statements are still safe thanks to the ledger and settlement systems implemented in transactions. In such attacks, it is not easy to find malware and erase it. EnergoBank should cut the all-financial transactions and restore the last solid dataset to protect financial statements.

Recover: In this case, there is no need to recover the system because hackers believed in erasing the malware. Nevertheless, the system must be controlled by system watchers and try to find any other malware that was undetected. Also, how that malware can get into the system should be investigated and prevented.

Lessons Learned: Hackers who use sophisticated and unique products to interfere with the systems intelligence services should investigate possible threats. A ledger and settlement system is the key to protecting financial assets. For the continuity of services, financial institutions should work with third-party experts to detect newly risen threats like Corkow. Also, all software versions should be updated to previous versions; most banks use outdated software solutions. Instead, depending entirely on endpoint antivirus solutions, email attachments should be verified in a different environment (sandbox). Setting up notifications from security systems and responding to them immediately is vital. Using security information and event management (SIEM) systems, security systems must be watched by a security operations centre (SOC). Multi-Factor authentication should be used to access. Internal network security should be strengthened. Financial institutions can prevent malware from downloading into the system with all those measures. Detecting malware in the system is much more complicated than preventing it from the system.

4.5.6 Case 6: Robinhood data breach

On 8 November 2021, Robinhood's commission-free investing application announced it experienced a data security incident through social engineering. Robinhood is classified as an A-class security firm, according to UpGuard (UpGuard, 2021).

Seven million subscribers are affected. Most persons affected had their identities and email addresses disclosed. Only 300 individuals' names, birth dates, and ZIP codes were disclosed. About ten clients' "more extensive account information" was compromised (Brown, 2021). Robinhood published a blog entry to notify its community. On the evening of 3 November, Robinhood encountered a data security issue. A small amount of private information pertaining to a subset of Robinhood's customers was accessed by an unapproved third party. According to their inquiry, Robinhood believes that no debit card, social security numbers, bank account numbers, or data were revealed, and no consumers have incurred a financial loss due to the event. The unauthorised user used the telephone to socially engineer a customer service agent and gain access to many customer support systems. Caleb Sima, chief security officer of Robinhood, stated, "As a Safety-First organisation, we owe it to our clients to be honest, and transparent." "After a thorough investigation, notifying the whole Robinhood community of this event is the proper course of action" (RobinHood, 2021).

According to insider news, the hackers requested a ransom payment (the firm did not reply to Insider's questions about whether it paid or plans to pay the ransom). Also, other hackers targeted Robinhood users last year, successfully accessing about 2,000 of its customers' trading accounts (Sonnemaker, 2021).

Following the discovery of the data breach, Robinhood's after-hours share price declined by approximately 3%. In reaction to a data breach on 3 November, Robinhood was struck with a class-action lawsuit in California Northern District Court. The lawsuit claims that Robinhood failed to protect current and previous customers' personal information from hackers, putting them in danger of identity theft for the rest of their lives.

Identify: On the evening of 3 November 2021, Robinhood's security team discovered a third party's unauthorised access to consumers' personal information. After holding the intrusion under control. The intruders demanded a ransom payment. Consequently, Robinhood informed law enforcement and began investigating the source of the breach with the help of outside cybersecurity firm Maidant. Having investigated the cyberattack's origin with law enforcement and Maidant. Robinhood asserted that the attackers exploited the phone to socially engineer a customer support agent and get access to multiple customer support systems. Robinhood announced nothing about whether they would pay the ransom fee to save the leaked data. According to Robinhood's blog post, the attacker could have simply exfiltrated millions of records during the data breach window or had the authorisation to do so. The trading platform indicates that the blackmail request was made after the security flaw was fixed. The trading platform will notify any affected individuals (Ikeda, 2021).

Protect: As soon as Robinhood's security team identified attacks, the firm contained third-party access to its servers. After starting to investigate whether there is a data leak or not? When the data pipeline to the attackers had been cut off, they demanded an extortion fee for data. As a result of that demand, Robinhood informed law enforcement to find attackers. Attackers have the email and passwords of 7 million users. Hence, Robinhood informed its community to use multi-factor authentication and change their passwords with a much stronger and remarkably different one. The blog announced that breach Robinhood shows how to keep accounts secure for its customers. "If you are a client looking for account security information, please click Help Center > My Account & Login > Account Security. When unsure, log in to view Robinhood messages—we will never include a link to your account in a risk notice" (RobinHood, 2021).

Detect: Robinhood started working with Maidant to ensure the security of its servers. Also, published forward-looking statements to detect threats beforehand. Once again advised them to use multi-factor authentication. Using that technique, security breaches can be detected easily. Restructuring the cyber security response team to counteract attacks. Also, that kind of leak can be caused by insider threats. Robinhood must ensure they have the right tools and plans to spot any unusual behaviour. HR plays a critical role in detecting insider threats since they have contextual data that can assist the firm in identifying who is in danger. Establish a whistleblower policy and collaborate with other departments. People with access to your most valuable assets should be closely monitored (Adams, 2020). John McClurg, senior vice president and chief information security officer of BlackBerry, states, "Using artificial intelligence-driven preventative tools, businesses may avoid data breaches and ransomware assaults in advance." Although the breach was ostensibly contained, exposed consumer information such as full names, ZIP codes, and birth dates can aid future assaults, such as phishing emails. By preventing cyberattackers during the exploitation phase, organisations can increase their resilience and protect the security of their customers and workers' data (Henriquez, 2021).

Respond: The Robinhood community informed customers about the breach and showed the precautions. Maidant and Law Enforcement got involved. Lisa Forte, a cybersecurity expert and partner at Red Goat Cyber Security, believes that Employee education on how to recognise and prevent social engineering assaults will help organisations combat these expanding dangers in the long run, but it is not a silver bullet, according to Forte. These strategies are deceptive and rely on human weaknesses to break organisational defences. As a result, robust processes should always be accompanied by education and awareness. Training is critical, but strong technical defences and procedures must accompany it. "On top of that, 'higher risk roles,' such as finance, HR, and executives, require more in-depth training because their positions are more likely to be targeted with sophisticated social engineering due to the access they have" (Paul, 2021).

Recover: Cutting the data pipeline to the intruders and containing the breach after being offered a ransom payment, contacting law enforcement to save data. Having an expert opinion from Maidant to prevent further attacks. Alerting the customer to take evasive action.

Lessons Learned: A regularly based security investigation is crucial to discover that kind of intrusion. Robinhood has been late to find the breach. It is too late to respond because 7+ million customers' data have been stolen. Educate all the teams about cybersecurity and ensure they know social engineering methods and threats. Robinhood failed to do so and caused that incident. Also, there are insider threats that can cause the same damage. Robinhood needs to create a network with the HR department to monitor its employee's behaviour. Multi-factor authentication should be mandatory, not optional. The incident happened on 3 November 2021 when Robinhood informed its customers on 8 November 2021. In those five days, customers were left vulnerable. Firms need to act quickly and be more transparent. Working with outside security experts can flourish the security infrastructure.

4.5.7 Case 7: Diebold Nixdorf

Diebold, headquartered in Canton, Ohio, controls approximately 35% of the global ATM business and is currently the leading provider in the United States. Additionally, the 35,000-person company develops software and point-of-sale systems utilised by numerous other retailers (Krebs, 2020). The American ATM manufacturer Diebold Nixdorf had "a brief IT systems disruption" on 25 April 2020, resulting from a ransomware assault. The attack had no impact on the company's ATMs, customer network, or the general public, but a system automatically dispatched field service technicians impacted (Rolfe, 2020).

Identify: On 25 April, the company was targeted by a ransomware attack that affected over 100 customers, as first reported by Krebsonsecurity.

Diebold Nixdorf, the most significant ATM supplier in the US, is considered to have a 35% market share worldwide. The corporation said that its ATMs, customer networks, and the general public were unaffected but that its system for automating requests for field maintenance technicians was (Rolfe, 2020). Businesses must safeguard their hardware and software assets against ransomware assaults. These are frequently the entrance points from which criminal actors launch ransomware assaults. The ATM and customer network of the organisation do not appear to have been harmed by this malware assault. Diebold has assessed that the malware's spread has been halted, the company claimed in a statement given to KrebsOnSecurity. The incident did not affect customer networks, ATMs, or the general public, and its effect on our business was negligible (Krebs, 2020).

Protect: Network segmentation can successfully shield IT systems from ransomware threats. It entails designing more compact subnets that are only partially interconnected to one another within a more extensive network. Network segmentation controls network flows across different subnets and restricts the attacker's lateral mobility to prevent unauthorised users from accessing the organisation's data and intellectual property (Packetlabs, 2021). Diebold Nixdorf appears to have accomplished this. The attack impacted a system that automates requests for field service technicians but did not impact customer networks, ATMs, or the general public (Krebs, 2020). "This serves as a reminder that ransomware may affect organisations of any size and technical prowess," says Erich Kron, advocate for security awareness at security training organisation KnowBe4. Diebold was lucky to have segregated its network in this instance, minimising the harm to the business network and saving other vital network systems and consumer effects. Kron noted that ransomware has persisted throughout the outbreak. "As a result, enterprises must ensure they are prepared for assaults of this nature by training people to recognise and report phishing attempts, the most typical method ransomware spreads, and by having effective endpoint protection and backups in place," he suggested. Consequently, employees and other users must regularly be trained on corporate cybersecurity policies and procedures (Riley, 2020). Data availability and regular backups help lessen the effects of ransomware. A routinely backed-up data set should always be kept offline. Regular backups tested and protected are crucial for a swift and effortless recovery from ransomware outbreaks. Secure backups should be kept online to prevent the system from being erased by ransomware or attackers. In the Respond section, we will examine how this protection is performed for Diebold Nixdorf. The businesses must determine the external information systems that connect to essential business operations and resources. How to contact partners in the case of a ransomware attack should be planned, and it may be necessary to disengage from external services temporarily. The businesses must decide which operations must always be maintained to be profitable. This could involve keeping a website running to collect payments, securely storing patient or customer information, or ensuring your business's data is always correct and accessible (Computer Security Resource Center, 2022).

Detect: To recognise the unusual activity, such as illegal entities and behaviours in networks and the physical environment, it is necessary to create and test methodologies and procedures. Larger or more complex organisations should buy and incorporate SIEM solutions with various sources and sensors to enhance network visibility, aid in the early detection of ransomware, and better understand how ransomware can spread throughout a network. These instruments must generate and record logs. Logs are essential for detecting irregularities in software and computers because they record communication channels and events, such as accounts and system modifications. Utilising software solutions that can collect these logs and search for out-of-the-ordinary network behaviour is essential. Brian Krebs reported that on Saturday, 25 April 2020, late at night, the Diebold Company's security staff discovered suspicious activity in its internal network. After suspecting a ransomware attack, Diebold started removing systems from that network right away to prevent the infection from spreading, according to the business (Guenni, 2020). Infrastructure needs to be watched over frequently. When harmful or suspicious activity is discovered on the network, detection mechanisms that set off alerts should be set up, and applications should be used to start the proper reaction. Identifying the ransomware variant is essential. Understanding any potential activities the ransomware may have performed and determining what cleanup steps need to be taken will be made more straightforward. Knowing the type of infection will also help identify a decryption key for encrypted data if a public file is accessible. The investigation revealed that the attackers used ProLock ransomware, which was once known as PwndLocker but changed its moniker in March after addressing a vulnerability that permitted the production of a free decryptor. The ransomware encrypts data on the victim's computer while appending ProLock to the filename. The infected must then pay a ransom to obtain a decryption key. Utilising malicious BMP files, the infection is disseminated (Rolfe, 2020).

Respond: To prevent the further spread of ransomware attacks, it should be a top priority to disconnect and isolate all affected devices from the network immediately. Diebold, anticipating a ransomware attack, quickly began unplugging systems on that network to prevent the malware's spread. To safeguard information confidentiality, availability, and integrity, businesses must manage their information and records (data) per their risk strategy. They must disengage from the network as necessary to secure critical data. Further research indicated that the attackers intended to install ProLock ransomware on the organisation's networks. This ransomware attack was contained by the company's prompt disconnection of business network systems. Diebold Nixdorf stated that although they did not pay any ransom, approximately one hundred customers were temporarily inconvenienced owing to the incident (Etbfsi, 2020). "Once we identified the issue, we promptly restored service to the most significantly affected systems. We also quickly contacted law enforcement and hired a prominent cybersecurity firm." the corporation said in an email statement (Kovacs, 2020).

Recover: Recovery requires effective communication. In order to make sure that everyone involved receives the information they need without spreading false information, recovery plans should carefully consider what, how, and when to release information about the ransomware incident to different stakeholders. It could be essential to communicate with internal and external stakeholders. "Diebold has assessed that the malware's spread has been halted," the company claimed in a statement given to KrebsOnSecurity. The incident did not affect customer networks, ATMs, or the general public, and its effect on our business was negligible (Krebs, 2020). Once the incident is under control and the virus has been completely eradicated, all parties should be involved, and things should return to normal. Much like reacting, planning for contingencies far in advance of an event is the first step in recovering from ransomware incidents. Businesses in this situation should have plans to patch vulnerabilities and bring back system functionality. Focus on procedures for determining the ransomware incident's impact, contacting the appropriate parties, and acting quickly to mitigate the problem (Computer Security Resource Center, 2022). "As soon as we identified the issue, we could immediately restore access to the most affected systems. We also immediately contacted law enforcement and a renowned cyber security firm." stated an email from the company to Security Week (Guenni, 2020).

Lessons Learned: In ransomware assaults, it is critical to act quickly. Guaranteed remedies had to be put into action right away. If Diebold had not promptly disconnected the systems on this network to stop the malware's propagation, it is possible that it could have done so. As previously stated, network segmentation is a powerful tool for defending IT systems against ransomware assaults. In many ways, network segmentation increases the security of our system. Diebold Nixdorf implemented this to stop the problem from spreading to ATMs. We know that Diebold called a cybersecurity company and swiftly resumed service to the affected systems. Additionally, they stated that they provided information to police enforcement (Kovacs, 2020). All this suggests that it would be better to be transparent about ransomware attacks. Being transparent on this issue will be very beneficial both at the point of restoration and in terms of taking quick action and explaining the attack to the relevant teams. If we are afraid and try not to announce the attack, this may increase the cost of the ransom or cause the software to spread further. Diebold personally connected with customers, reassuring them and keeping things from escalating. In such events, customers can be frightened and worried. Contacting the company will address their concerns. It will also prevent frightened users from using the malware unknowingly. Abrams of BleepingComputer stated that the timing of Diebold's attack – Saturday evening – is exceptionally typical and that ransomware distributor typically waits until the weekend to start attacks, as this is when most firms have the least number of technical employees available. The great majority of ATM skimming assaults also occur on weekends for the same reason (Abrams, 2020). Abrams stated that Friday and Saturday nights after hours are famous for ransomware attacks since the perpetrators want to launch the malware while no one is there. Several ransomware groups began obtaining sensitive data from victims before releasing ransomware as a virtual club to use against individuals who did not pay the ransom demand promptly. In order to threaten to disclose or sell data if targets refuse to pay, attackers may equip themselves with data about the victim or the victim company's partners or clients. In actuality, numerous significant ransomware gangs engage in this conduct, publishing blogs on the Internet and the dark web with identities and data collected without the victims' consent.

Diebold reported that no private information was taken. However, businesses occasionally try to conceal their payments. The fundamental difficulty here is that stolen or encrypted data could significantly exacerbate future difficulties. The issue can be fixed if there is a backup of the encrypted data. Backups, however, might also be encrypted in specific circumstances. Data theft can result in severe sanctions and reputational damage. On the other hand, encrypted data can make it difficult for businesses to conduct business and harm their reputation with customers. According to Bleeping Computer, hackers demanded ransoms ranging from $175,000 to $660,000 for the PwndLocker attacks that recently attacked several public and private businesses in the United States and other nations. PwndLocker was recently renamed ProLock after the cybersecurity company Emsisoft developed a method that allows customers to restore their files without paying a ransom (Abrams, 2020).

REFERENCES

Abrams, L. (2020). *New PwndLocker Ransomware Targeting US Cities*, Enterprises. [Çevrimiçi] Available at: https://www.bleepingcomputer.com/news/security/new-pwndlocker-ransomware-targeting-us-cities-enterprises/ [Accessed 10 June 2022].

Adams, D., (2020). *Digit News*. [Online] Available at: https://www.digit.fyi/the-insider-threats-an-interview-with-cybersecurity-expert-lisa-forte [Accessed 13 April 2022].

Akamai, (2019). *akamai.com*. [Online] Available at: https://www.akamai.com/newsroom/press-release/state-of-the-internet-security-financial-services-attack-economy [Accessed 22 April 2022].

Asmundson, I., (2011). *What Are Financial Services*. s.l.: s.n.

Bank for International Settlements, (2016). *bis.org*. [Online] Available at: https://www.bis.org/cpmi/publ/d146.pdf [Accessed 25 April 2022].

Bank for International Settlements, (2019). *bis.org*. [Online] Available at: https://www.bis.org/fsi/fsisummaries/cyber_resilience.pdf [Accessed 21 April 2022].

Bitmart, (2021). *BitMart Security Breach Update*. [Çevrimiçi] Available at: https://support.bitmart.com/hc/en-us/articles/4411998987419-BitMart-Security-Breach-Update [Accessed 10 June 2022].

BitMartExchange, (2021). *BitMart Bolster Security and Restore Promptly After the Challenge*. [Çevrimiçi] Available at: https://bitmart-exchange.medium.com/bitmart-bolster-security-and-restore-promptly-after-the-challenge-4e605f6d852d [Accessed 10 June 2022].

BitSight, (2019). *BitSight*. [Online] Available at: https://www.bitsight.com/sites/default/files/migration/documents/BitSight%2520CEFPRO%2520Report%2520-%2520Third-Party%2520Cyber%2520Risk%2520Financial%2520Services.pdf [Accessed 20 April 2022].

Brown, S., (2021). *CNET*. [Online] Available at: https://www.cnet.com/news/privacy/robinhood-data-breach-is-bad-but-weve-seen-much-worse/ [Accessed 12 April 2022].

Carnegie, (2022). *Timeline of Cyber Incidents Involving Financial Institutions*. [Çevrimiçi] Available at: https://carnegieendowment.org/specialprojects/protectingfinancialstability/timeline [Accessed 10 June 2022].

Chainalysis, (2022). *Lessons from the Wormhole Exploit*. [Online] Available at: https://blog.chainalysis.com/reports/wormhole-hack-february-2022/ [Accessed 10 April 2022].

Cisomag, (2020). *cisomag.eccouncil.org*. [Online] Available at: https://cisomag.eccouncil.org/cyberthreats-financial-service-providers/ [Accessed 21 April 2022].

Computer Security Resource Center, (2022). *Getting Started with Cybersecurity Risk Management | Ransomware*. [Çevrimiçi] Available at: https://csrc.nist.gov/csrc/media/Publications/white-paper/2022/02/24/getting-started-with-cybersecurity-risk-management-ransomware/final/documents/quick-start-guide--ransomware.pdf [Accessed 10 June 2022].

Conference Board of Canada, (2018). *Building Cyber Resilience*. Ottawa: Conference Board of Canada.

Etbfsi, (2020). *Diebold Nixdorf: ATM Manufacturer Diebold Nixdorf Affected by a Ransomware Attack*. [Çevrimiçi] Available at: https://bfsi.economictimes.indiatimes.com/news/blockchain/atm-manufacturer-diebold-nixdorf-affected-by-a-ransomware-attack/75733177 [Accessed 10 June 2022].

European Central Bank, (2018). *www.ecb.europa.eu*. [Online] Available at: https://www.ecb.europa.eu/paym/pdf/cons/cyberresilience/Cyber_resilience_oversight_expectations_for_financial_market_infrastructures.pdf [Accessed 18 August 2022].

Extropy, I.O., (2022). *Solana's Wormhole Hack Post-Mortem Analysis*. [Online] Available at: https://extropy-io.medium.com/solanas-wormhole-hack-post-mortem-analysis-3b68b9e88e13 [Accessed 11 April 2022].

Group IB, (2019). *Analysis of Attacks Against Trading and Bank Card Systems*. Central Region, Singapore: Group IB.

Guenni, (2020). *Diebold Nixdorf Victim of a Ransomware Attack*. [Çevrimiçi] Available at: https://borncity.com/win/2020/05/12/ransomware-bei-diebold-nixdorf/ [Accessed 10 June 2022].

Henriquez, M., (2021). *Security Magazine*. [Online] Available at: https://www.securitymagazine.com/articles/96492-robinhood-data-breach-impacts-seven-million-users [Accessed 13 April 2022].

Hubbard, R. G. & O'Brien, A. P., (2022) *Economics*. Harlow: Pearson.

Ikeda, S., (2021). *CPO Magazine*. [Online] Available at: https://www.cpomagazine.com/cyber-security/data-breach-of-robinhood-trading-platform-blamed-on-social-engineering-similar-to-2020-twitter-breach/ [Accessed 13 April 2022].

International Bank for Reconstruction and Development, The World Bank, & International Monetary Fund, (2005). *Financial Sector Assessment*. s.l.:s.n.

Kaspersky, (2016). *Kaspersky*. [Online] Available at: https://www.kaspersky.com/resource-center/threats/metel [Accessed 21 April 2022].

Kaspersky Labs, (2017). *New Technologies New Cyberthreats Analysing the State of IT Security in Financial Sector*, Moscow: Kaspersky Labs.

Kost, E., (2022). *UpGuard*. [Online] Available at: https://www.upguard.com/blog/biggest-cyber-threats-for-financial-services#toc-3 [Accessed 21 April 2022].

Kovacs, E., (2020). *ATM Maker Diebold Nixdorf Hit by Ransomware*. [Çevrimiçi] Available at: https://www.securityweek.com/atm-maker-diebold-nixdorf-hit-ransomware [Accessed 10 June 2022].

Krebs, B., (2020). *Ransomware Hit ATM Giant Diebold Nixdorf*. [Çevrimiçi] Available at: https://krebsonsecurity.com/2020/05/ransomware-hit-atm-giant-diebold-nixdorf/ [Accessed 10 June 2022].

Kudelski Security, (2022). *Quick Analysis of the Wormhole Attack*. [Online] Available at: https://research.kudelskisecurity.com/2022/02/03/quick-analysis-of-the-wormhole-attack/ [Accessed 10 April 2022].

Liquid, (2021). *What Are Blockchain Bridges and Why Do We Need Them?* [Online] Available at: https://blog.liquid.com/blockchain-cross-chain-bridge#HowDoBlockchainBridgesWork [Accessed 18 March 2022].

Muncaster, P., (2016). *InfoSecurity*. [Online] Available at: https://www.infosecurity-magazine.com/news/hackers-attack-shifted-ruble/ [Accessed 21 April 2022].

Neyret, A., (2020). *Stock Market Cybercrime: Definition, Cases and Perspectives*. Paris: Autorité des marchés financiers.

Norges Bank, (2019). www.norges-bank.no. [Online] Available at: https://www.norges-bank.no/en/knowledge-bank/financial-stability/why-are-banks-so-important/ [Accessed 21 June 2022].

Office of the Comptroller of the Currency, (2022). *www.occ.treas.gov*. [Online] Available at: https://www.occ.treas.gov/topics/supervision-and-examination/capital-markets/financial-markets/index-financial-markets.html [Accessed 14 August 2022].

Özarslan, S., (2022). picussecurity.com. [Online] Available at: picussecurity.com [Accessed 22 April 2022].

Packetlabs, (2021). *What Is Network Segmentation, and Can It Help with Ransomware?* [Çevrimiçi] Available at: https://www.packetlabs.net/posts/network-segmentation/#:~:text=Network%20segmentation%20is%20an%20effective,limited%20inter%2Dconnectivity%20between%20them [Accessed 10 June 2022].

Paganini, P., (2016). *Security Affairs*. [Online] Available at: https://securityaffairs.co/wordpress/44376/cyber-crime/metel-hackers-exchange-rate.html [Accessed 21 April 2022].

Paul, D., (2021). *Digit News*. [Online] Available at: https://www.digit.fyi/robin-hood-data-breach-7-million-customers/ [Accessed 13 April 2022].

Reisinger, D., (2016). *Yahoo Finance*. [Online] Available at: https://finance.yahoo.com/news/russian-hackers-spiked-currency-exchange-210644283.html?guccounter=1&guce_referrer=aHR0cHM6Ly93d3cuZ29vZ2xlLmNvbvbS8&guce_referrer_sig=AQAAAI6nQrOVfl1Feylo1nx4j91dm8Ia8glbkx845Wc8W8bmOoGWgJggBoz0xXuqdomYtmLO3ildWhkT7os-PQxFnOf [Accessed 20 April 2022].

Rekt, (2022). *Wormhole*. Rekt. [Online] Available at: https://rekt.news/wormhole-rekt/ [Accessed 10 April 2022].

Reserve Bank of Australia, (2022). *Financial Stability Standards for Securities Settlement Facilities*. [Online] Available at: https://www.rba.gov.au/payments-and-infrastructure/financial-market-infrastructure/clearing-and-settlement-facilities/standards/201212-new-fss-ris/pdf/attachment-5.pdf

RobinHood, (2021). *blog.Robinhood*. [Online] Available at: https://blog.robinhood.com/news/2021/11/8/data-security-incident [Accessed 11 April 2022].

Rolfe, A., (2020). *Diebold Nixdorf Suffers ProLock Ransomware Attack*. [Çevrimiçi] Available at: https://www.paymentscardsandmobile.com/diebold-nixdorf-suf-fers-prolock-ransomware-attack/ [Accessed 10 June 2022].

Saunders, A., Cornett, M. M. & Erhemjamts, O., (2022). *Financial Markets and Institutions*. New York: McGraw-Hill.

Salt Labs, (2022). *Understanding the Coinbase API Vulnerability*. [Online] Available at: https://salt.security/blog/understanding-the-coinbase-api-vulnerability

Sonnemaker, T., (2021). *businessinsider*. [Online] Available at: https://www.busines-sinsider.com/robinhood-data-breach-exposes-customer-emails-names-2021-11 [Accessed 12 April 2022].

Stealth Labs, (2021). *BitMart Falls Victim to a Crypto Heist*. [Çevrimiçi] Available at: https://www.stealthlabs.com/news/bitmart-falls-victim-to-a-crypto-heist-loses-usd-200-million-in-tokens/ [Accessed 10 June 2022].

SudoNull, (2016). *SudoNull*. [Online] Available at: https://sudonull.com/post/79597-Money-is-not-sleeping-who-wins-the-confrontation-between-hackers-and-financial-organizations-ITI-Cap [Accessed 21 April 2022].

The World Bank, (2016). *Financial Development*. [Online] Available at: https://www.worldbank.org/en/publication/gfdr/gfdr-2016/background/financial-development.

UpGuard, (2021). *UpGuard*. [Online] Available at: https://www.upguard.com/secu-rity-report/robinhood [Accessed 13 April 2022].

Wormhole, (2022). *Wormhole Incident Report - 02/02/22*. San Francisco, CA: Wormhole/Solana.

Yakovenko, A., (2017). *Solana: A New Architecture for a High Performance Blockchain*. v0.8.13, 5 November, p. 10. Available at: https://solana.com/solana-whitepaper.pdf

Chapter 5

Food sector

The food industry comprises a complex network of farmers and businesses that provide most of the food consumed by the global population. The phrase "food industry" does not have a sole definition, but it refers to everything related to the production and distribution of food. The word "food industries" refers to several industrial processes used in food product preparation, preservation, transportation, certification, and packaging.

Today's food sector is very diverse, with production processes ranging from tiny, traditional, family-run businesses requiring much labour to be massive, capital-intensive, and heavily mechanised industrial processes. Behind the scenes, the sector also works on improving food quality through research and development. The lobbyists and authorities who seek to guarantee that standards are routinely fulfilled and followed are also a part of the sector. Local agriculture, produce, or fisheries are the backbone of many food industries.

5.1 WHAT IS FOOD AS AN INFRASTRUCTURE?

The food infrastructure lies in the centre of humankind's daily activities with the fact that the residents rely on it for essential food needs and in the centre of the economy with the constitution of a supply chain between the consumer and the producer.

The food system is one of the critical infrastructures since it is directly related to fuelling the economy, creating jobs, advancing justice, and addressing climate change (Brown, 2021). It is possible to observe the influence of food infrastructure on the economy via CISA, and EESC reports that reported the food sector has accounted for roughly one-fifth of the US's economic activity and has been an essential contributor to the EU economy by generating 7% of GDP, respectively (CISA, 2022; EESC, 2015). Therefore, any development or alteration in this infrastructure could have significant consequences.

While evaluating the infrastructure of the food system, it should be noted that the food infrastructure depends on different infrastructures. It depends on many infrastructures, such as water, transportation, communications, and energy. However, the food system infrastructure is differentiated from those other infrastructures since it directly relates to consumer markets (Penders et al., 2014). While food provision has always become apparent in the market and market devices, water, gas, and electricity have recently opened up to the market competition. Food system infrastructure does not only rely on producers and consumers; it is intended to benefit large corporations related at every stage of the food chain (Brown, 2021). Moreover, the food infrastructure is directly related to social and political plans and policies adopted and implemented by the governments to strengthen their communities' food infrastructures. Enhancing food infrastructure is significant for food availability and efficient distribution to the population. For this reason, nations typically have elaborate plans to ensure national food production and supply to prevent times of crisis (Penders et al., 2014).

A study investigating the food sector indicates that it is crucial to understand that the food system infrastructure is based on the complexity of interrelated process components besides economic, social, and political contexts (Kasper et al., 2015). These components involve large systems that are interconnected with each other and responsible for the stages of production, processing and packaging, distribution and retailing, marketing, and capital, as shown in Table 5.1 (Cantrell, 2010).

- **Producing Food:** At this stage, the primary food production responsible includes seedling, growing, crops harvesting, and cattle raising and butchering. The basic food groups, often known as "food elements," are as follows: fruits, vegetables, legumes/beans/pulses, grains, tubers, meat, milk, poultry, eggs, fish, and other seafood (Eurostat, 2017). Secondary food production involves refining or purifying, extracting, and transforming the raw foods that are the products of primary food production into more usable or edible forms. Processed dairy, flours, edible oils, sugars/sweeteners, and starches could be examples of secondary food products.

Table 5.1 Stages of Food Infrastructure (Cantrell & Lewis, 2010)

Stages of Food System Infrastructure	
Producing	Includes primary and secondary food production, which are responsible for the growth and transformation of food
Processing and packaging	Include food preparation for raw and secondary production, as well as cutting, cleaning, packaging, storing, and refrigeration
Distributing and retail	includes actions related to supply, storage, sale, and trade
Marketing	Includes the promotion of produced products
Capital	Includes the financing of the food system

- **Processing and Packaging:** Processing and packaging include cutting, cleaning, packaging, storage, and refrigeration of raw and secondary production foods to keep them from spoiling before they reach the consumer. Milling wheat, pasteurisation of milk, and sorting and refrigerating meat are examples of primary processing, which are often required before food is consumed to ensure food safety (Dani, 2015).
- **Distributing and Retail:** The food services sector is the focus of distribution and retail, a tertiary activity in the food system infrastructure. This stage is in charge of managing primary and secondary food items safely via distribution, transportation, storage, sale, and trade in accordance with the requirements and needs of customers (EIT Food, 2022).
- **Marketing:** Marketing is the stage that relates to the promotion of produced products. Examples of marketing are billboards, coupons, advertising campaigns, packaging materials, and branding (Cantrell & Lewis, 2010).
- **Capital:** Capital is the final stage of the food system infrastructure responsible for financing through loans and investments. This financing stage provides intermediation among natural resources, human capital and social capital. As a result, the food infrastructure is maintained using natural resources like land, water, and other ecological resources, human resources like creativity, and labour, as well as education and training, social resources like churches, youth organisations, and business chambers of commerce, and financial resources like education and training (Cantrell & Lewis, 2010).

5.2 WHY IS FOOD INFRASTRUCTURE IMPORTANT?

As one of the essentials for life – air, water, shelter, and food – the food sector has an essential place in people's lives. Besides the fact that food is a necessity for survival, the food system's multifunctional nature implies it has far-reaching implications for a variety of other areas, including public health, social justice, energy, water, land, transportation, and the economy (Morgan & Sonnino, 2010). The food sector represents $10 trillion or over 12% of the global GDP today and over 40% of all jobs (Strauss, 2022). Aside from that, the agricultural sector employs 27% of the world's workforce (Worldbank, 2022). In addition, one-third of global greenhouse gas emissions, 70% of freshwater usage, and 80% of tropical deforestation, and habitat loss stem from agri-food systems. Global food consumption is estimated at $9 trillion; however, when the other areas affected by the food sector are included, such as public health, the environment, and financial costs, the actual cost of food reaches up to $20 trillion (Strauss, 2022).

These new and highly complex developments related to the food sector show how impactful the sector is over society, the economy, and the environment.

In 2007–2008, food prices increased dramatically, global wheat prices almost doubled, and rice prices almost tripled, driving formerly protected socio-economic classes into food insecurity, which now affects about 2 billion people. As a result of the food price surge, food riots occurred in more than 60 nations worldwide. After the incidents, G8 leaders convened their first-ever food conference in 2009.

The food sector has an impact on climate change. Increased levels of heat and water, and damaged ecosystems, are some consequences of climate problems, and these effects are predicted to be worse in the poorest countries, which are the ones that have contributed the least to the problem of global warming. Land disputes are intensifying as wealthy but food-stressed countries (such as Saudi Arabia and South Korea) try to purchase up arable land in Africa and Asia to ensure food security, triggering accusations of new colonialism. Cities are becoming increasingly concerned about how they feed themselves due to rapid urbanisation, as cities are the most politically sensitive geographies in most countries due to their sensitivity to food shortages (Morgan & Sonnino, 2010).

These factors indicate that improving public health, strengthening food security and resilience, supporting family farms, revitalising rural communities, redressing structural injustice, and mitigating climate change may all be accomplished through constructing infrastructure that supports sustainable food and agricultural systems. On the other hand, there has been intense industrialisation and digitalisation in the food sector in recent years. Chemical-intensive monocultures developed for animal feed, biofuels, processed foods, and industrial-scale livestock production dominate software-based agricultural systems. These farming techniques negatively impact the world's important soil, water, and biodiversity and produce unsustainable greenhouse emissions (Waterman et al., 2022).

5.3 KEY PLAYERS AND STAKEHOLDERS

Specific characteristics of the various stakeholders in the food sector are essential to comprehending the sector's cyber security capabilities. There are seven stakeholders in the food sector, which are explained below and demonstrated in Figure 5.1.

- Consumers: Price has a significant influence on consumer demand, but food security, prestige, animal protection, and environmental impact are also significant concerns (Baker et al., 2020). According to a 2018 National Farmers Union (NFU) analysis, the cost of food fraud in the UK food sector might be as significant as £12 billion per year. As a result, consumer trust is diminishing (NFU Mutual, 2018).

Figure 5.1 Elements of the food sector.

- **Farms:** Farms' structure provides hurdles for newcomers, promoting high levels of continuity among farming families and encouraging farmers to labour until they retire (Department for Environment, Food & Rural Affairs, 2013). Many farmers consider farming a culture, and as a result, they may make decisions that are only sometimes in their best interests (Baker et al., 2020). For this reason, agriculture's shift to digitisation and new technologies is hampered.
- **Processors:** In general, primary processing for bread, dairy, poultry, and potatoes is highly centralised, with large processor corporations able to exercise enormous influence over farmers through techniques such as contract farming (Baker et al., 2020). Auxiliary processors are mainly composed of several small enterprises and are less concentrated.
- **Retailers:** Retailers significantly and directly impact food regulations, representing customer interests and expectations.
- **Suppliers:** Original Equipment Manufacturers (OEMs) and agrochemical companies are collecting farming data to gain pricing power or generate new sources of revenue, such as supplying smart farming or equipment maintenance solutions.

- **Government:** The configuration of the food network is shaped by governmental policies and planning. Governmental organisations also use web applications to deliver critical operational functions.
- **Logistics:** The many organisations in the food nodes are linked via food delivery and storage. To minimise rotting and meet food safety regulations, this frequently necessitates using specialised trucks and facilities with controlled conditions (Baker et al., 2020).

As with many other critical infrastructures, we observe private and public sector participation and collaboration in the food and agriculture sector. The private sector side of the food and agriculture sector is represented in the United States by the Food and Agriculture Sector Coordinating Council (FSCC). In contrast, the public side is represented by the Food and Agriculture Government Coordinating Council (FAGCC). In addition, the United States Department of Agriculture (USDA) and the Department of Health and Human Services (HHS) have also been defined by PPD-21 as the Sector-Specific Agencies of the industry. However, HHS has delegated this task to the Food and Drug Administration (FDA).

FSCC is a structure that includes company owners, industry operators and trade associations in the food and agriculture sector aimed to share information, plan sectoral strategy, and establish communication with policymakers in line with the needs and demands of the industry. It consists of seven sub-councils, each represented by two designs and an alternate. These individuals attend FSCC meetings, express their views, and if all sub-councils make a joint decision, i.e., reach a consensus, the decision is put into action.

As stated earlier, FAGCC represents the public leg of institutions structured to collaborate in the critical infrastructure of food and agriculture. At the Federal and State, Tribal and Territorial (SLTT) level, FAGCC analyses, provides policy recommendations, determines procedures and strategies, and interacts with the private sector side of the industry on an annual basis to ensure the safety of food and agriculture critical infrastructure (FDA et al., 2015). The diversity of FAGCC's members is wide. It houses representatives from academia and representatives at the Federal, State, Tribal, and Territorial levels. While the USDA and FDA are of particular importance as they are designated SSAs for the food and agriculture industry, the FAGCC also covers a wide range of organisations, from the US Department of Homeland Security to the Association of Public Health Laboratories. The two key institutions of the FAGCC are the USDA and the FDA, which are leaders in infrastructure safety and resilience in the food and agriculture sector and are responsible for establishing a policy-making plan and ensuring cooperation among key players in the industry. The USDA and the Office of Homeland Security and Emergency Coordination supervise the health of plants and animals used in the food and agriculture sector and the food processing and packaging process compliance with specific standards. USDA also supports and establishes research and development activities to improve these processes. Another important task of the USDA is to ensure that the food and agriculture sector of the United States of America is opened to international markets and to be in a position to support international food aid programs. The FDA alone is responsible for the safety of 80% of all food consumed in the United States. Likewise, the FDA inspects the compliance of the products with public health standards in the food and agriculture sector, except for meat, poultry, and processed eggs, from the beginning to the end of the process, that is, until the sale of the product. The mandates and duties of the FDA and USDA are similar. Differences occur mainly in jurisdiction areas. For example, the USDA is the leading agency to regulate meat, including beef, pork, lamb, and poultry, while the FDA supervises mainly seafood products (Bakota, 2019).

5.4 CYBER RESILIENCE IN FOOD INFRASTRUCTURE

The food industry is willing to switch from analogue to digital systems. Using new technologies to control processing and manufacturing in the food industry provides higher quality, safer products, faster production, and advantages in storing data. In addition, farm management software can help farmers efficiently manage their farms' operations. Besides all these benefits, there are threats to the food industry because of its digital vulnerabilities. New technologies include traceability, insight and methods for increasing profitability and tracking and monitoring agricultural employees and equipment (Baker et al., 2020). Cyber assaults on these systems will have disastrous results. These results can be summarised as follows:

- Data leakage puts a company at a competitive deficit.
- Leakage of confidential information exploited by prospectors looking to buy unproductive land at a reduced rate.
- Leakage of information that supports organised criminal groups in plundering farm assets.

Cybercriminals target personally identifiable information, commercially sensitive information, financial assets, and IoT-Robotics systems when they attack Food Critical Infrastructures (Borchi et al., 2021).

- **Personally Identifiable Information:** Large amounts of data are produced and gathered daily due to their continual and complicated nature. Personal Identifiable Information (PII) such as full names, residences, dates of birth, legal papers, and contact information is included in some of this data. Staff, service providers, and industry partners' financial information are also included in PII.

- **Commercially Sensitive Information:** Records on production efficiency, livestock/poultry health, and crop yields are among the types of information hackers seek to benefit rivals, putting primary producers at a competitive disadvantage with the data about land values that may be utilised to acquire land at a discount (Borchi et al., 2021).
- **Financial Assets:** Hackers will target credit card information, online banking usernames and passwords when initiating cyber financial attacks.
- **IoT-Robotics Systems:** Hackers targeting IoT and robotics equipment in agriculture, fisheries, and forestry may be lured to turn them off, inflicting harm to primary producers and supply networks, and then demand a ransom to turn them back on (Borchi et al., 2021).

Moreover, in the agri-food sector, the software is an essential component of the digital infrastructure, and security flaws in software systems continue to be common (Capgemini Consulting, 2016). Because process control systems, in particular, are difficult to upgrade, it leads to risks related to a lack of IT sustainability. Furthermore, the agri-food industry is heavily chain-focused because it operates in chains and networks. The consequences of any breakage in the chain may put food safety in danger (Capgemini Consulting, 2016). As a result, organisations should extend their food defence culture to cyber resilience to decrease the negative impact of the breakage of the chain. Cyber resilience flaws and failure to implement the cyber resilience framework steps may cause workflow malfunction to preserve food safety. Moreover, the food sector OT personnel are experts trained in food safety and production, not cybersecurity, which causes vulnerabilities in this sector. Therefore, the Food Protection and Defense Institute (FDPI) recommends increasing interaction between organisations' OT and IT personnel to understand better how ICSs and IT systems communicate (2019). As a result, they can improve processes and procedures to safeguard systems that benefit everyone, which provides mitigation against cyber incidents. According to FDPI, transnational criminal organisations are heavily involved in large-scale food-related crimes; for example, criminals hack into cargo systems to obtain information on targets, steal business credentials, and generate fraudulent bills of lading and manifests to allow bogus pickups and cargo thefts. These are the most frequently encountered types of cyber assaults (2019). At the same time, the sector adapts to smarter technologies and IoT, and the attack surface increases. For example, in a ransomware attack, attackers steal sensitive data and sabotage the process of business. Attackers disrupt business, incur financial loss, and harm the supply chain due to ransomware incidents. To mitigate the impacts, organisations should manage risk assessments that include inventorying both ICSs and IT systems and know how to protect the hardware and software. This implementation provides the first step of cyber resilience: the Identify function. Also, they should consider having third-party cyber security assessments performed on their process controls, ensuring protection against security vulnerabilities from unauthorised third-party individuals. Additionally, the Federal Bureau of Investigation (FBI) emphasises ransomware attacks in the food and agriculture sector and recommends some actions to mitigate the impact of cyberattacks (Federal Bureau of Investigation Cyber Division, 2021). Most of the actions are considered general cyber resilience actions, such as using a strong password and multi-factor authentication, keeping operating systems and software up to date, subdividing the network into several subnets, setting up production software for malware and virus, blocking hyperlinks in emails, and using secure networks (Federal Bureau of Investigation Cyber Division, 2021).

Cyber resilience is important in the food sector as it is responsible for providing essential goods and services that are critical to public health and safety. The sector relies on technology to manage supply chains, manufacturing processes, and distribution channels. Any disruption to these systems can have severe consequences for public health, economic stability, and food security.

The importance of cyber resilience in the food sector can be summarised as follows:

Protection of critical infrastructure: The food sector's infrastructure, including food processing plants, storage facilities, and distribution centres, is a critical component of national infrastructure. Cyber resilience measures help to protect this infrastructure from cyber threats, such as cyberattacks or ransomware, which can cause physical damage, disrupt operations, and compromise the safety of workers and the public.

Maintaining food safety and quality: The food sector is responsible for ensuring that food is safe and of high quality. Any disruption to the supply chain, such as cyberattacks or other cyber incidents, can have a significant impact on the quality and safety of food. Cyber resilience measures can help to ensure the integrity of the food supply chain, enabling organisations to detect and respond to cyber incidents quickly, and recover from them effectively.

Protection of sensitive information: The food sector collects and processes sensitive information, including customer data, supplier information, and intellectual property. This information needs to be protected from cyber threats, such as theft, espionage, or manipulation. Cyber resilience measures, such as access controls, encryption, and network segmentation, can help to protect sensitive information from cyber threats.

Compliance with regulations: The food sector is subject to various regulations and standards, such as the Food Safety Modernization Act (FSMA) and the Global Food Safety Initiative (GFSI). Cyber resilience measures help food organisations to comply with these regulations by providing a structured approach to managing cyber risks and ensuring the confidentiality, integrity, and availability of sensitive information.

In summary, cyber resilience is critical for the food sector as these organisations rely on technology to manage supply chains, manufacturing processes, and distribution channels. Cyber resilience measures help to protect critical infrastructure, maintain food safety and quality, protect sensitive information, and comply with regulations. The food sector should prioritise the development and implementation of cyber resilience measures to ensure they can effectively respond to cyber threats and protect their critical services.

5.5 CASE STUDIES

5.5.1 Case I: JBS

Computer networks of JBS, the world's largest meat processing corporation, were hacked in 2021, partially halting some deployments in Australia, Canada, and the United States, directly impacting thousands of employees. Hackers infiltrated a computer system and tried to intimidate by threatening to disrupt or delete data unless a ransom transaction was made (BBC, 2021). With partial redundancies at some of the company's operations and claims from farmers that their livestock deliveries were halted, the five-day stoppage jeopardised Australia's meat supply chain (Claughton & Beilharz, 2021). The meat manufacturer was forced to halt all cattle slaughtering at its US factories for a day, threatening to damage supply chain operations and raise food prices in the US, where labour shortages, high demand, and Covid-related interruptions were causing havoc (Makortoff, 2021). Even though the "great majority" of its facilities remained functional, the company paid the ransom due to the complexity of the attack (BBC, 2021).

Identify: Although there is no clear explanation about the implementation of this phase, considering that the company has spent more than $200m on IT and employs more than 850 tech specialists (Makortoff, 2021), it is estimated that the Identify phase has been present in identifying key elements, though not at a sufficient level.

Protect: Although this is a recent occurrence, there has been insufficient information available, and considering the severity of the cyberattack, it is reasonable to conclude that the Protect phase was not adequately performed in this case.

Detect: There is no clear information on this subject because the information regarding how the attack was detected is not shared with the public.

Respond: As soon as the intrusion was detected, the corporation stated it halted all affected IT systems, and its backup servers were not compromised (BBC, 2021). According to public remarks, the corporation has demonstrated reasonably effective performance, indicating that the response phase has been overcome.

Recover: The company circumvented this phase at the mercy of the attackers by paying the requested ransom. As a result, the Recover phase can be said to have been bypassed unfavourably.

Lessons Learned: The main issue, in this case, is that the Protect phase is not implemented correctly. Also, due to improper implementation of the Identify and Protect sections, the attackers were paid a ransom, causing financial harm to the company and the customers. In a scenario when all of the phases are perfectly implemented, no ransom payment is required, and customers are not inconvenienced.

5.5.2 Case 2: Schreiber foods

A cyberattack on the primary US cheese manufacturer in October 2021 caused a countrywide cream cheese shortage just before the holidays (Elkin & Shanker, 2021). The attack occurred during cream cheese demand's rush hours. Americans were preparing and buying more cakes for the holidays, and cream cheese was a popular dessert component. Manufacturers were already suffering from labour shortages and supply chain problems for raw resources, packaging, and transportation before the cyberattack and peak Christmas demand (Maruf, 2021). According to The Wisconsin State Farmer, ransomware perpetrators demanded $2.5 million from Schreiber Foods (Shepel, 2021). It was not disclosed whether this ransom was paid.

Identify: Details about whether the Identify phase was implemented were not shared with the public.

Protect: Although the Protect phase is not explicitly described, the company claims in its statements that the specialised response team takes the appropriate steps right away (Starks, 2021). Considering these statements, it can be implied that the Protect step was completed.

Detect: Since the information about how the cyberattack was detected is not shared with the public, we do not have enough information.

Respond: The company's special cyberattack response team quickly responded by taking the necessary actions as soon as possible. This way, things could be kept at controllable levels without going to more serious and risky dimensions. Although we do not know the technical details of the Response phase, it has been successfully implemented.

Recover: Schreiber Foods claims its specialists quickly accomplished the Recover phase by doing all the essential steps. The cybersecurity team performed a fantastic job of recovering and reconstructing the system, according to spokesman Andrew Tobisch (Starks, 2021).

Lessons Learned: Great harm was avoided because the organisation was aware of the possibility of a cyber assault, established a dedicated team, and implemented the essential procedures sufficiently. Although we need more information about the other phases, it was shared with the public that the Respond and Recover phases were successfully implemented. Therefore, the impact of this cyberattack was minimal, preventing both the company and consumers from suffering for a long time.

5.5.3 Case 3: JFC International

Asian culinary goods are widely distributed and wholesaled by JFC International. JFC International purchases branded goods from other foreign businesses in addition to its own products. In February 2021, a ransomware assault that affected numerous of its IT systems resulted in a cyber disaster. The JFC International Europe Group claimed that it has informed authorities, staff members, and business partners about the hack, which appears to have affected JFC International (Kovacs, 2021). JFC International Europe Group labelled the incident as a "data security incident." It is therefore possible that the attacker acquired some data as a result (Kovacs, 2021).

Identify: We do not know whether the Identify step was performed correctly since details about whether it was done using various frameworks before the attack was not disclosed to the public.

Protect: Given the attack's results, it is reasonable to assume that this step was implemented, albeit inadvertently, given the lack of significant implications. Official information concerning this phase, however, was kept a secret.

Detect: Unfortunately, because information about how the attack was detected is not shared with the public, we do not have any information regarding how this phase was delivered.

Respond: According to JFC International Europe Group's report, a complete forensic analysis by in-house professionals and exterior experts was quickly launched (Kovacs, 2021). Additionally, the corporation alerted the appropriate authorities and informed workers and business associates about the cyberattacks (Paganini, 2021). So, immediate action about informing officials and quick execution of forensic analysis was made as the right move for the response phase.

Recover: JFC International reports that after a temporary pause for security concerns, normal European commercial operations have resumed, and the impacted servers have been secured (Kovacs, 2021). So, this part is partially successful.

Lessons Learned: The primary purpose of the cyber resilience framework is to ensure that the company's business is running as usual at the time of an attack. Therefore, if all steps of the cyber resilience framework had been implemented, this operation pause might have happened elsewhere. Thankfully, impacted servers have been secured, and the business has resumed as usual.

5.5.4 Case 4: Harvest Sherwood Food Distributors

Harvest Sherwood Food Distributors was formed in April 2017 by the merger of Sherwood Food Distributors and Harvest Food Distributors. Harvest Food Distributors were serving independent food firms that lacked the size to self-distribute. Sherwood Food Distributors has become an outstanding independent meat and food distributor. In May 2020, a ransomware assault occurred, resulting in the disclosure of over 2000 confidential files, including cash flow analyses, insurance contracts, sub-distributor information, and proprietary vendor information (Kass, 2020). The hacker organisation *rEvil* gained access to the distributors' data using evasive ransomware known as "Sodinokibi" and threatened to release entire files unless the distribution businesses paid the $7.5 million ransom requested by rEvil (Clark & Merker, 2020). Some information has been made public, and the negotiation between the attackers and Harvest Sherwood Food Distributors did not succeed. This little leak appears to signal that the organisation accepted the attackers' requirements (Cyble, 2020).

Identify: Details regarding whether or not the Identify function was performed were unavailable.

Protect: Details of what kind of protection actions the organisation took were unavailable.

Detect: Information on how the organisation detected the cyberattack was not made public. All the information known is that the attackers established a note on 15 May, although the incident seems to have been known to the organisation's board since 3 May. Information about the detection process needs to be made available.

Respond: In this case, the response process was weak. The attackers demanded 7.5 million dollars, but the corporation was ready to pay 4.25 million. Negotiations failed miserably, and attackers disclosed additional sensitive material and increased the ransom to 42 million (Varghese, 2020). Moreover, the attackers said, "You have had much time that you have unfortunately abused with huge losses. In addition, you made a big mistake by contacting a company that misinformed you about negotiation experience" (Kass, 2020). This is an indication of a faulty response procedure.

Recover: Information about the process of recovery has not been made public.

Lessons Learned: The organisation needed a better response plan to manage the process. They were neither able to negotiate nor respond to the attack. Moreover, it is still being determined what the company did between detecting the hack and demanding the ransom between 3 May and 15 May. So, this process is not well managed.

5.5.5 Case 5: Crystal Valley Cooperation

Crystal Valley Cooperative, an agricultural supply and grain marketing cooperative based in Mankato, was targeted by a ransomware attack in September 2021, which impacted computers and disrupted operations. The co-op employs 260 full-time staff and serves 2,500 farmers and livestock producers in southern Minnesota and northern Iowa. The attack type typically includes cybercriminals threatening to reveal private information or prevent access to key files unless a ransom is paid (The Free Press, 2021). The attack made the company's networks, data, and automated processes inaccessible for weeks. According to the Cybersecurity and Infrastructure Security Agency, the criminal organisation responsible for the attack is probably connected to a Russian-speaking group that the FBI has accused of carrying out a ransomware attack on Colonial Pipeline a few months back (CHS, 2022).

Identify: There was no public information regarding the identification step.

Protect: According to the sources, the cooperation could not protect the systems against the attack.

Detect: The workers noticed the attack after facing breakdowns in the system. According to the investigators, the cyberattack most likely entered through a backup server that was still linked to the network and had been used to move the co-email op's services to the cloud. "It got forgotten because it was never really a requirement except for the email migration," says Langland (Vaas, 2022).

Respond: After the attack, the company had to sustain its automated operations manually. They used paper and pen to perform all digital activities. The company could not sustain its functions through digital systems for about ten days. Grain elevator workers in Crystal Valley recorded truck weights and moisture testing findings using paper and pen, which caused significant delays (CHS, 2022).

Recover: After a staggering amount of labour, Kienholz claimed that Crystal Valley operations were back up and running. The cooperative team rebuilt systems with the assistance of a business that specialises in recovering from cyberattacks, isolated certain areas of its network to make it more difficult for hackers to access all data, strengthened passwords and multi-factor authentication, reinstalled computers and servers, restricted administrative access to various systems, and made an investment in an endpoint detection and response system that watches for malicious activity (Vaas, 2022).

Lessons Learned: As stated in the recovery section, after the attack was neutralised and all the damage was determined, the company took all the necessary steps and made all the arrangements for its digital system. After these changes, the company projected to have much more cyber resilience to any cyberattack.

REFERENCES

Baker, L. et al., (2020). *Cyber Security in UK Agriculture*. s.l.: NCC Group.

Bakota, E., (2019). *FDA vs. USDA: What's the Difference?*. GovLoop. [Online] Available at: https://www.govloop.com/community/blog/fda-vs-usda-whats-the-difference/#:~:text=The%20USDA%20oversees%20over%20meat,bottled%20water%2C%20and%20whole%20eggs [Accessed 8 May 2022].

BBC, (2021). *JBS: Cyber-Attack Hits World's Largest Meat Supplier*. [Online] Available at: https://www.bbc.com/news/world-us-canada-57318965 [Accessed 14 May 2022].

Borchi, J., Melaine Woodcock, M. R. & Raniga, B., (2021). *A Threat-Based Assessment of the Cyber Resilience of the Australian Agricultural Sector*. s.l.: AgriFutures National Rural Issues.

Brown, A., (2021). *The Food System Is Critical Infrastructure*. Natural Resources Defense Council (NRDC). Available at: https://www.nrdc.org/experts/amy-brown/food-system-critical-infrastructure.

Cantrell, C. & Lewis, R. (2010). *Food System Infrastructure: Michigan Good Food Work Group Report No. 5 of 5*. East Lansing, MI: C.S. Mott Group for Sustainable Food Systems at Michigan State University. Available at: www.michiganfood.org.

Capgemini Consulting, (2016). *Cybersecurity in the Agrifood Sector*. [Online] Available at: https://edepot.wur.nl/378724 [Accessed 4 May 2022].

CHS, (2022). *What You Can Learn from One Co-op's Ransomware Attack*. [Online] Available at: https://www.chsinc.com/about-chs/news/news/2022/02/24/coop-ransomware-attack-story [Accessed 3 June 2022].

CISA, (2022). *Food and Agriculture Sector*. Available at: https://www.cisa.gov/food-and-agriculture-sector.

Clark, M. R. & Merker, N. R., (2020). *Weak Link in the Supply Chain: Why Distributors Need Cyber-Insurance*. [Online] Available at: https://www.lexology.com/library/detail.aspx?g=f863fea2-f902-4450-9958-f1329739fc80 [Accessed 15 May 2022].

Claughton, D. & Beilharz, N. (2021). *JBS Foods Pays $14.2 Million Ransom to End Cyber Attack on Its Global Operations*. [Online] Available at: https://www.abc.net.au/news/rural/2021-06-10/jbs-foods-pays-14million-ransom-cyber-attack/100204240 [Accessed 14 May 2022].

Cyble, (2020). *Distributors, the Largest Independent Wholesale Food Distributorship in the United States - Data Leak*. [Online] Available at: https://blog.cyble.com/2020/05/14/revil-ransomware-operators-breached-harvest-sherwood-food-distributors-the-largest-independent-wholesale-food-distributorship-in-the-united-states-data-leak/ [Accessed 15 May 2022].

Dani, S., (2015) *Food Supply Chain Management and Logistics: From Farm to Fork*, pp. 1–5. Koganpage Press. Available at: https://industri.fatek.unpatti.ac.id/wp-content/uploads/2019/03/261-Food-Supply-Chain-Management-and-Logistics-From-Farm-to-Fork-Samir-Dani-Edisi-1-2015.pdf

Worldbank (2022). *Employment in Agriculture (% of Total Employment) (Modeled ILO Estimate)*. Data. [Online] Available at: https://data.worldbank.org/indicator/SL.AGR.EMPL.ZS [Accessed 3 June 2022].

Department for Environment, Food & Rural Affairs, (2013). *Future of Farming Review Report.* s.l.: s.n.

EESC, (2015). *Food and Drinks Sector.* Available at: https://www.eesc.europa.eu/en/our-work/opinions-information-reports/opinions/food-and-drinks-sector.

Elkin, E. & Shanker, D. (2021). *Cream Cheese Is the Latest Casualty of Cyberattacks.* [Online] Available at: https://www.bloomberg.com/news/newsletters/2021-12-10/supply-chain-latest-cream-cheese-is-the-latest-casualty-of-cyberattacks [Accessed 14 May 2022].

EIT Food, (2022). *The Food System.* Available at: https://www.futurelearn.com/info/courses/food-supply-systems/0/steps/53648

Eurostat, (2017). *Output of the Agricultural Industry, EU-28.* Online source. Available at: https://ec.europa.eu/eurostat/documents/2995521/9380923/5-16112018-BP-EN.pdf/86dc9faa-616d-43d0-9933-e2f5d0af6d42

Federal Bureau of Investigation Cyber Division, (2021). *Private Industry Notification.* [Online] Available at: https://www.ic3.gov/Media/News/2021/210907.pdf [Accessed 4 May 2022].

Food and Drug Administration, United States Department of Agriculture, & Department of Homeland Security, (2015). *Food and Agriculture Sector-Specific Plan -2015.* Cybersecurity and Infrastructure Security Agency.

Kasper, C., Brandt, J., Lindschulte, K. & Giseke, U. (2015). Food as an infrastructure in urbanising regions. *7th International Aesop Sustainable Food Planning Conference Proceedings, Torino, Politecnico di Torino*, pp. 42–56. Available at: https://www.researchgate.net/publication/326914751_Food_as_an_infrastructure_in_urbanizing_regions.

Kass, D. H. (2020). *REvil Ransomware Attacks Food Distributor; Hackers Seek $7.5 M Ransom.* [Online] Available at: https://www.msspalert.com/cybersecurity-breaches-and-attacks/ransomware/revil-hits-food-distributors/ [Accessed 15 May 2022].

Kovacs, E., (2021). *Asian Food Distribution Giant JFC International Hit by Ransomware.* [Online] Available at: https://www.securityweek.com/asian-food-distribution-giant-jfc-international-hit-ransomware [Accessed 15 May 2022].

Makortoff, K., (2021). *World's Biggest Meat Producer JBS Pays $11m Cybercrime Ransom.* [Online] Available at: https://www.theguardian.com/business/2021/jun/10/worlds-biggest-meat-producer-jbs-pays-11m-cybercrime-ransom [Accessed 14 May 2022].

Maruf, R. (2021). *The Surprising Reason You Can't Find Cream Cheese Anywhere.* [Online] Available at: https://edition.cnn.com/2021/12/18/business/cream-cheese-cyberattack-schreiber-foods/index.html [Accessed 14 May 2022].

Morgan, K. & Sonnino, R. (2010). The urban foodscape: World cities and the new food equation. *Cambridge Journal of Regions, Economy and Society*, 3, pp. 209–224. doi:10.1093/cjres/rsq007.

NFU Mutual, (2018). *Food Fraud Report.* s.l.: s.n.

Paganini, P., (2021). *Distributor of Asian Food JFC International hit by Ransomware.* [Online] Available at: https://securityaffairs.co/wordpress/115150/malware/jfc-international-ransomware-attack.html [Accessed 15 May 2022].

Penders, B., Frohlich, X., Jauho, M. & Schleifer, D., (2014). *Preface: Food Infrastructures,* Limn. Available at: https://limn.it/articles/preface-food-infrastructures/.

Shepel, J., (2021). *Schreiber Foods Hit with Cyberattack; Plants Closed.* [Online] Available at: https://www.wisfarmer.com/story/news/2021/10/26/schreiber-foods-hit-cyberattack-plants-closed/8558252002/.

Starks, T., (2021). *'Cyber Event' Knocks Dairy Giant Schreiber Foods Offline Amid Industry Ransomware Outbreak.* [Online] Available at: https://www.cyberscoop.com/schreiber-foods-cyber-event-ransomware-agriculture-food/ [Accessed 14 May 2022].

Strauss, T., (2022). *How Can We Protect Food Systems Against Global Shocks? Here's What Business Leaders Say.* World Economic Forum. [Online] Available at: https://www.weforum.org/agenda/2022/05/protect-food-systems-against-global-shocks/#:~:text=They%20are%20also%20central%20to,tropical%20deforestation%20and%20habitat%20loss [Accessed 3 June 2022].

The Free Press, (2021). *Crystal Valley Co-op Hit by Cyberattack.* Available at: https://www.mankatofreepress.com/news/local_news/crystal-valley-co-op-hit-by-cyberattack/article_ee0a6786-1b24-11ec-a41a-1b3c14d1d303.html

Vaas, L., (2022). *Crystal Valley Farm Coop Hit with Ransomware.* Threatpost.com. [Online] Available at: https://threatpost.com/crystal-valley-farm-coop-hit-with-ransomware/174928/ [Accessed 2 August 2022].

Varghese, S., (2020). *REvil Gang Ups Ransom Demand After Negotiations with Food Firm Fail.* [Online] Available at: https://itwire.com/business-it-news/security/revil-gang-ups-ransom-demand-after-negotiations-with-food-firm-fail.html [Accessed 17 May 2022].

Waterman, C., Feldman, M. & Kraus-Polk, J., (2022). *Filesforprogress.org.* [Online] Available at: https://www.filesforprogress.org/memos/food-procurement-and-infrastructure.pdf [Accessed 3 June 2022].

Chapter 6

Government sector

A government is a system through which a state or area is governed (Voegtlin & Scherer, 2017). The moment and location of the origin of human governance are unknown, although ancient government structures are known. The first minor city-states emerged about 5,000 years ago. Indus Valley Civilisation, Sumer, Ancient Egypt, and the Yellow River Civilisation had all increased the size of the areas they dominated by the third to second millennia BC (Weiss & Courty, 1993). Most of the terminology used to describe governments, including monarchy, oligarchy, and democracy, have Greek or Roman origins (Blythe, 1992).

6.1 WHAT IS GOVERNMENT AS AN INFRASTRUCTURE?

When looking at the changes taking place in the world, the infrastructure and how these changes can be protected, it is essential to understand the fundamental roles of that infrastructure. Most individuals only interact with the government by paying taxes and choosing their representatives in the political arena. However, in reality, a government may play various responsibilities as the infrastructure itself. It is crucial to comprehend them to appreciate what is to be protected from cyberattacks. Understanding governments' responsibilities as infrastructure are necessary, especially in a world where we face daily economic crises, the rise of tech giants, and many cyberattacks on different infrastructures. Typical responsibilities of governments can be listed as follows:

1. Providing non-rivalling goods and services without letting trade-offs in order to supply consistent and stable availability and utilisation of them to the citizenries.
2. The management of and interference with externalities are significantly debated issues because of holding both positive and negative effects. Usually, state-owned companies or heavily regulated public/

private corporations are in charge of managing positive externalities. Using rules and laws and adopting norms can frequently eliminate the bulk of negative externalities.

3. Allocating funding and redistribution is another responsibility of the government for any governmental functions required to be spent on infrastructure, such as providing public goods like education or allocating income. Furthermore, the government's job is to determine the taxation system and how it affects the economy, social equality, and other factors like competitiveness.

4. Social security is another critical issue than ever because of growing concerns over modern colonialism and rising social inequality. In many countries, social security also provides coverage for unemployment, medical costs, and other forms of assistance in various situations. In light of the digital age, the basic-income movement is expanding because many are concerned that the sizable IT sector would lead many people to lose employment and jeopardise their primary income.

As can be seen, governments have a wide array of interests to take care of as an infrastructure. In addition to those mentioned, the responsibilities of governments as infrastructure are also changing a lot today. For example, building cyber resiliency precautions for country-wide infrastructures and protecting citizens from cyberattacks are gaining more importance nowadays since the rapid spread of technology into every sector of society has caused a considerable change in how people live, work, and do business and how governments serve the people they represent (Ndou, 2004). Furthermore, exponential technological improvements and falling prices have connected the world more. This has led to many new opportunities, progress, and innovation. The Covid-19 pandemic has sped up this trend, but, likely, we are still in the initial phases of a long-term fundamental change. The growth of cyberspace on a global scale is changing how we live, work, and talk to each other, as well as how our most critical infrastructure is built. Since the government is directly responsible for these essential services, any possible problem significantly impacts governments everywhere (Dunleavy & Margetts, 2006).

Governments' use of information and communication technology (ICT) to promote the streamlining of public administration is growing (Bonina & Cordella, 2009). ICT influences most public service ideals by enabling and embedding them (Bannister & Connolly, 2014). In the sense that it makes otherwise impractical acts or activities possible, it serves as an enabler. It is called an embedder because it makes it easier to put ideas into systems. In the public sector, ICT ethics and values discussions tend to focus on a few core ideas, especially privacy (Poel & Christen, 2020).

6.2 WHY IS GOVERNMENT INFRASTRUCTURE IMPORTANT?

Cyber incident response, the battle against cybercrime, and the protection of the critical information infrastructure (CIIP) are essential elements of the national cyber posture (Brunner & Suter, 2008). A paradigm for assembling these elements into a working and well-coordinated national cyber system must be developed by policymakers. The institutional setting for cyber incident response and CIIP differs from country to country, even though the above policy sectors are equally crucial for national cyber resilience. The interior ministry, court system, and law enforcement are typically responsible for addressing cybercrime.

Due to the interdisciplinary characteristics of cyber incident response and CIIP, nations have devised various approaches for integrating these capabilities into their institutional architecture (Skopik et al., 2016). Others have created a specialised national cyber agency that operates as a CIIP and incident response centre, while some countries have integrated this capability within their internal security apparatus. In European nations, the telecom sector regulator, an IT agency, an intelligence organisation, the interior ministry, a defence institution, or a cabinet office are just a few of the organisations that may be linked to a national Computer Emergency Response Team (CERT).

An essential set of topics includes industrial and trade strategies and refers to the economic elements of cybersecurity (Kshetri, 2013). One-sided trade routines and economic damage resulting from cyber theft of intellectual property are emerging concerns for public policy communities. To determine cyber theft's effects, it is vital to have tight contact with significant industrial players (Abomhara & Køien, 2015). In addition, the policy response toolkit to combat intellectual property theft is still in development and would require national and international components. For example, cyber theft could be punished through suitable international trade processes in response to unfair economic practices.

6.3 KEY PLAYERS AND STAKEHOLDERS

The provision of services to government infrastructures is one of the most crucial functions of a state for understanding the citizens' perception of the role and effectiveness of government (Lau & Carrasco, 2020). Since the government infrastructure facilitates the delivery of public services, it has mutual maintenance relations with other infrastructures in terms of governance of the current working system in between the rest of the infrastructures. In this respect, identifying key players and stakeholders of the government infrastructure is essential for better outcomes.

The quality of government infrastructure is linked with the budget and investment management for creating public services as much as the province's affluence. For instance, the rise of Asia is related to the fact that, as a percentage of overall government spending, Southeast Asian governments invest more in infrastructure (16.7%) than OECD members (7.6%), according to the OECD study Government at a Glance Southeast Asia 2019 (Lau & Carrasco, 2020; OECD/ADB, 2019). Therefore, one deterministic way to observe critical players in government infrastructure is by analysing where the government expenditures are distributed among the stakeholders. In a nutshell, where the government expenditures go is the matter.

The stakeholders of the government infrastructure could be distinguished into five headings according to the modes of infrastructure delivery. One of them is Public–Private Partnerships (PPPs), which are prolonged contracts between the government and a partner from the private sector. PPPs can deliver public services for social and infrastructure assets such as roads, bridges, hospitals, utilities, and prisons. PPPs also risk being exploited by omitting government obligations and spending from total debt and deficit calculations. Furthermore, the lengthy nature of PPPs may also be too expensive, inflexible, cumbersome, and flexible for the changing demands of the public sector and developing technologies (OECD/ADB, 2019). The other mode is state-owned enterprises (SOEs) entirely or partly owned by the government, mainly in network industries such as energy, water and public transportation. If an SOE can get financing, the government may hand over infrastructure investments to the latter. However, if the investment choice has budgetary repercussions, the government may still control the investment (OECD, 2015; OECD/ADB, 2019).

In the typical purchasing manner, a government agency gets agreements with private participants to acquire services and services related to infrastructure. In order to design, develop, build, operate, and maintain infrastructure assets, the government will enter into separate contracts with designers and constructors (OECD, 2015). In the privatisation mode of infrastructure delivery, private companies must offer the most effective system. Private companies choose infrastructure assets to invest in and create. Sectors with market failures, like water and electricity, have been privatised frequently. Governments have increased regulatory control in the sectors in question when privatisation has been chosen as the best solution (OECD, 2015). Lastly, the mode of direct provision of infrastructure entails the government being in charge of all facets of delivery, including finance, building, and future service provision. In this mode, the level of control over the infrastructure asset that the government has is at its highest (OECD, 2015).

The US government infrastructure is a dynamic system with a wide range of governance types differentiated by the federal, state, municipal, and tribal governments to provide physical facilities and the protection of their assets (CISA, 2022). The system works harmoniously among these stakeholders and provides efficient governance to ensure long-term economic growth and societal well-being. An OECD study has demonstrated the countries which adopted the mentioned stakeholders. The countries ensuring absolute value for money from infrastructure projects in all modes are the UK, Germany, Italy, France, and Australia. The countries that also provide capital for all cases above a certain value threshold are Hungary, Ireland, Japan, New Zealand, Norway, Turkey, and Korea. The government of Mexico ensures finance for only PPPs (OECD, 2017).

Some institutions and inter-governmental organisations, i.e., NATO, OECD, and UN, have influenced the development of government infrastructures. Furthermore, various national frameworks serve a vital role in improving government infrastructures. For instance, The World Bank created the Infrastructure Governance Framework, or InfraGov for short, to assist nations in overcoming these governance roadblocks and help them maximise the benefits of their infrastructure investments (Hawkesworth, 2022).

6.4 CYBER RESILIENCE IN GOVERNMENT INFRASTRUCTURE

Government critical infrastructures are attractive and strategically essential targets for local and international criminal organisations and groups. Moreover, unlike other sectors, the government stores more sensitive data than the private sector. The major challenge is implementing a high-level protection plan against these attackers while simultaneously providing full-time and uninterrupted access to citizens and other country elements.

Economic, domestic, and national security issues are interconnected, and policy options in these spheres may conflict. This creates a complex decision-making environment for policymakers (Yannakogeorgos & Lowther, 2013). A large-scale cyber governance model created to assess competing for policy agendas and capable of balancing national interests in cyberspace would benefit nations that want to be cyber-savvy (Dean & McDermott, 2017). The national cyber policy impacts the following: industrial and economic policy, domestic policy, international policy, security and defence policy, research, education, and technical development policy.

Safeguarding ICT networks that underpin the delivery of essential services is a significant challenge for policymakers today. As cyberspace evolves at the rate of innovation and expansion generated by private enterprises, governments have various degrees of capacity to adapt appropriately to this dynamic sector. Governments must adapt rapidly to comprehend the dynamics of digital change and maintain the requisite levels of innovation, training, and investment. In addition, they must build the capacity to investigate and prosecute cybercrime and improve their national incident response capability, which must encompass critical corporate and public sector organisations (Dennis et al., 2014). These policy areas provide the triangle base of a minimal national cyber system capable of protecting critical services, combating cybercrime, and providing adequate incident response capabilities. Policymakers must frequently talk to the private sector. Cybersecurity policymakers at the national level should set up a strategic vision, clarify policy options, and, most importantly, invest more money to reach their goals (Tiirmaa-Klaar, 2016).

Senior decision-makers should have a method to seize control of any successful national cyber system. It is responsible for directing, controlling, and funding national cyber activities. To make cyber security a high national priority, the cyber security leadership structure, which may resemble a National Cyber Security Council, should ideally submit to the supreme authority on national security or strategic planning and be near the cabinet of ministers (Warner, 2012). The leadership framework should also develop and revise national strategies and policies and monitor the execution of key national policy objectives. Senior public employees from cyber incident response, cybercrime, and a larger group of top civil servants should make up the national cyber regulating system. Diplomats, the defence community, and decision-makers in research and education, trade and industrial policy. Business sector organisations must be included alongside the interior and justice departments (Tiirmaa-Klaar, 2016). Many interested parties would help people understand the different parts of national cyber security policy and how they relate to other digital issues.

Traditional methods such as firewalls, preventing intrusions, and monitoring ports may need to be more efficacious against novel cyber threats. In order to implement an in-depth cyber resilience concept, other states and people who are well-skilled in the cyber security domain. With the help of the business sector, other actors, and persons with expertise in the cyber security arena, government organisations may execute a comprehensive cyber resilience concept:

- **Identify:** Government organisations should *identify* all the critical or essential services, prioritise them based on that criticality, and mark their importance. Accordingly, all the IT/OT assets, systems, and requirements or capacities have to be marked as prioritised based on these services. Moreover, organisations should also understand both the cyber and the risks, physical and risks. Combining all these risk portfolios or the threat surface scenario of these total IT/OT assets, government organisations must adequately define the threat scenarios as an event, incident or crisis to identify a particular situation as a crisis scenario. They can communicate appropriately to all the key stakeholders per the proper plan they have developed for identifying and addressing the specific critical assets for these services. In order to realise this, government organisations need a proper coordination matrix where all the key stakeholders have to be identified, and they have to be mapped to all the asset-related ownership and responsibility.

- **Protect:** Government organisations should *protect* their data storage network and all the critical systems and assets based on that criticality prioritisation. They should manage the device vulnerabilities, provide the right set of access as per the least privilege, and have a zero-trust requirement across architecture components; it is not only about the network but across all the systems. Moreover, regular backups should be conducted so that if there is a ransomware threat scenario, organisations can still get their critical services up and running from the backups. Furthermore, government organisations should train all the users with the policies and procedures regarding resiliency operations, their roles and responsibilities.

- **Detect:** Government organisations can have the ability to *detect* unauthorised activity by continuous monitoring of those critical devices and services. Therefore, they need to look into the continuous monitoring of logs and combining the threat intelligence from external environments and mapping that to the internal environment, how things are happening internally and how they can address the evolving threat scenarios from the external environments.

- **Respond:** Government organisations should develop and implement all the appropriate activities to address an event detected with the necessary services required for this *response* function. In order to do this, organisations need a proper standard operating procedure with all the necessary steps for on-time response and identifying all the critical stakeholders for communication. Furthermore, there should also be a proper communication strategy marked with all the critical responders who will be active in a crisis scenario. Thus, organisations must activate an internal crisis management team at the right time when defining or addressing the crisis scenario.

- **Recover:** Government organisations should have a proper *recovery* plan with all the necessary service level agreements defined, addressed, and effective through proper drills. In addition, organisations should have proper recovery time objectives for all their critical IT/OT assets supporting their critical services. Moreover, their architecture should have proper redundancy to fail in crisis scenarios. All this will be supported with proper exercise and evaluation plans so that in terms of there is a contingency or there is a post-incident requirement of learning about how they have done there, those things have to be continuously updated, and that should be shared with all the key stakeholders so that these stakeholders who are taking part in these activities of developing the resiliency of the total system or responding to these functions should always be up-to-date.

Cyber resilience is critical in the government sector as government agencies are responsible for providing essential services to the public, managing sensitive information, and maintaining national security. The sector relies heavily on technology to support its operations, making it vulnerable to cyber threats that can compromise its ability to provide critical services and jeopardise national security.

The importance of cyber resilience in the government sector can be summarised as follows:

Protection of critical infrastructure: The government sector's infrastructure, including energy grids, transportation systems, and communication networks, is a critical component of national infrastructure. Cyber resilience measures help to protect this infrastructure from cyber threats, such as cyberattacks or ransomware, which can cause physical damage, disrupt operations, and compromise national security.

Maintaining public safety and national security: Government agencies are responsible for maintaining public safety and national security. Any disruption to these services, or breach of sensitive information, can have severe consequences for public safety and national security. Cyber resilience measures can help to ensure the continuity of critical services, enable organisations to detect and respond to cyber incidents quickly, and recover from them effectively.

Protection of sensitive information: Government agencies collect and process sensitive information, including personal and financial data, classified information, and intellectual property. This information needs to be protected from cyber threats, such as theft, espionage, or manipulation. Cyber resilience measures, such as access controls, encryption, and network segmentation, can help to protect sensitive information from cyber threats.

Compliance with regulations: The government sector is subject to various regulations and standards, such as the Federal Information Security Management Act (FISMA) and the National Institute of Standards and Technology (NIST) Cybersecurity Framework. Cyber resilience measures help government agencies to comply with these regulations by providing a structured approach to managing cyber risks and ensuring the confidentiality, integrity, and availability of sensitive information.

In summary, cyber resilience is critical for the government sector as government agencies are responsible for providing essential services to the public, managing sensitive information, and maintaining national security. Cyber resilience measures help to protect critical infrastructure, maintain public safety and national security, protect sensitive information, and comply with regulations. The government sector should prioritise the development and implementation of cyber resilience measures to ensure they can effectively respond to cyber threats and protect their critical services.

6.5 CASE STUDIES

6.5.1 Case 1: SolarWinds

SolarWinds is an American company that develops software for the public and private sectors to meet the needs of these sectors in the cyber domain, such as network management and information technology. In December 2020, the company experienced one of the most significant cyberattacks in history, affecting the US Federal Government, NATO, the UK government and the European Parliament (Symantec, 2021). In the program 60 minutes, Microsoft president and vice chair Brad Smith said, "This is most likely the largest and most effective attack the world has ever seen." (Cerulus, 2021). Orion IT performance monitoring system, a product of SolarWinds company, was targeted by cyber actors (Oladimeji & Kerner, 2021). Orion has full access to the log and system performance data of the organisations it serves. For this reason, while it is an attack area for cybercriminals, it also has critical importance within organisations. The importance of the SolarWinds hack is its impact on a global scale. Thousands of private organisations, including major tech companies, such as Microsoft, Intel, Cisco, Deloitte, and FireEye, discovered and named the malware *sunburst*, and government agencies, such as Homeland Security, State Department, Commerce Department and Treasury Department, were affected.

Identify: Developed by cyber criminals, backdoor malware accidentally infected organisations' networks after an Orion update by SolarWinds company. In September 2019, the SolarWinds network system became vulnerable to cyber threat actors. In October 2019, cyber threat actors tested the Orion system with their malware. In February 2020, the malware infected the system. Finally, in March 2020, SolarWinds inadvertently began sending malware-containing Orion software updates to private organisations and government agencies (Oladimeji & Kerner, 2021). Identification of such vulnerabilities is of critical importance.

Protect: On 12 December 2020, SolarWinds was informed of the cyberattack. The company contacted law enforcement, intelligence agencies and governments to protect customer data and investigate the breach (Ramakrishna, 2021).

Detect: FireEye, a cyber security company, publicly announced the SolarWinds attack for the first time in their report. The report states that the malware developed by cyber criminals executes various commands to ensure that forensic tools and firewall detection systems are not running before it is infected the company's network system (Eckels et al., 2020). In a report published by Crodstrike, another cyber security firm, it was determined that it took for malware to remain undetected on the organisation's network was 95 days (Culafi, 2020).

Respond: FireEye found that specific DNS replies were causing the malware to self-destruct and stop further network activity. The domain used to resolve DGA domains has been modified to refer to a sinkhole server controlled by Microsoft with the assistance of Microsoft Threat Intelligence Center and GoDaddy's Abuse Team (Eckels et al., 2020).

Recover: By blocking and isolating the malware-containing version of Orion, companies disconnected threat actors from their network systems.

Lessons Learned: Organisations should adopt modern monitoring and collaboration software and ensure that firewalls and detection systems are always active. Moreover, organisations should be aware of the constantly evolving and sophisticated hacking methods and provide the highest possible protection for their critical assets. Lastly, they should search for vulnerabilities in their systems on 7/24.

6.5.2 Case 2: 2016 Clinton Campaign Data Leak

The Obama government openly accused Russia of interfering with the 2016 elections by hacking the Democratic National Committee and other political parties. The Office of the Director of National Intelligence and the Department of Homeland Security stated in response to mounting pressure from within the administration and from some lawmakers to publicly identify Moscow and hold it accountable for actions that were ostensibly meant to sow discord prior to the election. According to a joint statement from the two agencies, "the US Intelligence Community is satisfied that the Russian Government forwarded the recent intrusions of the emails of US individuals, institutions, and political organisations." The purpose of these thefts and exposures is to destabilise the American electoral system (Nakashima, 2016).

Identify: On 25 September 2015, an FBI agent told the DNC Information Technology manager in charge of the DNC network of anomalous network activity and mentioned the "Dukes," a well-known nickname for Russian government cyber agents. In October 2015, November 2015, and December 2015, an FBI agent called the DNC and urged the contractor to "confirm, to investigate particular conduct emerging from the DNC network that the FBI had recognised as potentially criminal" (CrowdStrike, 2020). The Department of Homeland Security stated that Russian intelligence agents launched attacks on voting systems in December 2015, including scanning a "widely used vendor of electoral equipment." The attacks lasted until June 2016. In April 2016, the GRU "...stole thousands of documents from the DCCC and DNC networks, including large volumes of election-related material...." The stolen information includes internal strategy documents, fundraising information, opposition research, and emails from DNC employees' work inboxes (CrowdStrike, 2020). On 14 April 2016, three days after the original breach, GRU agents downloaded rar. exe onto the DCCC's document server. The next day, the GRU inspected a compromised DCCC computer for data including search phrases such as

"Hillary," "DNC," "Cruz," and "Trump." On 28 April 2016, the DNC contractor reported odd behaviour on the DNC network. "We observed activity on one of our Windows servers that any authorised users could not have carried out." Accessing many separate password vaults of different people was the type of activity we were looking at, which is not something anyone would do. As a result, that set up an alarm for us..." The DNC's outside counsel contacted CrowdStrike on 30 April 2016 to explore a possible breach (CrowdStrike, 2020).

Protect: CrowdStrike moved swiftly upon entering the DNC. Falcon, a two-megabyte agent, launched on devices without a reboot, was used to examine every program-level action on the DNC's hundreds of computers. The unusual behaviour of a program or the transmission of millions of documents could be a sign. "We are not looking at personal information, documents, or emails," clarifies Co-Founder Alperovitch. "All we do is observe what is happening" (Walker, 2017). The DNC network was repaired between 10 June and 13 June 2016. CrowdStrike and DNC outside counsel informed the FBI on 13 June 2016 that Russian actors had been identified on the DNC network. CrowdStrike discovered indicators of intrusion (malicious code) on the computer network of the DNC, and the FBI sought forensic information, including these indicators. CrowdStrike continued to distribute breach-related information, such as "digital pictures" or copies of hard drives, with DNC permission until December 2016. On 14 June 2016, the DNC formally reported the hack of its network to CrowdStrike and detailed its findings. On 29 July 2016, the DCCC publicly confirmed that Russians had hacked it. Separate cyberattacks on state election systems continued until 29 December 2016. It was then determined that the Russians had scanned at least 21 state electoral infrastructures (CrowdStrike, 2020).

Detect: Every system action on the DNC's networks was logged and checked against CrowdStrike's historical intelligence database (the company processes 28 billion computer events daily). "Almost quickly, Falcon began revealing several indicators of DNC network intrusions," argues Alperovitch (Walker, 2017). Someone was investigating the DNC's servers, as one question had been answered. CrowdStrike evaluated its records to see if the hacking techniques were equivalent to any previously documented. They achieved success. According to allegations, two businesses concealed Donald Trump-related materials, including private conversations, email databases, and opposition research files. Alperovitch recalls, "We recognised that we had seen these actors before." Several minor but substantial signs support this conclusion, including information sent to an IP address associated with the hackers, an incorrectly spelt URL, and Moscow-related time zone variations. We may ascribe FANCY BEAR and COZY BEAR to the Russian government due to their nicknames (Walker, 2017). Both groups' rap repertoires were broad. COZY BEAR has already infiltrated the White House and the US Department of State and has been present in the DNC's system since the summer of 2015. After independently breaching the network in April 2016, FANCY BEAR hacked people across the globe, including the German Bundestag (Walker, 2017). The GRU stole more than 300 GB of data from the cloud account of the DNC. The GRU began generating copies of the DNC's data on 20 September 2016, utilising a capability designed to allow users to create data backups (referred to as "snapshots" by [redacted]). "The GRU stole these photographs by transferring them to a GRU-controlled (redacted) account, from which GRU-controlled devices received duplicates. This categorisation acknowledges that the United States election infrastructure is so essential to the American way of life that its impairment or destruction would have catastrophic consequences for the nation" (CrowdStrike, 2020).

Respond: Having contacted law enforcement and outside security firm CrowdStrike, the DNC initiated the scan for possible breaches. CrowdStrike started its Falcon software detection process, and the FBI searched for forensic information. After confirming the breach, CrowdStrike successfully isolated the system from hackers.

Recover: The DNC network was fixed after the breach was identified. However, it is too late to recover the stolen data. FBI and US law enforcement are still trying to determine who is responsible and prevent further damage to the DNC.

Lessons Learned: Users are having difficulty determining whether or not an email is legitimate. This issue is related to how email clients are designed (User Experience) and how the email protocol is developed in some respects. Users require additional real-time information after receiving an email to determine whether the communication is legitimate (IronScales, 2016). Fully automated phishing response systems should be used. Using cloud services with multifactor authentication increases the security of the data. Also, protecting physical systems such as laptops with remote access technology may have prevented kompromat attacks.

6.5.3 Case 3: Bundestag Hack

Germany claims to have thwarted a cyberattack on critical ministries, but it has refused to acknowledge media accusations that the perpetrator was the Russian intelligence unit responsible for election meddling in the United States. An Interior Ministry official said Wednesday, "We can verify that the Federal Office of Information Security (BSI) and intelligence services are investigating a cybersecurity incident involving the information technology and networks of the federal government." German officials blamed Fancy Bear for a May 2015 hack of the Bundestag and further cyberattacks aimed at Chancellor Merkel and others (Neuman, 2018). MPs got an email from the address UN.org in January 2015 that looked like a UN News Bulletin. The malware was installed on the machine once the user clicked on the link in the email. The malware was able to spread and eventually compromise the parliament's networks (Cyberlaw, 2015). Merkel said that she had concrete evidence implicating Russia in the outlandish cyberattack on the German parliament. In answer to questions raised in the Bundestag, the German chancellor revealed that the 2015 hacking attack that occurred in November, aimed at her parliamentary email address, "obviously disrupts a trusting relationship" with Russia (Burchard, 2020). The European Union sanctioned two Russian intelligence agents and a military intelligence organisation GRU division, for their actions in the 2015 cyberattack on the German parliament (Cerulus, 2020).

Identify: Hackers broke into the "Informationsverbund Berlin-Bonn" (IVBB) network of the government, a platform for communication set up apart from open networks for ostensibly greater security. It is only used by the Chancellery, the German parliament, the Federal Audit Office, federal ministries, and various security organisations in Berlin and Bonn, the former capitals of Germany where several ministries still have offices (Neuman, 2018). Unintentionally, Claudia Haydt detected the cyberattack. Haydt, the office manager for politician Inge Hoger of the Left Party, was shot while writing an email to a friend called René. She was unable to get beyond the greeting, however. The accent above the é would not be seen. Haydt tapped the key, but nothing happened. She tried repeatedly. Nothing. Haydt finally contacted 117, the technical support hotline for the Bundestag, and described her issue. She remembers the technician recommending a computer restart. Likewise, this was ineffectual. It was the afternoon of 8 May 2015, on Friday. The issue with René's name resurfaced on Monday, then again on Tuesday. A computer specialist from the Bundestag reinstalled Claudia Haydt's programs, but her accent remained. The technical staff of the German parliament then discovered something was amiss. They were unaware that they had previously lost control of Bundestag's computer network. On this day in May 2015, a digital conflict started that would last weeks and was unprecedented in Germany. It was as if a group of foreign guerrilla attackers had infiltrated the parliament building, taken its core systems, and burst into the Bundestag offices, except that the conflict was digital. At least 16 lawmakers' offices were inspected, mailboxes were copied, hard drives were checked, and potentially classified internal information was stolen (Beuth, 2017).

Protect: The Federal Ministry of the Interior partners with the Federal Office of Information Security to offer adequate IT security (BSI). Germany established its Cyber Security Strategy on 23 February 2011. As components of this strategy, the National Cyber Response Centre and the National Cyber Security Council were to be formed, among other things. As global networks grow increasingly linked, mishaps in other nations may affect the IT security in Germany. Consequently, the Federal Government interacts with international partners to enhance cross-border IT security, primarily within the European Union but also with the Organisation for Economic Cooperation and Development (OECD) and the Group of Eight (G8) (G 8) (Federal Ministry of the Interior and Community, 2011). Experts who work in the German internal intel agency (BfV) at the government's cyber defence centre detected the espionage attempt almost immediately and notified the Bundestag administration (Reuters, 2015).

Detect: The attack's effect and perpetrators' abilities should not be underestimated, despite the simplicity of the instruments obtained from the hack. From a strictly operational perspective, a tunnel and a control execution tool are sufficient for an attacker with the necessary rights to traverse a network unimpeded. Noting that Artefact #2 was collected on "22 April 2015" suggests that the settlement may have just lasted a few weeks. Since the attackers did not care about covering their tracks or keeping access for a long time, they did not try to create more network administrator accounts). The operation was meant to be done quickly to get as much data as possible (NetzPolitik, 2015). Two servers of the Die Linke network have yielded two suspicious artefacts. One is an open-source application that permits a Linux host to issue remote commands to a Windows host. The second is a proprietary weapon that, despite its modest size, possesses a specific capacity and works as an underpass that attackers may employ to sustain themselves within a compromised network. The combination of both malware has enabled the attackers to maintain a foothold within the network, collect data, and retransmit any information deemed worthwhile. The characteristics of one of the artefacts and intelligence obtained on the attackers' infrastructure indicate that Sofacy, a state-sponsored organisation, was behind the attack (APT28). However, it is possible that harmful artefacts have yet to be discovered. According to research conducted by the security firm FireEye in October 2014, the group may have originated in Russia (NetzPolitik, 2015). Artefact No. 1 was found in a Die Linke-operated File Server. This file is a 64-bit binary version of the open-source application Winexe. Similar to the more popular PSExec, Winexe allows system managers to perform actions on remote servers. Winexe is simple to use and necessitates no installation or configuration, unlike commercial alternatives such as Symantec pcAnywhere, which offer a more robust feature set. Winexe's Linux client is one of its advantages over PSExec. PSExec does not have a Linux client. For lateral movement across infiltrated networks, attackers utilise Winexe and PSExec more frequently. Antivirus and other commercial security tools generally safelist these applications so they do not arouse suspicion. Winexe is a Windows service that may be configured to automatically activate at system startup and await receiving commands through a specified pipe. Windows implements interprocess communication using named streams. Processes can connect and share data across a network via named pipes. Network computers can connect to the pipe server by opening a file handle on "ServerNamepipeahexec." Once a person or programme is connected to the pipe, they can swiftly deliver the information needed to execute orders (just as they would typically through a command line). The supplied data is subsequently transmitted to a "CreateProcessAsUserA" call, which executes the specified command. Using Artefact #1 alone, an attacker may be able to execute instructions, download or develop more scripts, and retrieve data while inside the network (for instance, through FTP) (NetzPolitik, 2015). Artefact #2 was discovered in Die Linke's Admin Controller. Despite its large download size, this is a handcrafted virus with limited capabilities (1,1 MB). The second artefact provides the attacker with a backdoor into the exploited network. The characteristics of the artefact suggest that the malware's creators named it "Xtunnel." As its name implies, the artefact looks to serve as a tunnel, granting the attacker persistent direct access to the internal network. Following activation, the artefact will attempt to establish a connection by creating a socket. If it fails, it will hibernate for 3 seconds before attempting again. The IP address with which the malware attempts to communicate is hardcoded in plaintext within the programme, indicating that the malware's developers did not attempt to disguise or obfuscate code. The method through which the object attempts to connect to the IP address is "176.31.112.10" (NetzPolitik, 2015).

Respond: After the onslaught was finally repulsed, German federal prosecutors opened an espionage probe, and Merkel warned of "hybrid warfare." Because the administration was sure that the invaders were operating on behalf of a foreign power, employees at the Chancery considered conducting counterattacks. They thought they came from Russia, namely from APT28, or "Fancy Bear," a unit of the country's military intelligence organisation (Beuth et al., 2017).

Recover: The computer system of the German parliament was shut down for four days for repair, and new safety procedures were added. Following investigations by the German intelligence service, it was determined that the attack was carried out by a 'foreign intelligence service' (Cyberlaw, 2015).

Lessons Learned: The hack in Germany proved that there is usually a need to bridge the gap between policies and actions. Organisations must ensure that on-the-ground actions are in sync with the goals of cybersecurity strategies. Operational employees in charge of security activities should be familiar with the strategies and procedures, but they must also conceal the goal and logic so that they can act in accordance with the practices' intent as situations arise. It is widely suggested that firms "prepare for a huge blow" concerning cyberattack practice planning. Do more than prepare for little occurrences. Prepare for large-scale attacks that are not tech-driven and will not be solved by your core team but instead require coordination across organisations and with outsiders (Bail, 2020).

Another vital aspect of addressing is communication during and after cyberattacks. Organisations must balance the necessity for rapid communication with the urgency of dealing with the current issue and getting the facts straight. Another essential point to remember is that communication is not only about the media when an assault or breach is made public. It must be in the broadest sense of communication, so it is also about internal communication to keep employees informed and possible communication with regulators and those affected by the breach. You must plan to address them ahead of time (Bail, 2020).

The Triton assault vector would not have spread throughout the Middle Eastern system without human error. Triton, designed to function as a Remote Access Trojan (RAT), requires programming control to execute actions on the targeted machine. This model emphasises training workers to be vigilant to potential dangers (Bail, 2020).

Antivirus is a must-have, but endpoint management and protection are even more beneficial. Endpoint security is essential in protecting your company from cyber threats such as ransomware. Antivirus software and other traditional endpoint security technologies have flaws. In any event, scan your frameworks and, at the very least, physically repair the most fundamental weaknesses (Bail, 2020).

6.5.4 Case 4: Aadhaar Hack

Aadhaar is a unique 12-digit identifying number given to each Indian resident by the Indian government. The Unique Identification Authority of India (UIDAI), part of the Indian Planning Commission, manages Aadhaar numbers and ID cards. A consumer's whole profile, including demographic and biometric data, is linked via their Aadhaar card, which serves as a single, distinctive identifying document or number. Although it can be utilised as the only method of identification when applying for services that require it, the Aadhaar card/UID does not substitute other forms of identification. Additionally, it serves as the basis for the Know Your Consumer (KYC) regulatory standards that banks, financial institutions, and other institutions that keep track of customer data employ. In addition, unlike passwords, biometric data cannot be altered; therefore, hackers may damage the victim severely with no redress if they successfully impersonate a fingerprint (Johar, 2017). The word Aadhaar card is now common to every Indian. About 1.2 billion persons in India now hold this 12-digit unique identity number. This identification number has gone a long way since its establishment and has had its ups and downs. The future does not appear to be any better. With breaches in the news regularly, it is a topic that all of us are concerned about. If the Aadhaar database is breached, the lives of 1.2 billion people could be jeopardised (Cybervie, 2019). A three-month investigation by HuffPost India claims that a software patch that deactivates crucial security features of the software used to register new Aadhaar users has allegedly undermined the data stored in India's contentious Aadhaar identifying database. Over 1 billion Indians' biometric data and private information are at risk, according to this debate. The patch, which is still widely used and can be downloaded for as cheap as Rs 2,500 (about $35), enables unlawful individuals from any country to produce Aadhaar numbers at will (Racha Kharia, 2018). Installing the enrolment application on a personal computer and upgrading a folder containing Java libraries using Control C and Control V cut-and-paste instructions are all required to utilise the patch (Racha, 2018).

Identify: Orlando Padilla, the founder of a specialised cybersecurity company NoMotion Software LLC, claims that the hackers created 26 different code-level changes to the registration software, confirming concerns that the hack resulted from knowledgeable and sophisticated adversaries with a well-defined plan. According to Padilla, the application also disables the biometric security features connected to enrolment supervisors, who supervise the actions of registration operators (Sethi, 2018). A malignant patch enables an individual to generate unauthorised Aadhaar numbers by circumventing crucial security measures such as the biometric authentication of registration operators. The patch bypasses the enrolment software's built-in GPS security function, which is intended to determine each enrolment centre's precise position, allowing users to be registered from any place in the world, such as Karachi, Beijing or Kabul. The patch diminishes the sensitivity of the enrolling program's iris-recognition technology, allowing them to impersonate the software using an image of a registered operator instead of their physical presence (Sethi, 2018).

Protect: The UIDAI adopts the following precautions to ensure the security of Aadhar Data. According to UIDAI, the Aadhaar database in CIDR has never been compromised since its inception. Some organisations have published their beneficiary information, including Aadhaar details, on their websites to comply with the transparency regulations. However, the UIDAI guarantees that Aadhaar is not utilised in unnecessary ways. The UIDAI employs cutting-edge security technologies to safeguard the data of Aadhaar Cardholders. In addition, they continually enhance them to counter various hazards and obstacles (Garg, 2021). According to Ministry of Electronics and Information Technology guidelines, agencies cannot store sensitive personal information, including passwords, biometric information, financial data (bank account, debit card, credit card, and other payment instrument details), medical records and history, physical and mental health, and sexual orientation, without encryption. By preventing the host computer from saving user biometric information, the possibility of using saved biometric information for authentication without user agreement is eliminated (Johar, 2017). Anand Venkatanarayanan, a cyber security specialist and software developer for HuffPost India who revealed his findings with the NCIIPC, claims that the patch was made by grafting code from older, less secure versions of the software onto more recent versions of the software (Racha, 2018).

Detect: The current onslaught arises from an action taken in 2010 to allow private agencies to register citizens in the Aadhaar system to expedite the process. The Enrolment Client Multi-Platform (ECMP), developed by Mindtree, a Bengaluru-based business, was installed on the hundreds of computers maintained by these private operators in the same year. In addition to private enrolling businesses, the UIDAI has enrolment contracts with "common service centres," which are computer kiosks located in villages and provide access to commonly used e-government services like pensions and student financial aid. By the end of February 2018, 180 million Indians had been enrolled at these facilities. According to cyber security expert Bjorksten, installing the software on every enrolment workstation "puts the operation of crucial Aadhaar components in the control of the system's adversaries" (Racha, 2018). According to UIDAI, the ECMP is an "offline client" responsible for enrolling users and updating their data without requiring a network connection in a peasant area with limited access. The software stores change on a local scale on the device installed before transmitting them when an internet connection exists. An essential security aspect of the ECMP is that Aadhaar enrolments and changes must be "approved" by an authorised operator and, if applicable, her supervisor, who must place their fingers against a biometric scanner. The ECMP creates an enrolment packet file when the operator or supervisor approves, which is then forwarded to UIDAI servers. According to UIDAI, their back-end software evaluates the enrolment packet and the associated meta-data cluster. According to publicly accessible UIDAI documentation and discussions with professionals who have analysed the enrolment client, the meta-data is probably a recording of an offline procedure in which the enrolment operator's biometric signature is compared to her biometrics stored locally on the hard disk of the computer performing the enrolment. The software patch addresses this flaw: Enrolment packets generated by compromised software are indistinguishable from authentic ones during biometric sign-off, an offline process (Sethi, 2018). Padilla's analysis revealed that most changes were done by modifying four ".jar" files in the Java library of the enrolling software. HuffPost India has concealed the jar files' names to safeguard the software's remaining security. The subsequent functional changes are the outcome of the confirmed code alterations (Sethi, 2018):

- All biometric authentication has been turned off.
- Operators do not need to use biometric authentication to log in.
- Biometric authentication by the supervisor can also be bypassed.
- Operators can now log in even if their authentication fails due to a bug in Login Failure.
- Operator iris authentication has been disabled.
- Operators can log into the enrolling software continuously with deleted login time-out sessions.

- Timezone functioning has been affected by several modifications. In particular, a feature that checked if the program was using Indian Standard Time, enabling the program to determine location, has been inactivated.
- A device that tallied the count of mismatched fingerprints has been eliminated.
- The program now validates the correctness of enrolment packets and syncs with UIDAI servers in three ways.
- The system now recognises the Aadhaar numbers with the prefixes 0 and 1. The alteration is puzzling because real Aadhaar numbers do not start with 0 or 1.
- A Java integrity check that determines whether the software library has been modified has been amended.

Respond: The assertions have been denied by the UIDAI as absolutely false. In response to the charges, the UIDAI stated that no operator could create or update an Aadhaar card unless an individual provided biometric information. The UIDAI stated that before issuing an Aadhaar, it matches all of the biometrics of a person enrolling for Aadhaar – ten fingerprints and both iris – with the biometrics of all Aadhaar holders and that the claims of inserting information into the Aadhaar database were "absolutely false" (BusinessToday.In, 2018). Despite these charges and wrangling, UIDAI officials have been working on various approaches to strengthen the Aadhaar system. A 16-digit virtual ID has been introduced. The virtual ID is stated to be transient and can only be generated by an Aadhaar cardholder individually. After a specific amount of time has passed, the virtual ID can be altered (Cybervie, 2019). UIDAI has taken steps to eradicate bogus websites and apps that give information to attackers. It also barred 5000 officials from using the portals without permission (Tech2, 2018).

Recover: According to the experts interviewed by HuffPost India, the weakness results from a technology decision taken at the program's inception. Therefore, addressing it and any potential future flaws will alter Aadhaar's fundamental structure. Gustaf Bjorksten, a Chief Technologist in a global technology policy and advocacy organisation, namely Access Now, and one of the professionals who reviewed the patch at the request of HuffPost India, stated, "Whoever created the patch was highly determined to undermine Aadhaar." Bjorksten continued, "There are undoubtedly several criminal, political, domestic, and international individuals and organisations who would benefit sufficiently from this Aadhaar compromise to justify the expense of installing the patch" (Racha, 2018). To have any chance of protecting Aadhaar, the system's design would need to be drastically revised.

Lessons Learned: A more trustworthy option would be a web-based strategy with all software placed on the UIDAI's servers and enrolling operators having a username and password to access the system. An analogy would be the distinction between Microsoft Word, which is used by installing it on computers, and Google Documents, which hosts online and is accessible to users with only logging in (Racha, 2018). According to the software architect B. Regunath, who led the Mindtree team working on the project because Internet access was inadequate in many parts of the country. To make up for effectively handing over management of the enrolment process to tens of thousands of operators distributed throughout the nation, Regunath's team added security safeguards to the program. The most prominent security feature obligated all operators to log into the software by initially procuring a fingerprint or iris scan. Each laptop must also be enrolled with UIDAI (Racha, 2018). Controlling access to third-party data is necessary. Improve the administration of API access and intrusion prevention solutions. Regular reviews of security measures ensure that the e-hospital infrastructure is not compromised (Tech2, 2018). Aadhaar may only be modified in a restricted manner. It will probably increase privacy concerns. Lack of government supervision and data usage policies could worsen the issue (Agrawal et al., 2017).

REFERENCES

Abomhara, M. & Køien, G. M., (2015). Cyber security and the internet of things: Vulnerabilities, threats, intruders and attacks. *Journal of Cyber Security and Mobility*, 4, 65–88.

Bail, S., (2020). *LinkedIn*. [Online] Available at: https://www.linkedin.com/pulse/lessons-learned-from-cyber-attack-german-authorities-2015-bail/ [Accessed 10 June 2022].

Bannister, F. & Connolly, R., (2014). ICT, public values and transformative government: A framework and programme for research. *Government Information Quarterly*, 31(1), 119–128.

Blythe, J. M., (1992). *Ideal Government and the Mixed Constitution in the Middle Ages*. Princeton: Princeton University Press.

Bonina, C. M. & Cordella, A., (2009). *Public Sector Reforms and the Notion of 'Public Value': Implications for Government Deployment*. S.l.: AMCIS.

Brunner, E. M. & Suter, M., (2008). *International CIIP Handbook 2008/2009: An Inventory of 25 National and Seven International Critical Information Infrastructure Protection Policies*. Zürich: Center for Security Studies (CSS), ETH Zurich.

Burchard, H. V. D., (2020). *Politico*. [Online] Available at: https://www.politico.eu/article/merkel-blames-russia-for-outrageous-cyber-attack-on-german-parliament/ [Accessed 5 June 2022].

BusinessToday.In, (2018). *Businesstoday.in*. [Online] Available at: https://www.businesstoday.in/latest/economy-politics/story/aadhaar-software-hack-uidai-data-ghost-entries-110677-2018-09-11 [Accessed 12 June 2022].

Cerulus, L., (2020). *Politico*. [Online] Available at: https://www.politico.eu/article/eu-sanctions-russias-fancy-bear-hackers-for-2015-bundestag-breach/ [Accessed 6 June 2022].

Cerulus, L., (2021). *Web.archive.org*. [Online] Available at: https://web.archive.org/web/20210215110722/https://www.politico.eu/article/solarwinds-largest-cyberattack-ever-microsoft-president-brad-smith/ [Accessed 22 March 2022].

CISA, (2022). *Government Facilities Sector, Critical Infrastructure Sectors, Cybersecurity and Infrastructure Security Agency*. CISA. Retrieved from Government Facilities Sector.

CrowdStrike, (2020). *CrowdStrike*. [Online] Available at: https://www.crowdstrike.com/blog/bears-midst-intrusion-democratic-national-committee/ [Accessed 1 June 2022].

Culafi, A., (2020). *www.techtarget.com*. [Online] Available at: https://www.techtarget.com/searchsecurity/news/252476720/CrowdStrike-Intrusion-self-detection-dwell-time-both-increasing [Accessed 22 March 2022].

Cyberlaw, (2015). *Cyberlaw*. [Online] Available at: https://cyberlaw.ccdcoe.org/wiki/Bundestag_Hack_(2015) [Accessed 6 June 2022].

Cybervie, (2019). *Cybervie.com*. [Online] Available at: https://www.cybervie.com/blog/aadhaar-card-breach/ [Accessed 12 June 2022].

Dean, B. & McDermott, R., (2017). A research agenda to improve decision making in cyber security policy. *Journal of Law & International Affairs*, 5(1), 29–31.

Dennis, A., Jones, R., Kildare, D. & Barclay, C., (2014). Design science approach to developing and evaluating a national cybersecurity framework for Jamaica. *The Electronic Journal of Information Systems in Developing Countries*, 62(1), 1–18.

Dunleavy, P. & Margetts, H., (2006). New public management is dead-long live digital-era governance. *Journal of Public Administration Research and Theory*, 16(3), 467–494.

Federal Ministry of the Interior and Community, (2011). *Bmi.bund.de*. [Online] Available at: https://www.bmi.bund.de/EN/topics/security/it-cybersecurity/it-cybersecurity-node.html [Accessed 10 June 2022].

Garg, T., (2021). *Paisabazaar.com*. [Online] Available at: https://www.paisabazaar.com/aadhar-card/leaked-aadhaar-details-bank-account-cannot-hacked/ [Accessed 12 June 2022].

Hawkesworth, I., (2022). *Successful Infrastructure Projects Require Efficient Governance. World Bank Blogs*. Retrieved from https://blogs.worldbank.org/governance/successful-infrastructure-projects-require-efficient-governance.

IronScales, (2016). *Ironscales.com*. [Online] Available at: https://ironscales.com/blog/clinton-email-leaks/ [Accessed 4 June 2022].

Johar, A., (2017). *Economictimes.indiatimes*. [Online] Available at: https://economictimes.indiatimes.com/tech/internet/watch-out-aadhar-biometrics-are-an-easy-target-for-hackers/articleshow/61183055.cms?from=mdr [Accessed 13 June 2022].

Kshetri, N., (2013). Cybercrime and cyber-security issues associated with China: Some economic and institutional considerations. *Electronic Commerce Research*, 13(1), 41–69.

Lau, E. & Carrasco, B., (2020). *Why Infrastructure Governance Matters. Asian Development Bank*. Retrieved from https://blogs.adb.org/blog/why-infrastructure-governance-matters.

Nakashima, E., (2016). *Cs.brown.edu*. [Online] Available at: https://cs.brown.edu/people/jsavage/VotingProject/2016_10_07_USAccusesRussiaOfHackingElections.pdf [Accessed 1 June 2022].

Ndou, V., (2004). E-Government for developing countries: opportunities and challenges. *The Electronic Journal of Information Systems in Developing Countries*, 18(1), 1–24.

NetzPolitik, (2015). *NetzPolitik.org*. [Online] Available at: https://netzpolitik.org/2015/digital-attack-on-german-parliament-investigative-report-on-the-hack-of-the-left-party-infrastructure-in-bundestag/ [Accessed 6 June 2022].

Neuman, S., (2018). *NPR*. [Online] Available at: https://www.npr.org/sections/thetwo-way/2018/03/01/589787931/russias-fancy-bear-reportedly-hacks-german-government-networks [Accessed 6 June 2022].

OECD, (2015). *Towards a Framework for Governance of Infrastructure. Public Governance Committee*, Public Governance and Territorial Development Directorate, OECD. Retrieved from https://www.oecd.org/gov/budgeting/Towards-a-Framework-for-the-Governance-of-Public-Infrastructure.pdf.

OECD, (2017). *Getting Infrastructure Right: The Ten Key Governance Challenges and Policy Options*. Retrieved from https://www.oecd.org/gov/getting-infrastructure-right.pdf.

OECD/ADB, (2019). *Government at a Glance Southeast Asia 2019*. Paris: OECD Publishing. https://doi.org/10.1787/9789264305915-en.

Beuth, P., Biermann, K., Klingst, M. & Stark, H., (2017). *Zeit.de*. [Online] Available at: https://www.zeit.de/digital/2017-05/cyberattack-bundestag-angela-merkel-fancy-bear-hacker-russia?utm_referrer=https%3A%2F%2Fwww.google.com%2F [Accessed 6 June 2022].

Poel, I. V. D. & Christen, M., (2020). Core values and value conflicts in cybersecurity: Beyond privacy versus security. *The Ethics of Cybersecurity*, 21, 45.

Racha, K., (2018). *Huffpost.com*. [Online] Available at: https://www.huffpost.com/archive/in/entry/uidai-s-aadhaar-software-hacked-id-database-compromised-experts-confirm_a_23522472 [Accessed 12 June 2022].

Ramakrishna, S., (2021). *Oragematter.solarwinds.com*. [Online] Available at: https://orangematter.solarwinds.com/2021/01/11/new-findings-from-our-investigation-of-sunburst/ [Accessed 22 March 2022].

Reuters, (2015). *Reuters*. [Online] Available at: https://www.reuters.com/article/germany-cybersecurity-idINL5N0Y63P720150515 [Accessed 6 June 2022].

Oladimeji, S. & Kerner, S. M.., (2021). *TechTarget*. [Online] Available at: https://www.techtarget.com/whatis/feature/SolarWinds-hack-explained-Everything-you-need-to-know [Accessed 22 March 2022].

Sethi, A., (2018). *Huffpost.com*. [Online] Available at: https://www.huffpost.com/archive/in/entry/uidai-aadhaar-hack-new-analysis-shows-hackers-changed-enrolment-software-code-in-26-places_a_23525828 [Accessed 12 June 2022].

Agrawal, S., Banerjee, S. & Sharma, S., (2017). Privacy and security of aadhaar A computer science perspective. *Economic & Political Weekly*, liI, 93–102.

Skopik, F., Settani, G. & Fiedler, R., (2016). A problem shared is a problem halved: A survey on the dimensions of collective cyber defense through security information sharing. Computers & Security, 60, 154–176.

Eckels, S. & Smith, J. & Ballentin, W., (2020). mandiant.com. [Online] Available at: https://www.mandiant.com/resources/sunburst-additional-technical-details [Accessed 22 March 2022].

Symantec, (2021). Attacks Against the Government Sector. [Online] Available at: https://symantec-enterprise-blogs.security.com/blogs/expert-perspectives/attacks-against-government-sector [Accessed 22 March 2022].

Tech2, (2018). firstpost.com. [Online] Available at: https://www.firstpost.com/tech/news-analysis/aadhaar-security-breaches-here-are-the-major-untoward-incidents-that-have-happened-with-aadhaar-and-what-was-actually-affected-4300349.html [Accessed 12 June 2022].

Tiirmaa-Klaar, H., (2016). Building national cyber resilience and protecting critical information infrastructure. Journal of Cyber Policy, 1(1), 94–106.

Voegtlin, C. & Scherer, A. G., (2017). Responsible innovation and the innovation of responsibility: Governing sustainable development in a globalised world. Journal of Business Ethics, 143, 227–243.

Walker, C. S., (2017). Wired UK. [Online] Available at: https://www.wired.co.uk/article/dnc-hack-proof-russia-democrats [Accessed 4 June 2022].

Warner, M., (2012). Cybersecurity: A pre-history. Intelligence and National Security, 27(5), 781–799.

Weiss, H. & Courty, M. A., (1993). The genesis and collapse of third millennium north mesopotamian civilization. Science, 261(5124), 995–1004.

Yannakogeorgos, P. & Lowther, A. B., (2013). Conflict and Cooperation in Cyberspace: The Challenge to National Security. s.l.:CRC Press.

Chapter 7

Healthcare sector

The importance of health infrastructure in advancing health policy and welfare mechanisms cannot be overstated. The sector emphasises the need to provide healthcare facilities across the country. It has been defined that the health infrastructure is an essential provision for implementing productive and meaningful health activities for the public. The health infrastructure includes skilled labour, electronic information systems, public health organisations, resources, and research. When people pay attention to the growth of health infrastructure, they must also develop these components. One of the most significant considerations is that key actors within the health sector must detect flaws and deficiencies in medical and healthcare facilities. After these components have been recognised, professionals must devise methods to improve them. Furthermore, contemporary, scientific, and inventive ways must improve the health infrastructure. Health infrastructure advancements will substantially contribute to supporting the health and well-being of all people, independent of their age, community, or category.

7.1 WHAT IS HEALTHCARE AS AN INFRASTRUCTURE?

The health infrastructure is essential for determining a country's healthcare delivery and welfare mechanisms. The infrastructure has been regarded as the foundation for providing public health services. It denotes the investments and importance of infrastructure development in both the public and private sectors. The health infrastructure measurements in this section are divided into two groups: educational infrastructure and service infrastructure (National Health Profile, 2018). The definition and purpose of the health infrastructure can be described in the following three major components (Office of Disease Prevention and Health Promotion, 2020):

- Up-to-date data and information systems
- Trained and skilled personnel

DOI: 10.1201/9781003449522-7

- Organisations capable of analysing and reacting to public health requirements

The basis for carrying out the essential obligations of public health, which have been identified as the following critical health services, are provided by public health infrastructure (Public Health Functions Steering Committee, 1995):

1. Taking account of people's health so they can spot and solve community health problems.
2. Identifying and investigating community-wide health threats.
3. The need to inform and educate the community regarding health problems.
4. Mobilising community partnerships and action to solve health issues.
5. Creating strategies and programs to assist people in achieving their health objectives.
6. Regulating regulations safeguarding people's health and keeping the environment safe.
7. Providing critical healthcare to people and guaranteeing that health service is available.
8. Making sure the public and private healthcare employees are qualified.
9. Examine personal and social healthcare's efficacy, availability, and effectiveness.
10. Analysing to find new insights and answers to health concerns.

7.2 WHY IS HEALTHCARE INFRASTRUCTURE IMPORTANT?

The most crucial element within the health infrastructure is the continuity of health services. "The process through which the physician-led care team and the patient collaboratively participate in continuing healthcare management through the common goal of cost-effective, high-quality medical treatment," according to the American Academy of Family Physicians, describes the continuity of health service. In other words, the degree to which that series of discrete medical care events is experienced as connected, consistent, and coherent with the patient's medical requirements is defined as continuity. Mainly two factors differentiate continuity of care from other care approaches: Focusing on individual patients and care over time (Haggerty, 2003). The continuum of medical care has been crucial for general practice. Continuity results in better healthcare satisfaction rates and results. In addition, it enhances the cost efficiency of the health service (Jeffers & Baker, 2016). Continuity is divided by Haggerty (2003) into three main categories: Informational, Management, and Relational. Moreover, Access and Service continuities are also essential to mention.

Each type's value varies depending on the treatment environment and the providers. In addition, each can be evaluated from a people or disease-centred viewpoint.

- **Continuity of Information:** It is described as "the utilisation of information on personal circumstances and historical events to provide current treatment suited for each individual." Information that has been documented primarily focuses on the illness. Still, information about the patient's context, preferences, and values is crucial to connect disparate care events and guaranteeing that services are responsive to needs. When healthcare professionals interact with patients, this information accumulates in their memories.
- **Continuity of Management:** This type of continuity is critical in the case of complex or chronic clinical conditions that necessitate the treatment of many clinicians who may work at odds with one another. Continuity is established while services are given in a complimentary and timely manner. Care protocols or shared management plans help maintain administration consistency, giving clinicians and patients confidence and predictability in the future.
- **Continuity of Relationship:** Relational continuity can be explained as a therapeutic relationship between one or more healthcare suppliers and a patient. It creates a link between past and present healthcare and future healthcare. Primary and mental healthcare place the most priority on this. A stable core of personnel gives patients a sense of predictability and coherence even in situations when there is no expectation of developing long-lasting relationships with various caregivers, such as nursing home care and inpatient services.
- **Continuity of Access:** Continuity of access in mental health treatment refers to the idea that continuous communication is required to guarantee that administration objectives are adjusted and met and that supplies must often enable a wide variety of services. This type of continuity requires flexibility in adjusting care to changes in an individual's circumstances and requirements. Long-term care needs both flexibility and consistency for managerial continuity.
- **Continuity of Service:** The importance of continuity of service is also understood by the lack of it. Unfortunately, a cyber assault on a healthcare institution that interrupts its ability to handle patients could be detrimental to a community's handling of standard treatment and patient surges during disasters. There are three types of cyber assaults that influence healthcare institutions. In Figure 7.1, these categories are shown and explained briefly:

To conclude, the experience of the continuity of healthcare service for patients and their families is the notion that suppliers are aware of previous events, that various providers have agreed on management strategies and

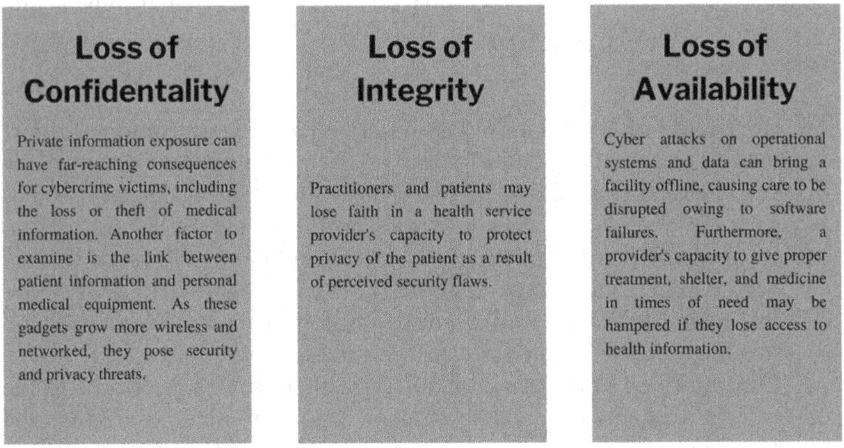

Loss of Confidentality

Private information exposure can have far-reaching consequences for cybercrime victims, including the loss or theft of medical information. Another factor to examine is the link between patient information and personal medical equipment. As these gadgets grow more wireless and networked, they pose security and privacy threats.

Loss of Integrity

Practitioners and patients may lose faith in a health service provider's capacity to protect privacy of the patient as a result of perceived security flaws.

Loss of Availability

Cyber attacks on operational systems and data can bring a facility offline, causing care to be disrupted owing to software failures. Furthermore, a provider's capacity to give proper treatment, shelter, and medicine in times of need may be hampered if they lose access to health information.

Figure 7.1 Classification of the impact of cyberattacks on healthcare facilities.

plans and that the healthcare service is provided for them in the future. Nonetheless, the continuity concept can vary in different contexts. The synthesis of each discipline will enable a provider to interpret how other providers understand this concept and eliminate misunderstanding by utilising universal terms accepted globally. It contributes to the goal of cost-effective and high-quality health service.

7.3 KEY PLAYERS AND STAKEHOLDERS

There are five key players and stakeholders in the health ecosystem that we have enumerated. These are classified as regulators, payers, suppliers, providers, and patients as shown in Figure 7.2 (Writers, 2019). As regulators, governments are responsible for providing and regulating health services. Governments must ensure that individuals, companies and groups in this industry act honestly and with integrity. Various institutions within the structure of countries are responsible for these regulations. For example, public institutions are responsible for the accreditation of doctors and private companies. Another stakeholder group in the health ecosystem is payers. There are many ways to finance health services. This financing can be obtained from patients who directly pay for the service received, from private sector commercial insurance companies or directly from public health services. Furthermore, suppliers are vital to the ecosystem (Wegener, 2022). Companies and groups provide the products, services, and facilities used in diagnosing, treating, and advising patients, collectively referred to as suppliers. These suppliers may be pharmaceutical and medical technology companies and construction companies that provide the infrastructure for

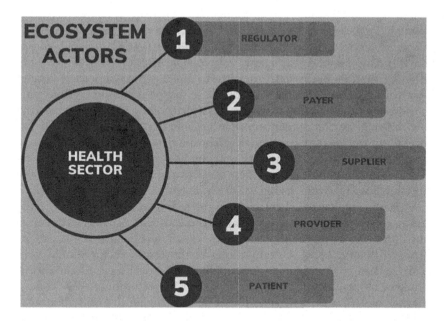

Figure 7.2 Health sector actors.

health services. The fourth key stakeholders are the providers of the health services, which are the healthcare workers. Healthcare workers consist of doctors, nurses, technicians, and secretaries. Healthcare workers can be employed in the public and private sectors or provide services voluntarily. Lastly, patients are one of the key players in the health sector. The World Health Organisation states that health services are a right, and every person has the right to be treated at the highest attainable health standard. Towards this, health services should be reachable on time, accessible, and affordable. Today, many countries place patients at the centre of the healthcare system's decision-making processes, promoting patient empowerment. The number of countries using this method is also increasing day by day.

7.4 CYBER RESILIENCE IN HEALTHCARE INFRASTRUCTURE

Cyber attacks in the health sector can be carried out on issues such as the shutdown of critical systems and the seizure of confidential information of studies on subjects such as vaccines or drugs. These attacks can disrupt the health system, disruption of first aid to people, or cause material shortages in epidemic situations. In such cases, when attacks occur, managers try to avoid malfunctions in the system or information leaks that may occur in the system instead of providing services to people. In this case, all the people waiting for service experience difficulties (Agrawal et al., 2022).

At least 560 healthcare institutions and providers' systems were taken offline by malicious attackers in 2020 alone, and they demanded payment to resume service delivery (Lehmann & Rosenblatt, 2022). These facilities, which tried to provide health services to people after the attacks, were in a difficult situation. In this case, they had to direct people who needed urgent intervention to other facilities. In this case, hospital administrations must consider how they will treat whom, what drugs they will give to patients, how they will protect patient information, and many other issues and produce solutions. This situation puts both hospital administrations and people in a difficult situation. Because they know how helpless they have left the health systems and how critical these services are, attackers are increasingly targeting hospitals, thus trying to get a ransom.

While the number of cyberattacks in the health sector is increasing daily, various measures must be taken against these attacks. Various steps can be taken on cyber resilience to ensure this security (Lehmann & Rosenblatt, 2022; Williams, 2010). Organisations in the health sector should work to strengthen corporate-wide security on cyber resilience. Organisations should be more resilient to attacks. Therefore, the importance of the concept of cyber resilience is increasing. It can be challenging to avoid all attacks, so organisations should equip themselves with prevention, preparedness, and response tools. This way, the risk of being affected by attacks will be reduced. Cyberattacks are accepted as a reality rather than an *if*. Thus, for cyber resilience practices, industries such as the health sector should prepare for what to do when an attack occurs. Healthcare organisations should implement risk management strategies. In addition, they should have an incident response plan. In order to ensure security, patient data must be securely encrypted. In order to achieve these, following and applying various cyber resilience frameworks is the most logical option to protect from or resist attacks (McKeon, 2021).

Cyber resilience is essential in the healthcare sector as healthcare organisations are responsible for providing critical services that directly impact patient care and well-being. The sector relies heavily on technology to support its operations, making it vulnerable to cyber threats that can compromise its ability to provide critical services and jeopardise patient safety and privacy.

The importance of cyber resilience in the healthcare sector can be summarised as follows:

Protection of critical infrastructure: The healthcare sector's infrastructure, including hospitals, clinics, and medical devices, is a critical component of national infrastructure. Cyber resilience measures help to protect this infrastructure from cyber threats, such as cyberattacks or ransomware, which can cause physical damage, disrupt operations, and compromise patient care and safety.

Maintaining patient care and safety: Healthcare organisations are responsible for maintaining patient care and safety. Any disruption to these services, or breach of sensitive information, can have severe consequences for patient care and safety. Cyber resilience measures can help to ensure the continuity of critical services, enable organisations to detect and respond to cyber incidents quickly, and recover from them effectively.

Protection of sensitive information: Healthcare organisations collect and process sensitive information, including personal and health data, financial data, and intellectual property. This information needs to be protected from cyber threats, such as theft, espionage, or manipulation. Cyber resilience measures, such as access controls, encryption, and network segmentation, can help to protect sensitive information from cyber threats.

Compliance with regulations: The healthcare sector is subject to various regulations and standards, such as the Health Insurance Portability and Accountability Act (HIPAA) and the General Data Protection Regulation (GDPR). Cyber resilience measures help healthcare organisations to comply with these regulations by providing a structured approach to managing cyber risks and ensuring the confidentiality, integrity, and availability of sensitive information.

In summary, cyber resilience is critical for the healthcare sector as healthcare organisations are responsible for providing critical services that directly impact patient care and safety. Cyber resilience measures help to protect critical infrastructure, maintain patient care and safety, protect sensitive information, and comply with regulations. The healthcare sector should prioritise the development and implementation of cyber resilience measures to ensure they can effectively respond to cyber threats and protect their critical services.

7.5 CASE STUDIES

7.5.1 Case 1: Magellan Health

In April 2020, one of the most significant cyberattacks in the healthcare sector took place. In this attack, the attacker obtained the credentials of Magellan Health's employees through social engineering. It then used these compromised credentials and malware to access more accounts and networks. This way, the attacker leaked sensitive data on the system and then launched a ransomware attack (Seals, 2020). As a result of the attack, Magellan Health announced that 365,000 patient records, including information such as social security numbers, treatment records and employee payroll data, were affected by this attack. However, it was later determined that the data of approximately 1.7 million people were stolen due to this ransomware attack (Toms, 2020). This was the second attack on Magellan Health in a year. The conclusion reached as a result of the lawsuits was that Magellan Health did not follow the best security practices and did not invest enough in cybersecurity measures (McGee, 2020).

Identify: A critical task to do as part of this step is to train the workforce, identify high-risk populations, and conduct frequent phishing tests. Nevertheless, this application cannot be seen here. The company must determine which vendors have access to its networks and assess their level of security maturity to secure its security. The protect function needed to be carried out correctly in this instance. In this assault example, it is clear that the attackers used the employees' identification information to carry out the attack, which was not adequately safeguarded.

Protect: The attack is carried out by using the employees' identity information. The company's security system does not have a multi-factor authentication (MFA) system. This verification system is a vital defence tool for such attacks. The identify function was not conducted for this case, nor could the protect function be exercised.

Detect: Another step that institutions should take to ensure their security is to ensure that the unusual behaviours occurring in the system are detected in real-time. In case of such detection, their employees who may be disabled from accessing the system should be warned. In this example, these necessary steps have yet to be taken. In addition, another measure that can be taken is to use geolocation services to identify anomalies that occur during file transfer. In this way, the sources of the anomalies can be understood.

Respond: The deficiencies experienced in the identify part also negatively affect the response part. These definitions should be made within the framework of the precautions to be taken, and these identified vendors should be integrated into the incident response plan. However, since there is already a problem while identifying this integration could not be realised for the response part either.

Recover: No study has been conducted by the institution on the recovery step to strengthen cyber resilience.

Lessons Learned: The main issue, in this case, appears to be the inappropriate actions within the protect phase. Incorrect application of the Identify and Protect sections resulted in a ransom payment to the attackers, which lost the company and its clients' money. There is no need for a ransom payment, and customers are not inconvenienced if every step is carried out perfectly.

7.5.2 Case 2: United Healthcare Services

United Healthcare Services (UHS), located in 400 and 3.5 million clients throughout the United States and the United Kingdom, was the unlucky target of the most devastating ransomware attacks in the healthcare business in 2020. Ruyk, a popular ransomware variant in the worldwide healthcare industry during the last two years, was implicated in the event (Arctic Wolf, 2021). In September, the attackers took down the organisation's entire IT network in the United States, requiring employees to rely on offline activities such as paper documents, redirecting clients to other doctors and cancelling meetings. The total restoration of UHS's systems took approximately a month. The FB, the IUS Cybersecurity & Infrastructure Security Agency, and the Department of Health and Human Services (HHS) released a warning in October 2020, suggesting "their reliable knowledge told them that there was an elevated and impending cybercrime threat to US hospitals and healthcare professionals." Ruyk was one of the strains mentioned in the warning event (Arctic Wolf, 2021).

Identify: The identification step was not executed by the company.

Protect: The protection was not enough for the attack. After the attack, the IT team took all the files offline to prevent further attacks while the recovery and analyses were executed.

Detect: According to security experts, the attack most likely began using the phishing email trap, as there is no evidence of data leakage. The attack was found out by delays in the service when the machines and programs were not working as usual. The service should have had a cyber detection policy to prevent phishing attacks.

Respond: Ransomware can be tremendously detrimental to day-to-day activities for firms that have not guarded or are ready against this threat by barring connection to data and systems. The MS-ISAC Primer on Ransomware emphasises the critical measures that every company must take to strengthen their ransomware resistance by appropriately safeguarding their networks, systems, and end-users. Maintaining up-to-date backups and saving them offline is just advice in the Essentials to help secure their institution against ransomware (Center for Internet Security, 2020).

Recover: A US senator wrote to the company's CEO in October 2020, raising concerns about the health system's risk management strategy, including patch management, third-party risk management, partition, and other procedures. The incident cost the corporation $67 million in recovery expenditures, personnel costs, and missed revenue. (Cybersecurity and Infrastructure Security Agency, 2020).

Lessons Learned: After the attack, it was realised that the employees were not educated about cyber security, so the Pennsylvania Department of Health gave information on the importance of the cybersecurity of the health organisation and to be aware of the types of messages for the phishing attacks.

7.5.3 Case 3: Broward Health

The North Broward Hospital District Board of Commissioners is in charge of the public, non-profit hospital system known as Broward Health. Providing healthcare to all of the patients served by Broward Health is its most notable accomplishment. Additionally, they try to support the requirements of both employees and doctors. On 15 October 2021, Broward Health had a data breach. On that day, hackers gained access to the company's database through a third-party medical provider who gave them network access (Landi, 2022). Broward Health's computer network was breached in October, allowing access to the personal and financial data of 1.4 million patients and employees. Patients' complete names, dates of birth, addresses, phone numbers, financial information, social security numbers, insurance information, medical history and information, treatments and diagnosis, and more are among the data that have been compromised.

Identify: This step was not fully executed by the company.

Protect: Broward Health Company has many health facilities, employees, and data of numerous people in their databases. They were working with a third-party company to deliver the appropriate safety to their networks. There needed to be more staff training about cybersecurity and its importance. The lack of these led to a data breach that affected about 1.4 million people. Their system was vulnerable to cyberattacks because there were too few precautions.

Detect: The security breach was detected by the IT team of the company. The team worked with an independent cybersecurity company to detect the breach.

Respond: Since Broward Health discovered the invasion of the network and contained the hack on 19 October 2021, they immediately informed the Department of Justice (DOJ) and the Federal Bureau of Investigation (FBI). The company obliged all employees to reset their passwords and employed an independent cybersecurity firm to investigate the incident.

Recover: Broward Health Company has enhanced security and prevented similar incidents. Some precautions are taken against very similar cases. One of them is to implement MFA, for every user and establish the least possible security requirements for all devices with access to its network that Broward Health's information technology department does not manage. Measures for security breaches will create the intended results.

Lessons Learned: With this attack, 1.4 million people's private information and personal data were acquired. The institution does not have adequate protective measures in place as part of attempts to increase cyber resilience, which is the first of the reasons why this assault was successful. MFA and network security are part of this stage. However, because these assessments were not done, hackers could readily obtain much information and breach the system. Even if it had been entered into the system, the information collected would have been restricted if such safeguards had been taken. Results from the tasks in the Detect section allowed to identify this assault. With the enhancements that will be made in this area, it will be much simpler and more effective to identify the assault and take action quickly when it surpasses the security wall, even though this attack was discovered after accessing the data of 1.4 million individuals. Additionally, this attack may be resisted with reaction and recovery procedures when detection is provided. The system can be swiftly restored to its initial condition if an assault impairs its functionality.

7.5.4 Case 4: Boston Children's Hospital

In 2014, a hacker group called Anonymous launched a DDoS attack on Boston Children's Hospital. In response to the hospital's recommendation, one patient was placed in a state ward and had custody taken away from her parents. According to the physicians, the kid's parents were pressing for needless therapies for an illness the youngster did not have, who thought the child suffered from a psychiatric disorder. The hospital was thrust into the centre of this issue due to the custody dispute, and some people, including Anonymous members, saw this as a violation of the girl's rights. DDoS assaults were executed by Anonymous, causing parties on the network to lose Internet access. The connection loss affected the patients and the medical staff, causing problems in the appointments, tests, and accounts (Center for Internet Security, 2022a).

To render a system inaccessible to the intended user(s), such as by blocking access, is known as a denial of service (DoS) attack. A successful DoS attack uses up all of the network or system resources, which typically causes a server to slow down or fail. A DDoS assault occurs when several sources launch a DoS attack together. Attackers that transmit a sizable volume of distorted network traffic directly to a target server or network are committing a standard DDoS assault. Using a botnet to deliver the traffic is one method an attacker might do. A botnet is a collection of several zombies or victim computers linked over the Internet, capable of communicating with one another and being managed from a central place. An evaluation when attackers submit genuine requests to legitimate public-facing servers while using a fake IP address to represent the intended victim, the assault is known as a DDoS. The replies to these requests come from dedicated servers and are transmitted to the targeted victim (Center for Internet Security, 2022b). There are various techniques to defend organisations or businesses from DDoS assaults. These strategies for preventing DDoS assaults are suggested by Andreja Velimirovic of PhoenixNap IT Solutions (PhoenixNap, 2021). Any DDoS attack attempt must be stopped by network security. Recognising a DDoS attack early on is crucial to reducing the damage since an assault only impacts if a hacker has enough time to accumulate requests. Furthermore, using several dispersed servers makes it difficult for hackers to target every server simultaneously. Other servers are unaffected and get more traffic while the targeted system is offline if an attacker performs the DDoS assault successfully against a single hosting device. In order to prevent network bottlenecks and single points of failure, institutions should host servers in data centres and colocation facilities in diverse geographic areas. Another option is a content delivery network (CDN). A CDN may disperse the load equally across numerous distributed servers since DDoS assaults function by overwhelming a server. Finally, to increase the effect of a DDoS assault, the hacker will likely send requests to every device connected to the network. The security team may foil this strategy by restricting network broadcasting between devices. A high-volume DDoS attack can be stopped by limiting (or, if possible, shutting off) broadcast forwarding. They could also give personnel instructions to turn off echo and charge services when they can.

Identify: The strategies employed during the Identify phase were not made public.

Protect: Information on the work to be done against DDoS attacks has been shared above. However, it will be understood from this attack that the work carried out by the hospital does not cover such protective measures. Therefore the desired protection could not be provided.

Detect: One of the essential steps of cyber resilience is the detection step, since knowing an attack is happening, or the detection of causes, is the first step of understanding and implementing the necessary measurements and cautions. After the attack, Daniel Nigrin accepted that they were flying blind, meaning they did not know when the attacks would happen. He also said they could not even recognise phishing scams while trying to recover from DDoS attacks.

Respond: When the hospital learnt about the original threat, it immediately mobilised its multidisciplinary incident response team. Which clinical and business operations would be impacted or lost if the hospital's Internet access was removed? That was the question the team had to answer. Notably, before to the assaults, the hospital had not carried out such an assessment. The group made three significant possible implications quite soon (Radware, 2022):

- Difficulty in digitally delivering medications to pharmacies
- Email outages in areas where email is crucial to business operations
- Difficulty in accessing electronics health records (EHRs)

Recover: The firm continued identifying recovery processes, but details were not publicised.

Lessons Learned: The technological expertise of the DDoS strikes on Boston Children's Hospital renders them negligible. Instead, they are essential because they show that anybody may be the target of a cyberattack, even healthcare organisations. Dr Nigrin's article in The New England Journal of Medicine states, "Such attacks might negatively impact patient care in clinical settings." In order to be ready to ensure and fight against these new risks, if and when they emerge, healthcare organisations should seriously consider allocating time and resources to operational best practices and IT security systems. Given the potential for a significant "domino impact" across Boston's vital infrastructure, that level of monitoring becomes even more crucial. The DDoS assaults could have negatively impacted BCH and possibly seven other hospitals. That may have endangered patients' lives and the delivery of medical treatment (Radware, 2022).

7.5.5 Case 5: Texas Hospital Network

When a worker at a Texas hospital used the hospital network to create a botnet to target competing hacking organisations, the insider victimised the facility. The individual was caught after documenting his own "infiltration" of the hospital network and making it available for public viewing on YouTube. The investigation revealed that the guard installed spyware on several computers, including nursing stations that housed patient data. He also installed a backdoor to the HVAC system that, in the event it failed, would have damaged pharmaceuticals and injured hospital patients (Center for Internet Security, 2022c).

> The greatest method to safeguard a company is to educate users and staff on how to spot and disclose insider risks or to stop them from unintentionally becoming one. We offer a few suggestions here (Netwrix, 2022):
>
> - Executing corporate-wide risk analyses. Understanding the essential assets, their weaknesses, and potential threats to them Include all of the hazards brought on by insider threats. After that, prioritise the threats and constantly improve the IT security infrastructure.
> - Policies and controls should be well-documented and consistently followed. Both security software solutions and appliances need configuration documentation and control policies. Establish guidelines for practically all staff interactions with the IT environment.
> - Create a secure physical environment at work. A competent security team that adheres to security guidelines to the letter should always be hired. They ought to keep suspicious individuals out of locations where there are virtual IT objects (such as server rooms or rooms with switch racks).
> - Implement strong policies and procedures for password and account management. Every user must connect to the systems using credentials that are exclusive to them; each user must have a separate login ID and password.

All endpoints, including mobile ones, are under the supervision and control of remote access. Install mobile data interception equipment and wireless intrusion detection and prevention systems. Examine if employees still need a mobile device and remote access. Ensure all remote access is turned off when a worker departs the company.

Identify: The strategies employed during the Identify phase were not made public.

Protect: Recommendations to protect an institution from cyber threats are revealed above. Since the institution did not follow these recommendations, the level of protection needed for this attack still needs to be achieved.

Detect: Other insiders are frequently the best source of insider threat detection. Therefore, identifying and preventing insider risks necessitates technology and human resources (Carnegie Mellon University, 2016). Individuals close to a person, such as family, colleagues, and coworkers, are helpful resources for spotting concerning behaviours. People working for the company frequently comprehend an individual's life events and stressors, and they may be able to explain any concerning behaviours (Cybersecurity & Infrastructure Security Agency, 2022).

Respond: The details of the response stage were not made public.

Recover: No clear recovery strategy has been shared.

Lessons Learned: Since many different cyber security dangers exist, it is difficult to identify and respond to insider threats alone. As a result, no solution can guarantee a complete reduction in risk. Organisations should instead aim to implement a layered strategy that includes a variety of security controls and procedures. Organisations should do yearly penetration tests to assist in discovering security flaws, conduct frequent risk assessments to understand the possible effect of insider assaults, regularly teach workers about security awareness, and closely monitor all accounts and privileges.

REFERENCES

Agrawal, R., He, J., Pilli, E. S. & Kumar, S., (2022). *Cyber Security in Intelligent Computing and Communications*, Vol. 1. Springer Nature, Singapore.

Arctic Wolf, (2021). The *Top 12 Healthcare Industry Cyberattacks*. United Healthcare Services. Available at: https://arcticwolf.com/resources/blog/top-healthcare-industry-cyberattacks [Accessed 2022].

Carnegie Mellon University Software Engineering Institute, (2016). *Common Sense Guide to Mitigating Insider Threats*. [Online] Available at: https://resources.sei.cmu.edu/asset_files/TechnicalReport/2016_005_001_484758.pdf [Accessed 3 May 2022].

Center for Internet Security, (2020). *Security Primer Ransomware*. Available at: https://www.cisecurity.org/insights/white-papers/security-primer-ransomware [Accessed 2022].

Center for Internet Security, (2022a). *DDoS Attacks: In the Healthcare Sector*. [Online] Available at: https://www.cisecurity.org/insights/blog/ddos-attacks-in-the-healthcare-sector [Accessed 3 May 2022].

Center for Internet Security, (2022b). *Guide to DDoS Attacks*. [Online] Available at: https://www.cisecurity.org/insights/white-papers/technical-white-paper-guide-to-ddos-attacks [Accessed 3 May 2022].

Center for Internet Security, (2022c). *Insider Threats: In the Healthcare Sector*. [Online] Available at: https://www.cisecurity.org/insights/blog/insider-threats-in-the-healthcare-sector [Accessed 3 May 2022].

Cybersecurity and Infrastructure Security Agency, (2020). *Ransomware Activity Targeting the Healthcare and Public Health Sector*. Available at: https://www.cisa.gov/uscert/ncas/alerts/aa20-302a [Accessed 2022].

Cybersecurity & Infrastructure Security Agency, (2022). *Detecting and Identifying Insider Threats*. [Online] Available at: https://www.cisa.gov/detecting-and-identifying-insider-threats [Accessed 3 May 2022].

Haggerty, J., (2003). Continuity of care: A multi-disciplinary review. *BMJ*, 327(7425), 1219–1221.

Jeffers, H. & Baker, M. (2016). Continuity of care: Still important in modern-day general practice. *British Journal of General Practice*, 66(649), 396–397.

Landi, H., (2022). *Hackers Hit Broward Health Network, Potentially Exposing Data on 1.3M Patients, Staff.* Fierce Healthcare. [Online] Available at: https://www.fiercehealthcare.com/tech/hackers-hit-broward-health-network-potentially-exposing-medical-data-1-3m-patients-staff [Accessed 3 May 2022].

Lehmann, T., & Rosenblatt, S., (2022). *How Healthcare Can Strengthen Its Own Cybersecurity Resilience.* Google Cloud Blog. Google. Retrieved 8 November 2022, from https://cloud.google.com/blog/products/identity-security/how-healthcare-can-strengthen-its-own-cybersecurity-resilience.

McGee, M. K., (2020). *Bank Info Security.* [Online] Available at: https://www.bankinfosecurity.com/magellan-a-14277 [Accessed 2022].

McKeon, J., (2021). [Online] Available at: https://healthitsecurity.com/news/5-strategies-to-improve-healthcare-cyber-resiliency [Accessed 6 August 2022].

National Health Profile, (2018). *An Overview of Educational Infrastructure and Service Infrastructure in the Health Sector in the Country.* Health Infrastructure.

Netwrix, (2022). *Insider Threat Prevention Best Practices.* [Online] Available at: https://www.netwrix.com/Insider_Threat_Prevention_Best_Practices.html [Accessed 3 May 2022].

Office of Disease Prevention and Health Promotion, (2020). *Public Health Infrastructure.* Available at: https://www.healthypeople.gov/2020/topics-objectives/topic/public-health-infrastructure#:~:text=public%20health%20services.-,Overview,(ongoing)%20challenges%20to%20health [Accessed 2022].

Public Health Functions Steering Committee, (1995.) *Public Health in America.* Available at: https://www.cdc.gov/nphpsp/essentialservices.html [Accessed 2022].

Radware, (2022). *Anyone is a Target: DoS Attack Case Analysis on Boston Children's Hospital.* [Online] Available at: https://www.radware.com/getattachment/Security/ERT-Case-Studies/771/Radware_Boston_Childrens_Hospital_Case_Study.pdf.aspx/?lang=en-US [Accessed 3 May 2022].

Seals, T., (2020). *Threat Post.* [Online] Available at: https://threatpost.com/healthcare-giant-magellan-ransomware-data-breach/155699/ [Accessed 2022].

Toms, L., (2020). *Global Sign.* [Online] Available at: https://www.globalsign.com/en/blog/cyber-autopsy-series-phishing-attack-magellan-health [Accessed 2022].

Wegener, E., (2022). *Transparency International Global Health.* [Online] Available at: https://ti-health.org/key-players/ [Accessed 2022].

Writers, T., (2019). *Techcanvass.* [Online] Available at: https://businessanalyst.techcanvass.com/us-healthcare-industry-key-players/ [Accessed 2022].

Williams, P. A. H., (2010). *Is Cyber Resilience in Medical Practice Security Achievable?* Western Australia, secau - Security Research Centre.

Chapter 8

Telecommunications sector

Telecommunications are defined by the Telecommunications Act of 1996 as "communications businesses using regulated or unregulated facilities or services," which includes the broadcasting, telecommunications, cable, computer, data transmission, software, programming, advanced messaging, and electronics industries. With the evolution of technology over the years, the telecommunications industry has gone far beyond its specific definitions. It has become an enormous sector divided into many sub-sectors, mainly the equipment, service, and wireless communication industry. The equipment industry comprises wireless equipment, broadcast network equipment, satellite equipment, and computer-networking equipment. The service sector includes wired and wireless services, the Internet, and other broadband services.

The telecommunication industry is classified as a sub-sector of the information sector in the North American Industry Classification System (United States, 2022). Furthermore, the telecommunication sector includes telephone companies, multiple service providers, Internet providers, cable system operators, wireless carriers, and satellite operators. Several sub-sectors of the telecom industry include processing systems, long-distance carriers, products, domestic, diversified communication services, and international.

8.1 WHAT IS TELECOMMUNICATION AS AN INFRASTRUCTURE?

The establishments principally engaged in this industry derive their revenue by operating, maintaining, and giving access to switch and transmission infrastructure and infrastructure that they own, as well as financing for the use of wired and wireless telecommunications networks. A single technology or combination can build transmission facilities. The examples of wired and wireless telecommunications carriers are shown in Figure 8.1.

Another aspect of this industry is telecommunications resellers and agents for wireless telecommunication services, which involves firms that purchase and resell access and network capacity from phone companies and other

DOI: 10.1201/9781003449522-8

Wired and Wireless Telecommunications Carriers	
Broadband Internet service providers, wired (e.q., cable, DSL)	Telecommunications carriers, wired, and wireless
Cable television distribution services	VoIP service providers, using own wired telecommunications infrastructure
Cellular telephone service carriers	Wireless Internet service providers, except satellite
Direct-to-home satellite system (DTH) services	Wireless telecommunications carriers, except satellite
Satellite television distribution systems	Wireless telephone communication carriers, except satellite

Figure 8.1 Wired and wireless telecommunications carriers.

Telecommunications Resellers and Agents for Wireless Telecommunication Services	
Agents for wireless telecommunication carriers	Wired telecommunications resellers
Cellular telephone stores, selling cellular phone service plans on an agent basis	Wireless phone service plan sales agents, selling on behalf of wireless telecommunications carriers
Mobile phone stores, selling mobile phone service plans on an agent basis	Wireless telecommunications resellers (except satellite telecommunications)

Figure 8.2 Telecommunications resellers/agents for wireless telecommunications services.

operators, either under agents or as vendors, or by companies that resell wired and wireless services to households and businesses. This sector cannot be referred to by the term "telecommunications carriers." The examples of telecommunications resellers and agents for wireless telecommunications services are shown in Figure 8.2.

The satellite telecommunications business comprises organisations that receive and send emails over a satellite network and primarily provide telecommunications services to the television and radio industries. This industry includes establishments that offer terminal stations and related facilities capable of giving, receiving, and relaying signals from and to one or more above-ground systems. Moreover, establishments in the industry are mainly concerned with providing specialised telecommunications services such as radar station operation and satellite tracking.

There are five main key sector components in the telecommunications sector. The first is the broadcast system, which uses free digital and wireless radio and TV transmitters to give programming, data, and other services. Broadcasters can broadcast multiple shows on one channel, completely switching to digital television and digital radio. Satellite stations and cable networks transmit their broadcasts and other program content over the Internet. Second, the cable industry comprises 7,700 cable systems that provide various services, from cost-effective programming to high-speed broadband. Combining coaxial cable and fibre allows for the transmission of intermittent signals to the client. The HFC network architecture divides the cable distribution system into multiple parallel networks. The HFC architecture enhances signal performance and bandwidth for commercial and residential clients. Typically, the HFC architecture in a community consists of three levels: a headend, one or more distribution hubs, and several fibre nodes. Third, the satellite platform is meant to transmit messages to the space station as it approaches. Signals transmitted by earth station antennas are amplified and returned to earth for reception by other earth station antennas. Numerous satellite functions, including event detection, timing, and navigation, are typically performed by a combination of space and ground components.

Moreover, another critical component is the wireless system. The term wireless stems from the fact that the wave of a single electromagnetic micro-wave signal carries a signal over a part or all of the communication path. Communication services provided by wireless technologies include personal communication services, wireless hotspots, commercial and private radio, unlicensed wireless, and cellular phones. It contains private company data and communication networks, the Internet's core, and the PSTN. Lastly, a wireline includes a packet-switched network made of copper, fibre, and coaxial transport media.

8.2 WHY IS TELECOMMUNICATION INFRASTRUCTURE IMPORTANT?

The importance of communication infrastructure continuity cannot be overstated. Even if the local power source collapses, the fixed telephone network should continue to operate. This misconception leads to discontent with modern mobile and Internet networks developed more commercially. All major telephone carriers have made enormous expenditures to assure the reliability and continuance of their infrastructures and services. The second point of failure comprises logic and system defects. To reduce dependence on a single system component, telecommunications companies will invest in redundant backup equipment and several transmission lines (redundancy). Consequently, the logical architecture of the service will be far more resilient than its features. However, these logical set-ups may fail to provide the anticipated resilience because of human error. Single points of failure should be avoided whenever feasible. Furthermore, software failure is a significant problem that needs to be minimised if it occurs. All telecommunications networks depend on software-managed hardware, and no software is resistant to errors and operational issues. In contrast to personal computers, a communications network should not break entirely and cease functioning. Systemic or 'common-mode' failure is a profoundly alarming software failure in which a software fault in one network node triggers the same problem in all linked nodes, leading to the 'runaway' collapse of the entire network. Finally, digital interference in network infrastructures, especially those increasingly dependent on IP technology, may be vulnerable to conditions entering the system via the network itself. They are becoming intentionally more violent. This category contains a wide range of dangers, such as wrong signals introduced by users at an excessively high voltage or incorrect frequency; Radio interference, such as amateur radio transmissions, can cause similar challenges with signal reception. DoS attacks are malicious attempts to disrupt a service, often via network traffic and traffic bottlenecks, which are sometimes exacerbated by advertising campaigns and television-based programming.

8.3 KEY PLAYERS AND STAKEHOLDERS

There are several key players and stakeholders within the telecommunications sector. The government is a critical stakeholder in the telecommunications industry. The policies and legislation being executed by the political power have been established and adopted by the government to benefit society. The government is concerned that services be provided to all citizens in a timely, high-quality, and cost-effective manner and that sector operations are conducted in the same lawful and orderly manner. The government is also interested in fostering a culture that will continue to attract investment in the business, ensuring that most people's aspirations are met.

A second key player within the industry is the customer. Customers of telecom goods and services have several expectations that must be addressed. The customer expects services to be available constantly and at all times. The customer expects high-quality services that are also reasonably priced. The customer wants to be safeguarded from being taken advantage of by service providers at all times. In short, the consumer of the telecom sector expects to be treated well, as in other sectors.

Moreover, infrastructure owners, shareholders, and investors also comprise vital players and stakeholders. A corporation or organisation that owns the telecommunications-related infrastructure and has the authority to engage in contractual agreements to supply communications-related services based on its infrastructure is called an infrastructure owner. In contrast, shareholders/investors are owners of telecommunications companies. They serve as a form of individual and corporate to protect investment and increase corporate value. These key players hold many decision-making positions affecting the industry and critical development interests. They can replace the general manager, overcome the issue of duality, elect non-candidate directors, vote for buying and selling decisions, and pay dividends.

New business models are emerging that combine online and offline delivery options. Furthermore, support from suppliers is essential for telecommunications organisations to supply a broad chain of products and services. This includes product manufacturers, service providers, content/application developers, and infrastructure equipment vendors. The latest developments in digitalisation will also change the relationship between companies in this sector – not only with each other but also with their customers and end-users.

Non-governmental organisations (NGOs) work with telecommunications companies to enable them to provide essential communications services in an emergency. Sustainable mentoring from rating agencies plays a leading role in the growth of telecommunications companies. Lastly, communities/NPOs are also essential actors.

8.4 CYBER RESILIENCE IN THE TELECOMMUNICATION INFRASTRUCTURE

Since the early 2000s, the telecommunication industry has expanded to become a significant economic and technical industry. In addition to being crucial to cultural, economic, political, and social growth, telecommunications also contribute to cyber security. This large-scale and indispensable relationship with other sectors has made telecommunications a target for cyber threats.

Telecom companies are a significant target for cyberattacks as they are large in scale and build, control, and operate critical infrastructure to transmit and store essential data. Considering that telecommunication companies control crucial infrastructures, it is inevitable that the impact of the attack is high, and the consequences are wide-ranging. Customer information is a high-impact target for cybercriminals. Telecommunications institutions typically store personal information such as customer names, addresses, and financial information. These sensitive data are tempting targets that cybercriminals and internal employees can use for extortion, identity theft, or counterproductive actions.

Another severe threat to the telecommunications industry is the attacks on modems and similar infrastructure devices used to access Internet Service Providers. After gaining unauthorised access to the device, hackers can use it for data theft, anonymous attacks, storage of retrieved data, or international phone calls.

THREATS TO THE TELECOMMUNICATIONS INDUSTRY FROM CYBERSPACE

- **Malware:** Malware is used by cyberattackers to target consumers and equipment connected to telecommunications services. They infect mobile devices with malware transmitted through unreliable and insecure applications. In most instances, malware attacks user accounts and exploits payment services to obtain financial and personal data.
- **SIP Hacking:** Voice-over-IP (VoIP) communications are most vulnerable to Session Initiation Protocol (SIP) hacking. Hackers may intercept VoIP calls, transfer SIP malware, or mess with the service without security measures.
- **Man-in-the-Middle Attacks (MITM):** By intercepting routes and misconfiguring services, cybercriminals assault telecommunications service providers. Hackers employ this method to spy on people, steal sensitive data, and disrupt services.
- **DDoS Attacks:** In the telecommunications business, a classic frontal attack is distributed denial-of-service (DDoS). While DDoS assaults are not exclusive to this industry, telecommunications companies face them higher than other industries. Cybercriminals utilise DDoS attacks to shut down networks and servers and disrupt service availability. In 2015, the DDoS attack on TalkTalk Group's telecoms company produced a distraction that allowed two hackers to steal the personal and financial information of 157,000 customers. As the number of connected devices in the sector increases, sophisticated DDoS attacks utilising smartphone-based botnets, international standards, and network protocols are being developed by hackers.
- **Social Engineering:** Cybercriminals employ social engineering and phishing techniques to infiltrate organisations and subscribers in the telecommunications sector. To obtain information, hackers impersonate service providers by making phone calls, which results in further penetration of company and consumer data.
- **Government Surveillance:** Government agencies intend to infiltrate telecommunications infrastructure and service providers to spy on citizens. Government actors have vast resources to execute advanced persistent attacks that can remain undetected, mainly when working with insiders.
- **User Device Threats:** Hackers prey on consumers and network equipment that are susceptible. The majority of subscribers connect with unpatched Android phones and routers. Constantly, cybercriminals investigate vulnerabilities that may be exploited to start attacks.

- **Insider Threats:** In 2015, a disloyal telecom employee, not a hacker, revealed 70 million jail calls. Fourteen thousand recordings were private conversations between attorneys and clients (Price, 2015). As noted previously, government actors and state-sponsored hacking groups recruit employees from telecommunications firms to assist in cybercrime and espionage. Cybercriminals blackmail or give financial incentives to insiders in exchange for unauthorised access to data and other company network resources.
- **Vendor and Supply Chain Risks:** Telecommunications firms outsource less vital processes to service providers. However, their suppliers' risk and security procedures may need to be revised compared to the organisation's. By penetrating a service provider's network, hackers may successfully steal data or disrupt service delivery.

Cyber resilience is vital in the telecommunications sector as the sector plays a critical role in the infrastructure of modern societies, providing essential services that enable communication, information exchange, and access to the Internet. Telecommunications infrastructure and services are highly dependent on technology, making them vulnerable to cyber threats that can disrupt operations, cause financial losses, and compromise the confidentiality and integrity of sensitive information.

The importance of cyber resilience in the telecommunications sector can be summarised as follows:

- **Protection of Critical Infrastructure:** Telecommunications infrastructure, including networks, data centres, and communication systems, is critical infrastructure. Cyber resilience measures help to protect this infrastructure from cyber threats, such as DDoS attacks, which can cause service disruptions, data loss, and financial losses.
- **Maintaining Service Availability:** Telecommunications services are essential to modern societies, enabling communication, information exchange, and access to the Internet. Any disruption to these services can have severe consequences for businesses, governments, and individuals. Cyber resilience measures can help to ensure the continuity of critical services, enable organisations to detect and respond to cyber incidents quickly, and recover from them effectively.
- **Protection of Sensitive Information:** Telecommunications organisations collect and process sensitive information, including personal and financial data, intellectual property, and proprietary information. This information needs to be protected from cyber threats, such as theft, espionage, or manipulation. Cyber resilience measures, such as access controls, encryption, and network segmentation, can help to protect sensitive information from cyber threats.

Compliance with Regulations: The telecommunications sector is subject to various regulations and standards, such as the Communications Act and the Cybersecurity Information Sharing Act (CISA). Cyber resilience measures help telecommunications organisations to comply with these regulations by providing a structured approach to managing cyber risks and ensuring the confidentiality, integrity, and availability of sensitive information.

In summary, cyber resilience is critical for the telecommunications sector as it plays a vital role in the infrastructure of modern societies, providing essential services that enable communication, information exchange, and access to the Internet. Cyber resilience measures help to protect critical infrastructure, maintain service availability, protect sensitive information, and comply with regulations. The telecommunications sector should prioritise the development and implementation of cyber resilience measures to ensure they can effectively respond to cyber threats and protect their critical services.

8.5 CASE STUDIES

8.5.1 Case 1: Nortel Networks Corporation

Formerly known as Northern Telecom Limited, Nortel Networks Corporation (Nortel) was a worldwide telecommunications and data networking equipment producer with headquarters in Mississauga, Ontario, Canada. The corporation was formed in 1895 as the Northern Electric and Manufacturing Company in Montreal, Quebec. At its peak in mid-2000, Nortel had approximately 90,000 worldwide, including 30,000 here in Canada. Led by the leadership of then-CEO John Ross, his stock reached a whopping $124 in Toronto, and the stock exchange rates more than one-third of all TSX companies. Sales of optical communication equipment reached a record high (Gillespie, 2021). In June 2009, Nortel Networks (Nortel), Canada, The largest company and recently number one in the world's communication equipment industry, announced that it would sell its entire business, effectively finishing operations for over 100 years with the unit. Many studies explain how the failed policies of the executive staff drove the company into bankruptcy. The subject of this case is how a systematic cyberattack that started in 2004 and then stretched back to the 1990s was noticed by the company's employees and how companies might face problems due to the poor digital resilience environment.

Relevant information to provide is the APT attack type. Advanced Persistent Threat refers to an attack in which an unauthorised user gains access to a system or network and remains undetected for a significant period (Chen et al., 2014). It typically includes network hacking, avoiding detection, planning attacks, mapping corporate data to identify the most accessible locations for the data of interest, and collecting sensitive corporate data from the organisations (Lord, 2018).

Identify: The strategies employed during the Identify phase were not made public.

Protect: In 2004, Nortel's specialist for cybersecurity, Brian Shields, investigated a severe breach of a network of telecommunications companies. At the time, 70% of all Internet traffic was carried out by Canadian technology, which was Nortel's fibre optic equipment (Cooper, 2020). That year, a Nortel Employee noticed that the file was downloaded to the company's "LiveLink" database (Blackwell, 2020). The employee says he can help with the downloaded material by emailing his executive (McFadden), but the executive does not understand what the employee is talking about (Blackwell, 2020). Nortel cyber security guards in Raleigh, North Carolina, were immediately warned. Raleigh's Larry Bill pointed out an annoying fact. According to the system records investigation, even if he is not physically present, McFadden has logged into the Nortel system from numerous locations around the globe, as indicated by the logs (Blackwell, 2020). Identification information of a critical executive attacked to pass a document about an attack. It turned out that this attack was not a small one. Security consultant Brian Shields found that seven Nortel executives (including CEO Frank Dunn) were hacked instead of one, and hackers extracted a surprising amount of confidential material from the database (Blackwell, 2020).

Detect: Shields analysed the numerical domain names of the servers that collected Nortel's data and discovered that they were concentrated in cyberspace like pinpricks (Cooper, 2020). According to Shields, Shanghai Faxian Corporation owns all website addresses. According to Shields, the registered company, which is unaffiliated with Nortel, was a front desk with no operations in China (Cooper, 2020). He traced the majority of hacking incidents to Chinese IP addresses. Typically, the content obtained from Nortel was delivered to an ISP in Shanghai (Blackwell, 2020). These files, according to him, contain documentation explaining current Nortel tech and the future of various products. Included in sales proposals are price and network design (Blackwell, 2020). Shields discovered another critical clue in Nortel's network traffic logs on Saturday, 24 April 2004. According to Shields, the Shanghai fax address downloaded 779 documents from Nortel's CEO Frank Dunn's account in just 7 hours of the day. The breach occurred four days before Dan's suspension while he was investigating accounting fraud. This revealed to Shields that cybercriminals in Shanghai were aware of the plans of Nortel's board of directors and the exact time to extract a massive record (Cooper, 2020). At the end of the investigation, Shields said it could track over 1,400 document thefts from LiveLink servers and that his boss allowed him to monitor the theft for only six months. He found evidence that Nortel's intrusion into the internal computer network began in 2000, perhaps in the 1990s. He claims it continued after his 2009 release (Blackwell, 2020).

Respond: Nortel's cyber security team has prepared a report to be presented to company executives. Shields says executives were indifferent and thought that simply changing the password for the manager account would solve this problem (Cooper, 2020). He asserts that he prioritises annual profits and innovative expenditures over safeguarding Nortel's significant research. It was desired to reach the company's critical information using social engineering techniques beyond cyberspace. According to an expert talking to National Post, he says there was practical detail to identify people, methods, and goals. People were captured, equipment was found, and back doors dated back to the Chinese. No clear response plan has been made public.

Recover: No clear recovery strategy has been shared.

Lessons Learned: Shield says the intellectual properties of Nortel company were stolen by cybercriminals (Cooper, 2020). Global News has analysed strategy documents titled "Roadmap Values and Challenges for Nortel" and "Value Chain Dynamics and Industry Structure" (Cooper, 2020). In addition, the stolen R&D documents include names like "Photonic Crystal and Large-Scale Integration," "Large-scale Integrated Optical Circuit Switching and Coordination," and "Universal Mobile Communication Service Speed Data" (Cooper, 2020). These Nortel documents relate to 2004's world-leading fibre optic equipment and future innovations in 3G, 4G, and 5G technologies, allowing them to broadcast highly detailed media on the Internet around the world (Cooper, 2020). The cyber resilience culture in the telecommunication sector should be applied correctly based on various frameworks and mounted following the company's structure. Moreover, board members should take the issue of cyber resilience seriously and give informative seminars to all company employees, including themselves. Besides education, telecommunication organisations should create cyber response teams that monitor their networks 24/7 and react quickly if any cyberattack occurs. In order to be prepared for a cyberattack, computers and mobile devices of executives who have the opportunity to access critical data of the organisation, in particular, should be updated at regular intervals, their passwords should be changed, and protection systems should be kept up-to-date.

8.5.2 Case 2: T-Mobile

T-Mobile is a subsidiary of Deutsche Telekom AG, a German telecommunications firm that supplies consumers in numerous countries with wireless voice, message, and data services (Grelg, 2021). After acquiring Sprint for $26 billion in 2018, the business became the second-largest U.S. telecommunications provider, after Verizon, with more than 104 million users (Dignan, 2018). In 2021, the company was subjected to a serious-scale cyberattack – roughly 50 million user data stolen by a 21-year-old American. The Wall Street Journal said that he utilised an insecure router to access millions of client details (McMillan, 2016). The Wall Street Journal reports that cybercriminals have examined Mobile Internet addresses for security vulnerabilities. He could view over one hundred of the company's servers after gaining access to a data centre near East Wenatchee, Washington. By 4 August, he had gathered millions of records (McMillan, 2016). Accessing the information servers of millions of people took nearly a week.

Identify: Since the appropriate cyber resilience frameworks were not applied, the identify function did not operate, and the necessary actions could not be executed during the event.

Protect: Unit221B LLC, a cybersecurity firm, warned T-Mobile of the hack on 16 August and stated that client data is being sold on the dark web (McMillan, 2016). The corporation instructed its clients to reset their passwords and PINs (Greig, 2021). T-mobile reached an agreement with the cyber security firm Mandiant and the consultancy KPMG to prepare a long-term defence and action plan against possible cyberattacks (Greig, 2021).

Detect: T-Mobile announced on 17 August that its systems had been infiltrated by a cyberattack that exposed the personal information of millions of users, former customers, and prospective customers. There was no access to customers' financial data, bank account numbers, credit card information, or other payment details. However, certain SSNs, names, residences, dates of birth, and driver's licences/credentials were exposed, as was the case with numerous past breaches.

Respond: The company hired Mandiant, which provides cyber security services. According to the research of the security experts of the Mandiant company, it was determined how illegal access to the servers was. After that, all the access points were closed.

Recover: The company made various suggestions to its customers to minimise the possible consequences of loss of reputation and avoid such an attack again. T-Mobile offered two years of complimentary identity theft protection services via McAfee's Identity Theft Security Service and encouraged clients to enrol in "T-free Mobile's scam-blocking protection via Scam Shield" (Dignan, 2018).

Lessons Learned: To meet their security needs, telecommunications companies should constantly seek technical support from security service companies and consulting companies. Additionally, Telecommunication companies should identify their critical assets and infrastructures and need to know their vulnerabilities.

8.5.3 Case 3: NTT Communications Corporation

NTT Communications Corporation is a global provider of network services in over 70 countries and 190 regions. NTT Com stated on 28 May that certain information, but not consumer customer information, was likely leaked externally on 11 May due to unauthorised access to NTT Com facilities on 7 May (NTT Com, 2020).

Identify: The procedures utilised during the Identify phase were not made public.

Protect: On 7 May, the NTT Com internal IT department discovered unauthorised remote Active Directory (AD) server access in a log. On the same day, the department swiftly stopped the AD operation server that the attacker had exploited to enable remote operation. NTT Com performed one inquiry. Therefore, the BHE/ECL service administration server, which could be accessed from the AD operation server, was promptly shut down. No external communication was permitted from the AD server on the internal segment. In addition, connectivity with external sites utilised by the attacker to install malware was blocked.

Detect: On 11 May, it was revealed that some information might have been leaked after monitoring the access records of internal systems. Since this illegal access was obtained through the operation server, a forensic analysis of the operation server was carried out. The findings revealed illegal access to the construction information management server, which was utilised to administer BHE/ECL services. On 13 May, it was found that some files on the construction management information server had been leaked after reviewing the server's access record.

Respond: In facilities transitioning to new services, security measures designed for the most current attack methods were deployed until they were physically removed. It also began blocking all communication channels that became redundant when customers stopped using them.

Recover: The company started investigating the attack and increased its efforts to strengthen the systems of its infrastructures against cyberattacks.

Lessons Learned: For telecommunication companies to respond quickly to cyberattacks, they must be able to instantly respond to attacks without system interruption through the cyber security units they have established or the cyber security companies they work with.

8.5.4 Case 4: LightBasin

LightBasin is a cyber threat group that has been actively targeting the telecommunications industry since 2016. They are experts in building custom tools and have in-depth knowledge of Telecom Network Architecture. LightBasin is not associated with any country up until now. They are also called UNC1945 (Harries & Mayer, 2021). LightBasin organises cyberattacks on critical telecommunication infrastructures running on Linux and Solaris operating systems (Harries & Mayer, 2021). According to the report published by a cybersecurity firm called CrowdStrike, this group emulates telecommunications protocols to facilitate command and control (C2) tools. It uses scan/packet capture tools to get specific information from the mobile telecommunications infrastructure (Harries & Mayer, 2021). LightBasin has demonstrated proficiency and comfort in using new tactics, methods, and procedures (TTP) in a Unix environment (Mandiant, 2021). CrowdStrike said that 13 telecommunications companies across the world were hacked by LightBasin (Harries & Mayer, 2021). LightBasin accessed the first DNS server that was compromised via SSH from one of the other compromised telecommunications companies, with evidence indicating that the attempted password swap was used to facilitate the initial compromise.

LightBasin scythe off system credentials to a text file following their slap-stick PAM back door deployment. To further their access across the net-work, LightBasin started with some systems and moved on to set up more of the SLAPSTICK back doors. LightBasin went back into the DNS service from the compromised telecommunications company to deploy an ICMP signalling implant as PingPong, an implant that CrowdStrike tracked.

Identify: A proper cyber resilience framework was not applied, which prevented identification capabilities from functioning and required actions to be taken during the event.

Protect: LightBasin's ability to modify its roaming agreements with other telecommunications companies stems from allowing all traffic between these organisations without identifying the required protocols. Mandiant experts suggest that any company that owns or operates a network that handles traffic on the Internet should insist on rules in place to restrict traf-fic to protocols that it should be allowed to travel to, such as the web or networks that support Linux and other operating systems.

Detect: Firewalls are used to keep out external Internet access, but PingPong most likely has to be sent from other compromised network infra-structure. The threat actor continues his attempts to hide their activities as legitimate traffic. CrowdStrike Services noticed that the shell from the implant was sending information to a server in another part of the world. LightBasin uses a new technique that uses SGSN to support C2 activities in conjunction with TinyShell. When tunnelled via the telecommunications network, the adversary can access the network using the GPRS network access points.

Respond: According to the Mandiant report, if LightBasin can utilise standard telecommunications protocols for command and control, there are better solutions than limiting network traffic, as it will not solve the problem. CrowdStrike recommends an incident response investigation that includes reviewing partner systems with the organisation.

Recover: Telecommunication companies have implemented incident response plans, but a specific recovery plan against the novel techniques of LightBasin has yet to be successful.

Lessons Learned: Telecommunication Operators should follow strict rules from the GRX/GTP firewalls and log and monitor activities from the Unix system. Likewise, telecommunication operators should be periodic compromise assessments. Vendors and third parties must have restricted remote access to be adequately audited.

8.5.5 Case 5: Syniverse

Syniverse is a global telecommunications company providing mobile net-work operators with solutions enabling mobile service delivery. Syniverse has a portfolio of products and services that helps mobile operators to connect with their customers. More than 1,500 mobile operators use Syniverse's products and services in more than 200 countries. In May of 2021, a data breach at Syniverse compromised two million persons' personal information. The colossal scale of the breach resulted in exposing a broad number of sensitive data, such as addresses, names, birth dates, and telephone numbers. The Spanish Hackers are a group of hackers responsible for the Syniverse data breach. The hackers used a "SQL injection" technique to access the company's database. SQL injection is an attack that allows attackers to execute malicious code on a database. This type of attack is relatively easy to carry out, and it can have devastating consequences.

Identify: Since the necessary frameworks for cyber resilience were not present at the site, the identify function was not practised, and the necessary actions could not be taken during the incident.

Protect: According to the SEC filing, Syniverse found no evidence of an intent to disrupt or monetise the activities of its clients, nor did it attempt to do so. Thematic impact on Syniverse's day-to-day operations and services or access to data will not be a consequence of these events.

Detect: Syniverse said that an individual or group noticed unauthorised access to its technical systems in May 2021. The unauthorised access began in May 2016 and prevented the team from using it on multiple occasions. There was a problem with the information that allowed access to the electronic data transfer (EDT) environment.

Respond: Syniverse adopted the security incident response strategy and enlisted the assistance of a premier forensics firm for its internal investigation. The corporation has also alerted law enforcement and is collaborating with them. Even though they were not captured in the event, all the customers had their credentials reset or taken away.

Recover: Syniverse has put in several extra safeguards to protect its systems and customers. The customer was communicated with who would likely be affected by the problem, and a defence action plan was put in place to deal with it.

Lessons Learned: SQL injection attacks occur due to code flaws in web applications or because the applications input field unexpectedly allows SQL statements directly to the user (Information Security Office, 2022). In order to prevent this situation, telecommunications companies' critical websites or applications should be created in a way that does not include coding errors.

8.5.6 Case 6: Orange SA

Orange SA, the French-based telecommunication company, experienced a cyberattack during the summer of 2020. Cybercrime group Nefilim claimed responsibility for the attack targeting the company's customer data. The Nefilim cyberattack group has accessed 20 Orange Pro/SME customer data. The stolen data, including emails, aeroplane schematics, and files from a French aircraft manufacturer, was shared on a data leak site named "Orange_leak_part1.rar" On 15 July 2020.

Identify: Orange Business Services might be critical in providing integrated communications products and services for corporations worldwide. However, the strategies used in the Identify phase were not formally notified to the public by Orange SA. Nefilim ransomware has targeted the Orange Business Services division.

Protect: According to the Privacy Policy for Orange Business Services Corporate Customers and Prospects, Orange restricts access to customer data to agents, employees, and third parties in case of unauthorised access or unintentional data loss (Orange, 2018). Orange only allows these parties to process consumer data per company instructions (Orange, 2018).

Detect: Nefilim ransomware was detected by the Orange cyber security team between 4 July and 5 July. Ransomware has been categorised as a cryptovirus-type computer attack.

Respond: Orange cyber security team started to investigate the source of the cyberattack and apply all requirements for the security of their systems. The company notified customers affected by the data breach and continued investigating and monitoring.

Recover: There was no large-scale recovery on Orange systems, where the attack was only about data found on one of the Neocles Bt platforms, "Le Forfait Informatique."

Lessons Learned: The Multi-Layered approach protects the system network with different layers and provides an isolated defence against cyberattacks (AMDH Services Limited, 2021). In order to protect against crypto virus ransomware, telecommunication companies should focus on a multi-layered approach.

8.5.7 Case 7: Telefonica

Spanish telecommunication company Telefonica suffered from a cyberattack on a Friday morning in 2017. Cybercriminals have demanded $550.000 in Bitcoin from the company so that the company can access its systems. The company has experienced an outage in 85% of its systems.

Identify: The attack has focused on Windows systems inside the company network. Company network systems might be identified as critical infrastructure in this case. A known ransomware attack WannaCry was the main element of this malicious attack. WannaCry enciphered most of the company archives and related system files.

Protect: Cyber security researcher Kafeine confirmed the attack and indicated that Windows SMB vulnerability has caused access to system files to be restricted.

Detect: The company could not detect the cyberattack on time. As a result, nine out of ten company computers were affected by WannaCry, and some employees had to leave their positions in the company. Anti-Malware product Malware Hunter first detected the attack, named version 2.0 of WannaCry.

Respond: The company cyber security team warned employees and wanted them to shut down their computers to prevent the cyberattack from infecting a deeper company network.

Recovery: As the ransomware randomly created encrypted and temporary files, not all files could be recovered. However, the system information was turned off before recovering the encryption process (ElevenPath, 2017).

Lessons Learned: Telecommunications companies should keep their backup files offline and check to see if it is working as expected. In addition, to ensure the security of offline backups, companies should store critical data separately from each other.

8.5.8 Case 8: Verizon

American-based wireless carrier company Verizon experienced a data breach in 2017. A configuration error on an Amazon Web Services storage exposed the personal data of around 14 million clients.

Identify: Amazon Web Services S3 might be identified as critical infrastructure in this case. The data leak was caused by the Israeli software company NICE Systems, which provided Amazon Web Services S3 with technical services. However, the strategies used in the Identify phase were not formally notified to the public by Verizon.

Protect: Typically, Amazon provides data access following identity and security controls. However, Verizon partner NICE Systems made the Amazon Web Services bucket publicly available due to human error.

Detect: A software company UpGuard primarily informed Verizon on 13 June about the data breach. However, the Amazon Web Services repository was locked down on 22 July. The exposed data included phone numbers, names, and PIN codes of customers.

Respond: After the data breach was detected, it was first investigated whether it was a cyberattack. Verizon said in its press release that the data breach affected 6 million customers, not the result of a cyberattack.

Recover: NICE Systems started to work in law enforcement to solve problems caused by data breaches. In addition, Verizon's investigations found that the data in the system could not be accessed by any external parties (Larson, 2017).

Lessons Learned: No matter how well the systems are protected, human error continues to be the leading cause of data breaches in the cyber domain. Telecommunication companies should take this factor seriously. Companies should provide regular training to their employees and raise the awareness of their employees about the cyber domain.

REFERENCES

AMDH Services Limited, (2021). *The Importance of Multi-Layered Security.* AMDH Services Limited. [Online] Available at: https://www.amdhservicesltd. com/the-importance-of-multi-layered-security#:~:text=What%20is%20 multi%2Dlayered%20security,your%20ICT%20infrastructure%20and%20 services [Accessed 2 August 2022].

Blackwell, T., (2020). *Exclusive: Did Huawei Bring Down Nortel? Corporate Espionage, Theft, and the Parallel Rise and Fall of Two Telecom Giants.* National Post. [Online] Available at: https://nationalpost.com/news/exclusive-did-huawei-bring-down-nortel-corporate-espionage-theft-and-the-parallel-rise-and-fall-of-two-telecom-giants [Accessed 12 March 2022].

Chen, P., Desmet, L. & Huygens, C., (2014). A study on advanced persistent threats. In *IFIP International Conference on Communications and Multimedia Security,* pp. 63–72. Berlin, Heidelberg: Springer.

Cooper, S., (2020). *Inside the Chinese Military Attack on Nortel – National.* Global News. [Online] Available at: https://globalnews.ca/news/7275588/inside-the-chinese-military-attack-on-nortel/ [Accessed 12 March 2022].

Dignan, L., (2018). *The T-Mobile and Sprint Merger: The Numbers and Assumptions You Need to Know.* ZDNet. [Online] Available at: https://www.zdnet.com/article/the-t-mobile-and-sprint-merger-the-numbers-and-assumptions-you-need-to-know/ [Accessed 12 March 2022].

ElevenPaths, (2017). *Telefónica WannaCry File Restorer: How Can We Recover Information Deleted by WannaCry?* Think Big.

Gillespie, A., (2021). *Nortel - A Decade Later.* The Canadian Business Journal. [Online] Available at: https://www.cbj.ca/nortel_a_decade_later_former_ceo_dunn_and_two_others_stand_trial/ [Accessed 15 March 2022].

Greig, J., (2021). *T-Mobile Hack: Everything You Need to Know.* ZDNet. [Online] Available at: https://www.zdnet.com/article/t-mobile-hack-everything-you-need-to-know/ [Accessed 13 March 2022].

Harries, J. & Mayer, D., (2021). *A Roaming Threat to Telecommunications Companies.* CrowdStrike. [Online] Available at: https://www.crowdstrike.com/blog/an-analysis-of-lightbasin-telecommunications-attacks/ [Accessed 13 March 2022].

Information Security Office, (2022). *How to Protect Against SQL Injection Attacks.* [Online] Available at: https://security.berkeley.edu/education-awareness/how-protect-against-sql-injection-attacks [Accessed 6 September 2022].

Larson, S., (2017). *Verizon Customer Data Leaked Through an Online Security Hole.* CNNMoney. [Online] Available at: https://money.cnn.com/2017/07/12/technology/verizon-data-leaked-online/index.html [Accessed 1 August 2022].

Lord, N., (2018). *What Is an Advanced Persistent Threat? APT Definition.* Digital Guardian. [Online] Available at: https://digitalguardian.com/blog/what-advanced-persistent-threat-apt-definition [Accessed 14 March 2022].

Mandiant, (2021). *ThreatSpace Cyber Response Simulation Exercise.* [Online] Available at: https://www.mandiant.com/resources/datasheets/consulting-services-threatspace-cyber-response-simulation-exercise

McMillan, R., (2016). *Group Claims to Have U.S. Government Hacking Tools for Sale.* [Online] Available at: https://www.wsj.com/articles/group-claim-to-have-u-s-government-hacking-tools-for-sale-1471309022

NTT, (2020). *NTT Com Confirms Possible Information Leak due to Unauthorised Access*. [Online] Available at: https://www.ntt.com/en/about-us/press-releases/news/article/2020/0702.html [Accessed 1 August 2022].

Orange, (2018). [Online] Available at: https://www.orange-business.com/sites/default/files/201812_privacy-protection-policy-orange-business-services.pdf [Accessed 7 July 2022].

Price, R., (2015). *These 70 Million Leaked Calls Suggest That Jails Breach Prisoner-Lawyer Confidentiality All the Time* [Online] Available at: https://slate.com/business/2015/11/anonymous-hacker-released-70-million-jail-calls-indicating-routine-violation-of-attorney-client-privilege.html

United States, (2022). *North American Industry Classification System*. [Online] Available at: https://www.census.gov/naics/reference_files_tools/2022_NAICS_Manual.pdf

Chapter 9

Transportation sector

The transportation sector is a sector that provides services to transport people and loads, which is formed by the combination of many different sub-branches. According to the Global Industry Classification Standards (GICS), the transportation sector is technically a subgroup of the industrial sector. The transportation sector consists of four main sectors, namely the aviation sector, maritime transport sector, road transport sector and rail transport sector, and each industry continues its services with different infrastructures. Here, the four main sectors are divided into various sub-branches within themselves, and the service network is expanding. In this section, detailed information about each transportation sector is shared.

9.1 AVIATION TRANSPORT

The aviation industry has an extensive area. It consists of many aircraft that allow passengers and cargo to travel. Thanks to its large volume, this sector employs millions of people. From aviation to air traffic control, thousands of people work in this industry daily, from aviation to air traffic control. The aviation industry is also fragmented within itself. This sector consists of three different sub-sectors. These sub-sectors include commercial, general, and military aviation (National Aviation Academy, 2020).

Commercial Aviation: The commercial aviation sector, unlike other sectors, includes the operation of aircraft used for passenger and cargo transportation and leased for this purpose. If financing is provided for the flight to take place, these flights fall into a different category, and this transaction is considered a commercial transaction. Therefore, airline operations are included in the scope of commercial aviation. Scheduled airlines worldwide are classified according to the revenue they generate from operations. This classification is divided into significant airlines, national airlines and regional airlines. Commercial aviation is a form of transportation that allows a person to travel on a schedule for reasons such as visiting another city or state and taking a vacation. This is considered general aviation in cases such as pilot or aircraft charter (National Aviation Academy, 2020).

DOI: 10.1201/9781003449522-9

General Aviation: The general aviation industry generally accounts for a large portion of flights. This sector performs business and public services with more flexible needs than airlines. General aviation includes the provision of personal transportation or business transportation that does not use an airline. Fighting forest fires, spraying agricultural products, transporting medical supplies or humanitarian aid, and emergency medical evacuation are examples of general aviation. Airborne law enforcement and business or leisure flights, such as a business person flying their plane to see customers in another city, are also operations within the scope of general aviation. Although a distinction is made between public and commercial aviation, there may be some overlap between these two sub-sectors. An example of this is business aviation. Business aviation is positioned somewhere between commercial air transport (air ambulance operations, charter operations) and general aviation (corporate functions) (National Aviation Academy, 2020).

Military Aviation: Military aviation, on the other hand, is slightly different from the two sub-sectors mentioned. This sector includes using military aircraft or other machinery to enable countries' air warfare capabilities. This sector also comprises logistics aircraft carrying cargo for military purposes. Operations such as cargo transport, reconnaissance missions (intel gathering), training military pilots and other personnel, and air combat uses military aviation (National Aviation Academy, 2020).

9.1.1 What is aviation as an infrastructure?

Airports form the basis of the aviation industry. The infrastructures of these areas, which have an important place in this sector, typically consist of two categories. These are divided into airside infrastructure and landside infrastructure. Infrastructure elements located on the airside contain aircraft movements near the airport. In addition, this infrastructure includes airport lights and signs, taxiways, aircraft parking aprons, runways, and navigational and visual aids that are important to the airport.

On the other hand, the landside infrastructure accommodates the movements of vehicles and passengers on land. This infrastructure includes the access roads to the airport, the car parks, garages, aviation-related or non-aviation-related businesses used at the airport, support buildings and terminal buildings (Ploeger et al., 2015). The units within the scope of this infrastructure can be listed as follows in Table 9.1.

9.1.2 Why is aviation infrastructure important?

The aviation sector contributes significantly to the development of the modern world. The aviation sector, which consists of organisations such as airlines, airports and air traffic management, connects many different points of the world thanks to the flights that take place 24 hours a day. The developments

Table 9.1 Aviation sector infrastructure (Ploeger et al., 2015)

Airfield electrical vault	Airfield lighting	Airfield signs
Airfield visual and navigational aids	Airfield pavements	Airfield markings
Hangars	Terminals and administrative/office buildings	Maintenance and storage buildings
Fuelling facilities	Deicing facilities	Landside infrastructure
Airport-owned utilities	Obstructions to imaginary surfaces	Fencing and gates
Drainage	Turf and safety areas	Maintenance equipment and airport vehicles

in this technology make this sector stronger day by day. The air transportation sector provides direct employment to 11.3 million people worldwide and supports 87.7 million jobs. The aviation sector creates an economic value of 3.5 trillion dollars in global GDP. If the aviation industry were considered a country in its own right, it would be the 17th largest economy in the world, with an economy of $3.5 trillion, providing direct or indirect jobs to 87.7 million people. In addition, aviation provides support to other sectors. One of them is the tourism sector. The aviation industry makes tourism possible. Many people use the aviation industry for travel, and 58% of international tourists travel by air to their destination. In today's world, the global economy is growing in a much more interconnected way. The influence of aviation in the formation of this situation is an undeniable fact. Aviation is a factor that brings people together (Air Transport Action Group, 2020).

9.1.3 Key players and stakeholders in aviation

Emerging technologies and digitalisation provide deeper performance insights and connectivity levels. Businesses benefit from the advantages of these technologies. In this way, the world becomes faster, more flexible, and more efficient. These technological advances create a global ecosystem where physical and digital assets, from critical infrastructure assets to people and data, are increasingly interconnected. This formation brings with it various threats. Industry and state actors need to work together to prevent these increasing threats and reduce risks as much as possible. A common understanding and approach to be developed towards these threats are required. In order to prevent these threats, the units in the sector ecosystem should be defined, and necessary measures should be taken in line with this definition. Actors in the aviation sector are listed in Table 9.2. These definitions can determine possible locations of cyberattacks (World Economic Forum Committee, 2021).

Table 9.2 Aviation Ecosystem Actors

Airports	Government agencies	Satellite providers
Airlines	Manufacturing	Telecom providers
Engineering and maintenance	Military aviation	IT-OT providers
ANSP	Travel agencies	

9.2 MARITIME TRANSPORT

Maritime transport is a broad concept used to describe transport on water. Through maritime transport, goods (cargoes) or people are transported from one point to another using waterway. Although developments in aviation have reduced the importance of sea routes, a significant part of the transportation activities in the world is carried out by the sea. One of the most important reasons is that maritime transport is cheaper than air transport. According to UNCTAD data, maritime transport constituted approximately 80% of world trade in 2020 (Stopford, 1997). Countries can benefit significantly from this situation if they improve their transportation infrastructure. Thanks to the developments in transportation infrastructure, many new investment opportunities may arise, or existing businesses may increase their trade volumes. In addition, competition increased due to the increase in national and international trade, leading to the revival of the labour market. Depending on all these developments, macroeconomic productivity factors improve, regional development takes place, and in this case, the welfare level of the people of the region increases. In addition, the increase in these incomes will positively affect other sectors, such as health and infrastructure. Participation in global maritime trade is critical to attracting global finance.

9.2.1 What is maritime transportation as an infrastructure

Transport of people (passengers) or things (freight) through waterways is referred to as maritime transport (or ocean transport), hydraulic effluvial transport, or, more broadly, waterborne transport. Throughout recorded history, shipping has been a standard method of moving freight. Sea travel has been less significant for passengers with the development of aircraft. However, it is still used for quick excursions and leisure cruises. Despite changes, exchange rates, and a surcharge added to freighting costs for carrier businesses, known as the currency adjustment factor, shipping by water is less expensive than shipping by air. Also, maritime transportation is the foundation of international commerce and the world economy. The amount and value of international commerce transported by sea and processed by ports throughout the globe have increased, and more than half of it is now done so (Van Oord, 2022).

Maritime transport is possible over any distance by boat, ship, sailboat, or barge, across seas and lakes, via canals, or along rivers. Shipping may be done for business, entertainment, or even for defence. Even though substantial inland transportation is less vital today, the world's main waterways, including numerous canals, are still tremendously important and crucial to all countries' economies. Any substance may be transported by water, but it becomes impractical when the delivery of an item is time-sensitive, such as with different kinds of perishable food. Even so, shipping over the sea is very cost-effective for regularly scheduled cargoes like trans-oceanic consumer goods and notably for big loads or bulk cargoes like coal, coke, ores, or grains. The industrial revolution occurred most effectively in areas with affordable bulk transportation through canals, navigations, or shipping by all forms of watercraft on natural waterways.

9.2.2 Why is maritime transportation important?

Maritime transportation is a critical component of global commerce. Numerous industries are linked to it. Shipping conveys various goods, including food, medicines, and technological equipment. Cost-effective shipping methods promote growth and sustainable development, particularly in developing countries. No nation on Earth is self-sufficient without marine transportation. Because trade and commerce entirely rely on marine transportation, it becomes a critical component of the global economy. Our everyday items are delivered by water as raw materials or as completed goods. Regarding international trade, maritime transport is the most cost-effective mode of transit. Maritime transportation has a plethora of advantages. The primary benefit is that there are a large number of ships available for transport. Numerous items may be carried concurrently. The travel route is inexpensive in comparison to other types of transport. The sea does not need significant infrastructural improvements. No nation, save those with a vulnerable geographical position, does not trade with the rest of the globe through marine transport (BitNautic, 2020).

Due to the ships' efficient use of energy, maritime shipping is a superior alternative to other modes of material delivery. One of the most compelling reasons to choose marine transportation is its economic benefits. Economic considerations make it a viable alternative for business and trade. Security is the key worry with the assault of piracy and worldwide terrorism. We have seen throughout the years from studies that sea travel is more secure than other modes of transit in terms of commerce. Thus, it is favoured around the globe as a secure mode of moving commodities (Lane & Pretes, 2020).

One of the most significant benefits of marine transportation is its environmental friendliness. The shipping sector is concentrating on creating fuel-efficient ship engines that result in lower greenhouse gas emissions. When a ship travels a greater distance on the same quantity of fuel, carbon dioxide emissions are lowered. As a result, marine transportation is less damaging to the environment than other modes of transport (BitNautic, 2020). Additionally, according to Goleblowski, water transport is the most energy-efficient mode. However, marine transport's contribution to environmental effects may arise; thus, efforts should be undertaken to minimise maritime transport emissions and mitigate all negative environmental impacts (Gołębiowski, 2016). Finally, the strategic importance of marine transportation in international relations cannot be overstated. Due to the broad scope of marine transportation, several parties are engaged. Countries connected to sea trade routes have long benefited from a strategic edge in international affairs. Each country has economic interests in marine commerce. These factors contribute to the marine shipping industry's prominence in diplomatic relations with other nations.

There are also cybersecurity cases which damage the maritime industry deeply. The South African port operator Transnet was recently targeted by a cyberattack, forcing it to suspend operations for more than a week at essential container ports in Durban, Port Elizabeth, and Cape Town. Another instance occurred when HMM, South Korea's flagship carrier, was the target of a hack that continues to impair its email systems. These are only a handful of the many assaults on the marine sector recently due to digitisation's increasing penetration. Cybercriminals have recently targeted IMO, CMA CGM, MSC, Costco, and Maersk. WannaCry and NotPetya are two common malware threats in data breaches and phishing. Now, we will discuss the critical nature of cyber resilience in the marine business.

9.2.3 Key players and stakeholders in maritime transportation

Using cutting-edge technology and digitalisation in the marine industry improved performance insight. The significant actors in Table 9.3 participate in most processes together and help keep services running. These technological developments provide a global ecosystem with more linked

Table 9.3 Ecosystem actors in maritime transportation (CSMOIM, 2022; The Geography of Transport Systems, 2022)

Maritime ecosystem actors		
Maritime shipping lines	Rail carriers and terminal operators	Ports
Port terminal operators	Third-party logistics providers	Stevedores and terminals
Port authorities	Air freight carriers	Marine services
Commercial real estate developers	Freight forwarders	Support services
Maritime lock and canal operators	Ferries and ships	Maintenance equipment and maritime vehicles
Truck carriers	Tour boats	

physical and digital resources, from vital infrastructure to people and data. There are many dangers associated with this development. Business and government entities must collaborate to stop these growing dangers and minimise risks.

9.3 ROAD TRANSPORT

Road transportation is a crucial segment of the transport infrastructure, as the transportation of goods and people between locations using roads. A road is a built or upgraded path that allows powered and non-powered vehicles to travel between them. Driving has various advantages when compared to other types of transportation. The investment required for road transportation is relatively modest compared to other modes of transportation, such as railways and air travel. Building, operating, and maintaining roads is less expensive than trains (The Economic Times Writers, 2022). The International Transport Forum involves the following items as the elements of the road infrastructure in Table 9.4 (The International Transport Forum Committee, 2013).

9.3.1 What is road transportation as an infrastructure?

Road transportation is critical to the economy because it allows goods and passengers to be transported. As the Blending in the Transport sector article explains, the proper transportation system operation relies heavily on road infrastructure. Road transportation is advancing towards ecologically friendly concepts by focusing on energy-efficient automobiles that meet environmental criteria. Buses, taxis, and auto rentals provide efficient ways for passengers to get to their destinations, whereas trucks are mainly used for freight transportation. Leading stakeholders in global road transport will continue to focus their efforts in the next few years on reducing traffic congestion and maintaining mobility. Global transportation networks will also adapt in response to environmental demands. Greener modes of transportation are encouraged by legislative mandates. Governments will focus

Table 9.4 Elements of road infrastructure

Land	Pavement and ancillary works	Pre-pavement road works
Cuttings and drainage works	Buildings used by the infrastructure department	Toll collection installations, parking metres
Support and backfilling	Level crossings	Lighting installations
Engineering structures: bridges, overpasses, tunnels, avalanche and falling stone protection structures	Signalling and traffic signs, as well as telecommunications installations	

on bringing road and highway networks up to date, creating new networks to reduce existing congestion, and implementing significant road transport standards to safeguard the environment. In the context of road transportation, government attempts to stimulate economic growth will place a premium on safety (European Commission, 2016).

9.3.2 Why is road transportation important?

It was mentioned that road transport was one of the most significant transport infrastructure sectors. The most significant reason for the importance of road infrastructure is that it is the most worldwide transport method people use daily. Dostál and Adamec mention that road transportation is crucial for various reasons (Dostál & Adamec, 2011). Roads are the primary mode of transportation that are used every day to convey people and cargo all over the world. The usefulness of road transportation comes from how easily it allows people to go from one region to another for various reasons. Roads play an essential role in economic development and give significant social benefits.

People utilise roads for various purposes, including commuting to work, visiting friends, and visiting a town or metropolis for shopping, dining, and other entertainment. This has economic as well as social implications. People would have a considerably more difficult time moving about without roads. It is difficult for a country to thrive and prosper without highways. Roads are used to move products. Roads are critical for carrying products from farms to retailers and for deliveries. Roads can distribute fast food, while haulage companies utilise trucks to convey items between warehouses and retail locations. It would take much longer for products to move from point A to point B if there were no roads and hence no place for trucks and vans to travel. We need roads to offer us the freedoms we need to enjoy life as we know it, both in the tourism business and general. Good road infrastructure allows us to maximise our social and economic potential by allowing us to obtain essential items and services that we require as humans.

9.3.3 Key players and stakeholders in road transportation

The road transportation ecosystem currently holds key players and stakeholders that contain several organisations that construct, manage, run, and function mobility services in or between cities and urban locations. New players that rely on data in the infrastructure to provide services are also present. Each player is the producer of data regarding the tangible and intangible elements of the road transportation ecosystem. Table 9.5 shows the stakeholders and key players of the road transportation ecosystem. The travelling public is the ones that use their vehicles or travel in their possible ways. Governments and private franchisees can manage transport agencies. While the government is in charge of the city's inside plan and management, like

Table 9.5 Ecosystem actors in road transportation

Road transportation ecosystem actors		
Government/private franchisees transportation agencies	Mobility system and service provider	Public travellers
Information service provider	Emergency services	Payment gateway services

signs, rules, road network, vehicle number, and track, the private franchisees are included in the duty of public or private transportation like taxis, buses, or shuttles. These players contain real-time data on the road transportation sectors while they keep track of the route, location, or use applications. Mobility services are the car share providers that rent cars or use applications for taxis like Uber or other companies. They can be deeply in contact with the information service providers. One of the most prominent data collectors in the sector is the information service providers. As mentioned, mobility systems, while they are the physical workers and providers, the information services are the services that help them for better optimisation in their work. They can use maps for navigation systems and intelligent transportation system vendors. With this data, the transportation experience can be much easier for the user and the provider (Pena, 2019).

9.4 RAIL TRANSPORTATION

Rail transport is also described as train transportation. Railways have been the most frequent mode of transport. Moreover, technological advancements have opened up monorail and magnetic-levitation (Maglev) trains, a form of transport that uses vehicles operating on prearranged paths (railroads, rails). Rail transportation is among the most vital, extensively utilised, and economical freight and commute transport types through short and long distances. Rail transportation operates on metal (generally steel) wheels and rails. This offers reduced resistance due to friction, enabling the attachment of more cargo and wagons to be attached. The vehicle that enables rail transportation is called a "Train." They are generally propelled by locomotives that use either gasoline or electricity to power them. Several route networks and complex signalling systems (communication-based control systems, CBCS) are used. This type of transportation is not only the swiftest way; it is among the safest. From a safety perspective, rail transportation has established itself as one of the most reliable ways of transportation. Compared to other modes of transportation, vehicles used in rail transport are swift and are not affected by weather disturbances such as fog and rain as much as other modes of transport. Train transportation is better organised than other modes of transport. Timetables and routes are fixed. Its services are better in reliability, consistency, and predictability than other transportation types. The birth of rail transportation reaches back to the man-powered machines used in the ancient Greek civilisation. It has grown into a sophisticated, contemporary system utilised in cross-country (and continent) and metropolitan and long-distance networks. This transport type used to carry passengers and products is crucial to financial improvement. Commuter trains, underground/above-ground urban metro railroads, and freight trains can be examples of adaptations. Similar to other transportation types, this one also has its limitations.

One of the significant constraints is the high cost of rail transportation. The cost of this construction is high when trying to build a network of rails. Creating, managing, and maintaining a fully equipped transportation network is much more expensive than other transport types. In addition, this type of transportation is not suitable for door-to-door services due to its fixed path. Intermediate rail fastening (IRF) is more expensive, with extra tears, time waste, and wear (Karpuschenko et al., 2021).

Because of numerous tactics to be reached, train lines were created differently depending on the geographical conditions. While penetration lines enable access to resources, regional networks serve area economies, and settlements along transcontinental lines can gain territorial control. The first rail lines were portage portions inside canal systems or routes to supplement and replace service gaps in existing canals. Rail might displace canal services in inland transportation, becoming the primary engine of spatial change in the world's industrialising regions due to its cost and time benefits.

9.4.1 What is rail transportation as an infrastructure?

Transport hubs, infrastructure, railway stations, and junctions with technical equipment and transport methods for moving passengers or commodities make a railway transport system. In the upcoming section, it is shown that sidings/branch lines and locomotive depots/sheds make up the railroad infrastructure (OECD, 2013):

- Engineering structures are categorised as overpasses, such as culverts and bridges; underpasses, such as covered cuts and tunnels; structures for an avalanche, retaining walls, and falling stone
- Ground area
- Safety, signalling, and telecommunications installations which are in marshalling yards, in stations, and on open tracks; consist of facilities for producing, converting, and distributing electricity for telecommunications and signalling; buildings for such plants or installations; lighting systems for safety and traffic
- Supply cables between contact wires and supports and catenaries; facilities for converting and conveying electricity for train hauling

- Facilities utilised by the department of infrastructure, including a portion for transportation charge collection systems installed
- Level crossings, including devices to enhance the security factor of the road

Railway Cyber-Physical Systems (CPS): An examination of the cyber resilience of many commonly used Railway Telemechanic and Automation Communication-Based Control Systems (RTA CBCSs) identified flaws and vulnerabilities that allow an attacker to impair dependability and circumvent functional safety safeguards, as well as conduct attacks directly against traffic safety. Surprisingly, these systems comply with all essential IT security and functional safety regulations and possess all necessary international, national, and industry certifications. The primary difference between assaults on RTA CBCSs and regular unauthorised strapping is that the former may be carried out remotely (without requiring direct physical access), and the evidence can be readily concealed. The railway CPS (Gordeychik, 2019) is under attack from various directions. The following are the critical security threats that the railway CPS faces:

Physical Threat: An initial requirement for IT security is physical security. Physical threats to railroad CPS include earthquakes, fires, floods, system failure caused by environmental disasters, failure of the equipment due to a power outage that causes database information to be stolen, hardware loss, badly damaged data, data breaches, and data transmission disconnection that causes electromagnetic interference (EMI).

Virus Threat: The most common malware/virus spreading method is over the network. The effects of malware on railroad CPS might be devastating since it covers a broad variety of NAPs (Network Access Points), needs complicated network administration, and requires more skilled system operators (also called Sysop). Any virus-infected Wi-Fi array, like an embedded Wi-Fi network, will likely infect the whole network. The virus has the potential to deplete network resources, steal critical data, harm operating applications, and completely collapse their IT system.

Malicious Attacks: There are two types of malicious assaults: attacks from outside and within the system. Malicious assaults are primarily carried out through operating databases or system susceptibilities on the network. There are cases involving malicious manipulation, stealing essential data, and outright system paralysis.

Railroad transportation may give a variety of benefits to society that may or may not result in a straight monetary benefit. This frequently has multiplicative consequences; for example, increased usage of train transport reduces the demand for new motorways and traffic congestion; environmental effects are lessened, the safety of transportation advances, public health enhances, and so forth. Building new railways or refurbishing existing railways creates employment possibilities similar to those associated with speedway installation. The railroad business advances daily, and indirect and direct employment rates are rising. More widespread usage of railroad transportation positively influences railway firms and public and federal spending. They may be summed up as energy savings, a decrease in freight transport cost, a decrease in traffic congestion, reducing soil and water pollution, reducing public health issues related to noise, and reducing greenhouse gas emissions (Dolinayova et al., 2016).

9.4.2 Why is rail transportation important?

As mentioned before, railroad transportation guarantees the movement of people and goods in both time and space using wagons and locomotives that travel along established lines, called railways, per the planned timetable (Dinu, 2018).

Rail transportation has one up on other transportation types in several aspects. To begin with, the capacities of the freights and passengers are much more compared to different kinds of transportation. Most of the time, it is financed by the governments to support national economic improvement. These aspects brought some regulations by the governments since they funded the railroad systems. Moreover, it is one of the safest types of transportation. It is shown that reliance on automation causes incidents (Papadimitriou et al., 2020), and with the contribution of automation nowadays, rail transportation has become one of the safest transportation methods.

9.4.3 Key players and stakeholders in rail transportation

Digitalisation in the railway sector and the implementation of emerging technologies enhanced performance insight. The primary actors, seen in Table 9.5, are involved in most processes and contribute to the operation of services. Technological developments create an ecosystem in a world that is becoming faster, more connected, and more productive. As the ecosystem gets more interconnected, critical infrastructure which involves data and people also hangs by threats. In Table 9.6, the main actors of the rail transportation ecosystem are shown.

Table 9.6 Ecosystem actors in rail transportation

Rail transportation ecosystem actors		
Political authorities	Clients	Shippers
Regulatory organisations	Railroad undertakings	Operators of infrastructure
Railway wagon owners	Rolling stock industry	Non-governmental organisations
Rail transportation associations and workers	Technology associations and providers	

9.5 CYBER RESILIENCE IN TRANSPORT INFRASTRUCTURE

Today, technology development contributes to the transportation sector. These developments are experienced in all sectors, such as land, sea and air transportation. With these developments, digitalisation is increasing in all transportation sectors. Moreover, especially with the widespread use of autonomous vehicles, the number of vehicles connected to the Internet will increase. Although all these developments have positive aspects, there are also risks. This digitalisation brings with it cyber risks. Thanks to these digital systems, the traffic in the city can be optimised, or it can be made more accessible for vehicles to go from one place to another, but this also brings risks. Some of them are threats such as physical and large-scale attacks, accidental errors/malfunctions/failures, insider threats or nefarious activities and abuse. Many other threats can be added to these threats (Enisa, 2015). For this reason, it is necessary to provide cyber resilience to ensure that transportation systems can operate smoothly. In order to achieve this, all institutions and companies need to follow up-to-date threats and invest in protecting themselves from them to develop their technologies and have personnel with technical competence. In order to provide cyber resilience, companies and institutions must first ensure that the most basic steps, identify, protect, detect, respond, and recover, are carried out. In this way, they will provide basic security for the institution. In order to keep this security at a high level, constant updates are required.

Cyber resilience is vital in the transportation sector as it is responsible for the movement of people and goods, making it a critical part of modern societies. The sector relies heavily on technology to support its operations, making it vulnerable to cyber threats that can disrupt services, compromise safety, and cause financial losses.

The importance of cyber resilience in the transportation sector can be summarised as follows:

- **Protection of Critical Infrastructure:** Transportation infrastructure, including airports, seaports, railways, and highways, is critical infrastructure. Cyber resilience measures help to protect this infrastructure from cyber threats, such as ransomware or malware attacks, which can cause physical damage, disrupt operations, and compromise safety.
- **Maintaining Service Availability:** The transportation sector is responsible for providing essential services, such as air travel, maritime transportation, and land transportation. Any disruption to these services can have severe consequences for businesses, governments, and individuals. Cyber resilience measures can help to ensure the continuity of critical services, enable organisations to detect and respond to cyber incidents quickly, and recover from them effectively.
- **Protection of Sensitive Information:** The transportation sector collects and processes sensitive information, including personal and financial data, operational data, and proprietary information. This information

needs to be protected from cyber threats, such as theft, espionage, or manipulation. Cyber resilience measures, such as access controls, encryption, and network segmentation, can help to protect sensitive information from cyber threats.

- **Compliance with Regulations:** The transportation sector is subject to various regulations and standards, such as the Federal Aviation Administration (FAA) regulations and the International Maritime Organisation (IMO) regulations. Cyber resilience measures help transportation organisations to comply with these regulations by providing a structured approach to managing cyber risks and ensuring the confidentiality, integrity, and availability of sensitive information.

In summary, cyber resilience is critical for the transportation sector as it is responsible for the movement of people and goods, making it a critical part of modern societies. Cyber resilience measures help to protect critical infrastructure, maintain service availability, protect sensitive information, and comply with regulations. The transportation sector should prioritise the development and implementation of cyber resilience measures to ensure they can effectively respond to cyber threats and protect their critical services.

9.6 CASE STUDIES

9.6.1 Case 1: Transnet

On 22 July 2021, there was an assault known as the Transnet Ransomware attack. In this assault, ransomware was deployed. Transnet has declared force majeure at many important container ports, including the Port of Durban, Ngqura, Port Elizabeth, and Cape Town, resulting from the attack's aftereffects. Because of this assault, South Africa's fundamental marine infrastructure was harmed, and operational integrity was jeopardised for the first time in its history (Reva, 2021). This incident has been deemed unprecedented by the Institute for Security Studies (ISS). ISS authorities thought Transnet withheld information about the hack out of fear for national security and to avoid legal repercussions. According to the news from Bloomberg News, the attackers reportedly encrypted the files on Transnet's computer system, preventing firm personnel from accessing the company's data. These were followed by directions on how to start a ransom negotiation with the perpetrators. The ransomware employed in the assault, which was associated with the "Death Kitty," "Hello Kitty," and "Five Hands" attacks, most likely originated in Central Europe or Russia. Transnet client data was not impacted by the hack, according to a statement published by the Ministry of Public Enterprises (Gallagher & Burkhardt, 2021).

Identify: The institution's data, equipment, systems, and facilities must be specified to execute identification. The staff members and their scope of authority should also be specified. It was evident from this occurrence that the institution did not adhere to these standards and that access to the data was simple. Only until the attackers posted a ransom note on Transnet's systems did the assault take place. Transnet could only pinpoint the attackers' location, which may have been in Eastern Europe or Russia.

Protect: According to the incident study, it was determined that the attackers had obtained access to the institution's computers and encrypted its data to prevent its authorities from viewing them. Here, more precautions have yet to be taken to guarantee cyber resilience. People inside the organisation must have access to different places under their jurisdiction to carry out the protection phase. Access to these areas must be made via encryption which entails many processes. Because Transnet lacks such a mechanism, it has become an easy target.

Detect: Once the attack on the staff's emails has been discovered and neutralised, the attackers break into port offices to steal data from systems, including the staff's keyboard inputs and screenshots from their workstations. Only when containers started to vanish in their entirety was this assault discovered. Due to insufficient effort in detection, the detection process has been delayed.

Respond: Preliminary analyses, according to the Department of Public Enterprises, proved that Transnet and its customers' data had not been affected by the hack; as a result, the ransom discussions were turned down.

Recover: After reinstalling its automated terminal-operating system within a week, Transnet has completely resumed operations at the country's ports.

Lessons Learned: It is obvious that the necessary steps to achieve cyber resilience have not been taken in this case. People inside the company must have access to various places that fall within their purview to carry out the protection step, and access to these areas must be secured using encryption that entails several processes. Because Transnet lacks such a mechanism, it has become an easy target.

9.6.2 Case 2: Port of Antwerp

Malware attacks are a common type of cyberattack in which the victim's computer is used to perform illegal actions. Malware is frequently malicious software. Harmful software refers to various assaults, including ransomware, spyware, and command and control. Malware is created, utilised, and sold by cyberattackers for a variety of purposes, although it is most typically used to steal personal, financial, or commercial information. While cyberattackers' goals vary, they almost always concentrate their tactics, methods, and procedures (TTP) on obtaining privileged credentials and accounts to accomplish their purpose (Rapid7 CyberSecurity Co., 2022).

In 2013, the Port of Antwerp discovered that its cargo control system had been cyberattacked by a narcotics gang. Indeed, the port's computer network had been spied on since June 2011, when it was purportedly penetrated by malware, notably a keylogger (which enabled the hackers to record the loading/unloading operators' keystrokes and therefore collect usernames and passwords) (Stormshield, 2021). Antwerp's port finally re-secured its system by spending approximately €200,000 on countermeasures, including a new password management system (for container access) and new communication channels between port managers and customer services (Stormshield, 2021).

Identify: Despite the hazards of cyber assaults, various solutions have been explored, and 200,000 euros have been invested in this area, but the studies are not solid enough to support the identification step needed for cyber resilience. The assault happened as a consequence of the missing components. In this instance, the assault on the Port of Antwerp happened over two years. First, the attackers sent infected emails to port employees, gaining remote access to data that the criminal organisation used to locate and seize drug-smuggling vessels.

Protect: It is clear that necessary protection measures were not implemented since the attack started in 2011, yet released in 2013.

Detect: For two years, the assault could not be carried out. The attackers could access all of the usernames and passwords for all of Antwerp's officers' and systems' ports because of this cybersecurity negligence.

Respond: A firewall was erected to stop additional intrusions after the initial attack on port employees, and the following breach was detected, but hackers still gained access to the building and placed key-logging devices on PCs. The attackers then entered the port's offices and used devices with hidden computers to capture data from systems (Seatrade Maritime News, 2013).

Recover: The Port of Antwerp has re-secured its system by implementing a new password management system (for container access) and communication routes between port managers and customer care representatives.

Lessons Learned: It is evident that the Port of Antwerp struggled to detect the attacks. In this instance, the Port of Antwerp attack occurred over two years without the organisation's knowledge. To guarantee that the remaining stages are carried out as planned, it is essential to learn from this scenario that organisations must have a good detection step when applying cyber resilience principles.

9.6.3 Case 3: Rotterdam Port

Ransomware is a type of cryptovirology virus that threatens to divulge the victim's personal information or obstruct access until a ransom is fully paid. A method known as cryptoviral extortion is used by more sophisticated virus, whereas other ransomware may simply lock the device without compromising any data. The data of the victim is encrypted, rendering it unusable, and payment is required to decrypt it (Schofield, 2016; Mimoso, 2016; Young & Yung, 1996).

The Petya ransomware began to spread internationally on 27 June 2017 geared for Windows desktops, laptops, and servers. Using the same Server Message Block vulnerability that WannaCry used to infect unpatched devices and a credential-stealing method, it spread to non-vulnerable PCs.

It was a global cyberattack called Petya. However, during its June 2017 run, Ukraine received most of its attention (McAfee, 2022a). Petya takes advantage of the Server Message Block protocol implementation flaw CVE-2017-0144 in Microsoft. This attack first exploits the weakness before encrypting the master boot record (MBR) and other data. The system is unreachable once the user receives a notification telling them to reboot it. Due to the operating system's inability to locate and decrypt files, Petya is now known as a wiper rather than the ransomware it once thought to be (McAfee, 2022b).

Security experts first identified Petya in March 2016, which was the successor of NotPetya. The virus had caused fewer instances at the time. Researchers remarked that the virus continued to operate uniquely, warning many in the sector to watch for the sophisticated assault. By the time the cyberattack on the Port of Rotterdam occurred, several cybersecurity companies had previously been aware of the virus, published technical analyses, and developed devices that may have stopped the assault. For instance, McAfee Cybersecurity Enterprise published their technical analysis of the Petya and NotPetya attacks, served their product and environment, published their report on "How to Protect against Petya Ransomware in McAfee Environment," and reported on their consumer impacts prior to the attack on the Port of Rotterdam.

A version of the NotPetya ransomware called Petrowrap was used to assault Rotterdam's port on 30 June 2017. Two container ports managed by APMT, a division of Moller-Maersk, had all of their activities suspended. As part of a Smart Port initiative that blends the Internet of Things and artificial intelligence, Rotterdam has invested the most in fully automating its operational processes, making it even more reliant on the dependability of its IT systems (Stormshield, 2021). In order to improve the port's cyber resilience, inform stakeholders about cybersecurity issues, improve organisational training, and provide better risk management, the Municipality of Rotterdam, the police, and the port authorities worked together to establish a Port Cyber Resilience Officer (Stormshield, 2021).

Identify: The strategies employed during the Identify phase were not made public.

Protect: The Protect step is one of the most important steps to ensure cyber security. New attack methods are constantly emerging in the field of cyberattacks. Therefore, in order to provide cyber resilience, these developments must be constantly followed up to date. In this way, each attack can be protected according to its characteristics. At that time, it was predestined that Petya and, therefore, NotPetya attacks caused significant damage (McAfee, 2022c). However, as it can be understood from the failure to provide the necessary protection against this attack, the protection step required to provide cyber resilience needs to be updated more.

Detect: One of the ports that have invested the most in fully automating its operational processes is the Port of Rotterdam. While these expenditures contribute to greater efficiency, it is clear that some cybersecurity issues may occur more frequently. If the work done to provide cyber resilience cannot reach the speed of developing the port, it becomes difficult to detect attacks. Although the attack elements used in the attack are a new attack method, it is difficult to detect this attack. It should be done frequently. In this example, it turns out that the current situation is not followed, and the determination cannot be made accordingly.

Respond: The protection was not fully provided so the attackers could gain access to the system, and then the attack could not be detected because there were not enough updates. In this case, creating a response against the attack is impossible. Since it was an undetected attack, this attack could not be responded to.

Recover: There are deficiencies in the studies required for the recovery step, and they could not be achieved at the desired level.

Lessons Learned: The protect phase's improper implementation looks to be the significant problem in this instance. Additionally, the attackers received a ransom payment due to incorrect implementation of the Identify and Protect sections, which cost the business and its clients' money. When every stage is executed flawlessly, there is no need for a ransom payment, and consumers are not inconvenienced.

9.6.4 Case 4: San Francisco Municipal Transport Agency

In late November 2016, San Francisco Municipal Transport Agency (so-called SF MUNI or SFMTA), which is the city's light rail metro train system, was attacked by hackers. The message that appeared on all the infected computers mentioned that they were hacked and gave some additional contact information. The hackers wanted 100 bitcoins, worth about £59,000 or $73,000 at that time, to withdraw from the attack. More than 2,100 computers, which had Windows OS and were not up to date, were affected due to this attack. This malicious software, also known as Mamba or HDDCryptor, aims at the resources in network shares like folders, drives, and printers using Server Message Block Version 1 (SMBv1). In addition, it locks and encrypts the drive of the computers by writing the MBR again. The utilisation of open-source tools does the encryption process, which was the main feature of this malware.

Identify: Organisational understanding to manage the risk was developed by SFMTA. However, some missing steps, such as better staff training and keeping the computers up to date, were required. As a result of those missing parts, the attack occurred.

Protect: Luckily, the ransomware attack on SFMTA's front-office systems was contained. The backup plan of SFMTA took a critical role in this "Protect" part. As a result, there was no significant damage to the system and the public.

Detect: Unlike many cyberattacks on the critical infrastructure that shut down the networks, this attack turned off the ticket machines. Screens of the SF MUNI went black with information about the situation and contact info written on it. Moreover, email and payment services were shut down, but the core systems kept working, enabling all the passengers to ride without charge.

Respond: As soon as discovering this malicious software, SMFTA got in touch with the Department of Homeland Security (DHS) to identify and contain the virus (Holland, 2016). After that, they shut down all the kiosk machines to prevent the virus from spreading, cooperating with Cubic Transport System that operates SMFTA. Instead of stopping the service, they opened all the gates for the public and gave free rides throughout the weekend (Brewster, 2016).

Recover: Thanks to their backup system, they could recover the encrypted data without paying the ransom. Paul Rose, the spokesman of SFMTA, said there was no significant harm to the system because of their systematic backup (Kumerow, 2016). Moreover, they attached more importance to the training of their staff to prevent such emergencies.

Lessons Learned: This attack shows the importance of a backup plan and immediate action against the attack. An organisational understanding of critical systems helps to recover from an attack with minor damage.

9.6.5 Case 5: WannaCry Ransomware Attack

The WannaCry attack (also called Wanna Decryptor/WannaCrypt) occurred in May 2017 (What is WannaCry ransomware?, 2017). It is encrypted software utilised by criminals to demand ransom. A result of this encryption process is done by the locking of the victims' computers or valuable folders on them. Hence, victims are unable to view/read their documentation. The WannaCrypt attack captures the victims' data hostage and claims to let off the system when the ransom is paid, which was wanted in Bitcoins. The malicious software was designed to spread quickly among PCs that use the same network. It infected the computers that used Microsoft Windows OS (versions XP, 7, 8, Server 2003) and did not have the proper security patch (patch "MS17-010"), which was issued by Microsoft two months before the attack. However, the PCs that do not regularly get updated were affected due to this ransomware. A relatively small ransom, $300–$600 per affected computer, was wanted to unlock all the encrypted files. This ransomware also affected the rail transportation industry. Deutsche Bahn and Russian Railways were among the infected ones. Deutsche Bahn reported that their schedules usually ran (Data Protection Report, 2017). They did not shut down the systems. Deutsche Bahn got off cheap because its central operating systems were not affected. However, this cybercrime can be considered a "wake-up call" for the rail industry. On the other hand, the IT systems of Russian Railways were affected.

Identify: This part of the framework was not fully understood by Deutsche Bahn. For example, their systems storing critical data were not up to date, resulting in this cybercrime. An organisational understanding of cyberattacks was developed, which was ineffective in preventing the incident.

Protect: There were many organisational challenges, such as the incident management process and employee responsibilities. Nevertheless, like the identify section, Deutsche Bahn did not fully prepare this section. First of all, awareness of keeping the systems updated was low. In addition, it is known that this attack occurred due to a phishing campaign showing insufficient staff training. Protective technology and data security were not sufficient to protect critical systems.

Detect: This ransomware was detected when there appeared a red screen with information about the ransom and the time left to pay the ransom on the screens of Deutsche Bahn, telling the authorities to pay the ransom wanted. Technically detecting this ransomware is done by reviewing and monitoring DNS queries. Moreover, they checked the *iuqerfsodp9ifjaposdfjhgosurijfaewrwergwea.com* domain to determine whether their network was infected (Marsh, 2017).

Respond: As mentioned before, Deutsche Bahn kept working usually and was not affected much. Closing off the ports that WannaCry exploited was one of the crucial moves. In addition, they worked with third-party antivirus software providers.

Recover: After this cybercrime, the education of the staff became more critical. Organisations started to inform their staff about such situations. The computers operating the systems were isolated in a room, and nobody could use them, but after the incident, these computers and their software programs started to update regularly. Moreover, implementing cybersecurity in the general safety and security policy process speeds up (van Gompel, 2017).

Lessons Learned: WannaCry Ransomware Attack showed that clicking links sent from suspicious senders is risky. Moreover, the staff of the organisations should be aware of the risk of email attachments. For the last lesson, operating systems used in organisations should be updated regularly so that the latest security precautions can be taken against such attacks.

9.6.6 Case 6: Cathay Pacific Airways Cyberattack

Cathay Pacific is an airline based in Hong Kong. This company announced that a data breach incident occurred in 2018. Although the detection of this violation was made in March, the violation was announced in October. When this data breach was investigated, it was seen that the first data breach occurred in October 2014. As a result of the investigations, it was revealed that not one but two separate malicious actors existed in the system for four years.

As a result of the investigation by the Information Commissioner's Office (ICO), the main reasons for the occurrence of this cyberattack were determined as poorly protected backup, the presence of unpatched vulnerabilities and the lack of multi-factor authentication. As a result of all these shortcomings, 9.4 million records were compromised in the attack. These records include passengers' names, passport information and personal data such as travel history, e-mile address, and telephone number. In addition, 430 credit card information was stolen (Whittaker, 2018; Cowley, 2020).

Identify: Organisations need to foresee possible threats and make various definitions to ensure their cyber resilience. However, the Cathay Pacific cyber security team has not conducted a study on the definition of identify, which is included in the scope of cyber resilience and was made for the first time. Since such a study has not been carried out, no attack can be detected by the company team and systems (European Commission, 2020).

Protect: Every company must take various security measures to ensure cyber resilience. It should be determined where the data of the entire institution is kept and which data is located where. Backups should be made when necessary. This data should be limited to the access of authorised persons, and special encrypted security measures should be taken to protect it. There are no systems such as backup or encryption in the Cathay Pacific company database. Since there is no encryption, attackers can easily access customer data without hindrance. In this case, the customer data appears before the attackers in plain text, and it is effortless to obtain the information of the people from it. In this case, it caused the data to be stolen easily (Cowley, 2020).

Detect: In cyberattacks, attackers always aim for easy targets. Since Cathay Pacific had used a 10-year-old system with vulnerabilities, it has become an easy target for cyberattackers. Due to its old infrastructure, the company cannot detect new threats. It was also exposed to this attack because it could not detect these threats and their security vulnerabilities (Cowley, 2020). For companies to have more secure systems, they need to detect their security vulnerabilities in advance, determine the types of threats that may occur, and take precautions accordingly. In this way, they can increase their cyber resilience.

Respond: Since the cyber security infrastructure of Cathay Pacific company is not very strong, data was stolen due to this cyberattack. There is no incident response plan in the company security system. When this event occurs, the company officials do not have any guidance stating what they should do for this reason. Therefore, the people working in the company responsible for cyber security do not know what to do in the event of a violation, what is the least, what to do in the following steps, and what action to take (Cowley, 2020). That is why companies need to have a Respond plan. In this way, it is determined step by step how to respond in the event of an attack.

Recover: Organisations in the sector should define, implement and test the management procedure followed in cyber security incidents to prevent sectoral activities and ensure business continuity. However, Cathay Pacific did not realise the cyberattack for four years, and no recovery plan can be created after realising it in this way (European Commission, 2020).

Lessons Learned: In this attack, it is clear that Cathay Pacific Airways did no work for cyber resilience. As a result of not carrying out these studies, the cyberattack was carried out efficiently. Since no precautions were taken against this attack, no identify or protect activities could be carried out. The system has become an obvious target, using a system of about ten years. Since no steps were taken for the Detect step, it could not be detected at the time of the attack. Since these steps cannot be taken, it is not possible to take the response and recovery steps are impossible. One of the lessons that can be drawn from this attack is the necessity of keeping up with the dynamics of the developing world. Technology is developing rapidly, and if a ten-year-old system is used, it will be insufficient to counter today's threats. Therefore, cyber security infrastructure should be kept as up to date as possible, especially in sectors where there may be problems in terms of cyber security. This way, it will be protected from current attacks. In addition, careful monitoring of the existing steps to provide cyber resilience will help to maximise the desired security. For this reason, the infrastructure should be kept as up to date as possible to ensure cyber resilience, and every step should be followed meticulously for security. This way, 9.4 million data will be prevented from being stolen due to an attack.

REFERENCES

BitNautic, (2020). *Why Is Maritime Shipping Important?* [Online] Available at: https://medium.com/@bitnautic/why-is-maritime-shipping-important-6a1cd7cc99ef.

Brewster, T., (2016). *Ransomware Crooks Demand $70,000 after Hacking San Francisco Transport System – UPDATED.* www.forbes.com. [Online] Available at: https://www.forbes.com/sites/thomasbrewster/2016/11/28/san-francisco-muni-hacked-ransomware/?sh=c1e712047061 [Accessed 20 April 2022].

Comité Sectoriel de Main D'oeuvre de L' industrie Maritime, (2022). *Future Workers of the Industry- Stakeholders.* [Online] Available at: https://www.csmoim.qc.ca/en/future-industry-workers/the-marine-industry/stakeholders.

Cowley, M., (2020). *Integrity360.* [Online] Available at: https://insights.integrity360.com/cathay-pacific-data-breach-fine [Accessed 2022].

Data Protection Report, (2017). *WannaCry Ransomware Attack Summary.* [Online] Available at: https://www.dataprotectionreport.com/2017/05/wannacry-ransomware-attack-summary/ [Accessed 24 April 2022].

Dinu, A.-M., (2018). *The Importance of Transportation to Tourism Development, ZBW - Digitales Archiv: The Importance of Transportation to Tourism Development.* Available at: https://hdl.handle.net/11159/2887 [Accessed 9 November 2022].

Dolinayova, A., Kanis, J. & Loch, M., (2016). Social and economic efficiency of operation dependent and independent traction in rail freight. *Procedia Engineering*, 134, 187–195.

Dostál, I. & Adamec, V., (2011). Transport and its role in the society. *Transactions on Transport Sciences*, 4(2), 43–56.

Enisa, (2015). [Online] Available at: https://www.enisa.europa.eu/publications/good-practices-recommendations/@@download/fullReport [Accessed 2 August 2022].

European Commission, Directorate-General for International Cooperation and Development, (2016). *Blending in the Transport Sector*. Publications Office. Available at: https://data.europa.eu/doi/10.2841/56992.

European Commission, (2020). *Transport Cybersecurity Toolkit*. European Union. [Online] Available at: https://transport.ec.europa.eu/news-events/news/european-commission-publishes-cybersecurity-toolkit-raise-awareness-cyber-risks-and-build-2020-12-16_en

Gallagher, R. & Burkhardt, P. (2021). *'Death Kitty' Ransomware Linked to South African Port Attack*. [Online] Available at: https://www.bloomberg.com/news/articles/2021-07-29/-death-kitty-ransomware-linked-to-attack-on-south-african-ports#xj4y7vzkg

Gołębiowski, C., (2016). Inland water transport in Poland. *Transportation Research Procedia*, 14, 223–232. https://doi.org/10.1016/j.trpro.2016.05.058.

Air Transport Action Group, (2020). *Aviation: Benefits beyond Borders*. [Online] Available at: https://aviationbenefits.org/downloads/aviation-benefits-beyond-borders-2020/

Holland, K., (2016). *Update on SFMTA Ransomware Attack*. SFMTA. [Online] Available at: https://www.sfmta.com/blog/update-sfmta-ransomware-attack [Accessed 20 April 2022].

Karpuschenko, N., Velichko, D. & Sevostyanov, A., (2021). Effectiveness of intermediate rail fastenings on the railway sections of Siberia. *Transportation Research Procedia*, 54, 173–181.

Kumerow, L., (2016). *Three Lessons from the San Francisco Muni Ransomware Attack*. Cloudsecurityalliance.org. [Online] Available at: https://cloudsecurityalliance.org/blog/2016/12/22/three-lessons-san-francisco-muni-ransomware-attack/ [Accessed 10 April 2022].

Lane, J. M. & Pretes, M., (2020). Maritime dependency and economic prosperity: Why access to oceanic trade matters. *Marine Policy, 121*, 104180. https://doi.org/10.1016/j.marpol.2020.104180.

Marsh, J., (2017). *Identifying WannaCry on Your Server Using Logs | Loggly*. Log Analysis | Log Monitoring by Loggly. [Online] Available at: https://www.loggly.com/blog/identifying-wannacry-server-using-logs/ [Accessed 24 April 2022].

McAfee, (2022a). *How to Protect Against Petya Ransomware in a McAfee Environment?* [Online].

McAfee, (2022b). *New Variant of Petya Ransomware Spreading Like Wildfire* [Online].

McAfee, (2022c). *What Is Petya and NotPetya Ransomware?* [Online].

Mimoso, M., (2016). *Petya Ransomware Master File Table Encryption*. threatpost.com.

National Aviation Academy, (2020). *National Aviation Academy*. [Online] Available at: https://www.naa.edu/sectors-of-aviation/ [Accessed 2022].

OECD, (2013). *Understanding the Value of Transport Infrastructure*. Itf-oecd.org. [Online] Available at: https://www.itf-oecd.org/sites/default/files/docs/13value.pdf [Accessed 10 April 2022].

Papadimitriou, E., Schneider, C., Aguinaga Tello, J., Damen, W., Lomba Vrouenraets, M. & Ten Broeke, A., (2020). *Transport Safety and Human Factors in the Era of Automation: What Can Transport Modes Learn from Each Other?, Accident; Analysis and Prevention.* US National Library of Medicine. Available at: https://pubmed.ncbi.nlm.nih.gov/32629228/ [Accessed 9 November 2022].

Pena, B., (2019). *A Taxonomy of Actors in the Hidden Ecosystem of Transportation Information Infrastructure - The Information They Collect and Hold.* Available at: https://medium.com/@benjiedlp/a-taxonomy-of-actors-in-the-hidden-ecosystem-of-transportation-information-infrastructure-the-df95e4aab076

Ploeger, D. C., Chapman, R. B., Peshkin, D. G. & Speidel, D. J., (2015). *Preventive Maintenance at General Aviation Airports.* Volume 1, Primer. Washington, DC: The National Academies Press. https://doi.org/10.17226/22117

Rapid7 CyberSecurity Co., (2022). *Malware Attacks: Definition and Best Practices.* [Online] Available at: https://www.rapid7.com/fundamentals/malware-attacks/.

Reva, D. (2021). *Cyber Attacks Expose the Vulnerability of South Africa's Ports.* [Online] Available at: https://issafrica.org/iss-today/cyber-attacks-expose-the-vulnerability-of-south-africas-ports

Ryan, G. & Burkhardt, P., (2021). *'Death Kitty' Ransomware Linked to South African Port Attack. www.bloomberg.com.* Bloomberg News.

Schofield, J., (2016). How can I remove a ransomware infection?. The Guardian.

Seatrade Maritime News, (2013). *Record volumes for Port of Antwerp in 2013.* [Online] Available at: https://www.seatrade-maritime.com/europe/record-volumes-port-antwerp-2013

Skorobogatova, O. & Kuzmina-Merlino, I., (2017). *Transport Infrastructure Development Performance*, 178, 319–329.

Stopford, M., (1997). *Maritime Economics.* Psychology Press, New York.

Stormshield, (2021). *Cybermarétique: A Short History of Cyberattacks Against Ports.* [Online] Available at: https://www.stormshield.com/news/cybermaretique-a-short-history-of-cyberattacks-against-ports/

The Economic Times Writers, (2022). *The Economic Times.* [Online] Available at: https://economictimes.indiatimes.com/definition/road-transport [Accessed 2022].

The Geography of Transport Systems, (2022). *Major Commercial Actors in Freight Distribution.* [Online] Available at: https://transportgeography.org/contents/chapter1/transportation-and-commercial-geography/commercial-actors-freight-distribution/.

The International Transport Forum Committee, (2013). *Understanding the Value of Transport Infrastructure.* OECD. [Online] Available at: https://www.itf-oecd.org/sites/default/files/docs/13value.pdf

van Gompel, M., (2017). *WannaCry Virus Was 'Wake-Up Call' for Railway Industry.* RailTech.com. [Online] Available at: https://www.railtech.com/digitalisation/2017/12/11/wannacry-virus-was-wake-up-call-for-railway-industry/?gdpr=accept [Accessed 10 April 2022].

Van Oord, (2022). *Realising and Improving Maritime Infrastructure for Thriving Economy.* [Online] Available at: https://www.vanoord.com/en/expertise/maritime-infrastructure/.

Whittaker, Z., (2018). *Techcrunch*. [Online] Available at: https://techcrunch.com/2018/10/24/cathay-pacific-passenger-data-stolen-breach/ [Accessed 2022].

www.kaspersky.com, (2017). *What is WannaCry Ransomware?*. [Online] Available at: https://www.kaspersky.com/resource-center/threats/ransomware-wannacry [Accessed 24 April 2022].

Young, A. & Yung, M., (1996). Cryptovirology: Extortion-based security threats and countermeasures. *IEEE Symposium on Security and Privacy*, Oakland, CA.

Chapter 10

Water sector

The water sector, which includes the supply of drinking water and the collection and treatment of wastewater, is essential and indispensable. Every system of the economy, politics, society, and environment uses or consumes water, participates in its management, or is affected by its abundance. Besides being a source of life, numerous businesses make substantial use of water as a raw element. It might be a mass transfer agent to remove pollutants from process streams like washing or stripping. Water is also frequently used in the food industry as a heat transfer medium, an intriguing aspect of its use as a mass-transfer agent. Sanitation is a further application of the water business and is crucial in halting the spread of disease. The water sector is experiencing fast transformation and climate change-related adaptations. Industry and academics are under much pressure to create technology and strategies for sustainable water management.

10.1 WHAT IS WATER AS AN INFRASTRUCTURE?

Water distribution, purification, storage, management of water resources, flood prevention, and hydropower systems all fall under the scope of water infrastructure. Water-based transportation networks, such as canals, are also included in the terminology (John, 2017). All artificial and natural structures that transfer clear water are included in a society's water infrastructure. Water infrastructure can be considered into three main categories: drinking water, wastewater, and stormwater. Table 10.1 shows the properties of these infrastructure elements. Most of these systems and infrastructures can be owned by the public, private sector, or both, depending on the country, state, and geography.

Table 10.1 Components of the water infrastructure (EPA, 2022)

Water infrastructure		
Drinking Water	*Wastewater*	*Stormwater*
Lands near water sources	Pipes and gathering systems	Basins for collection
Storage and reservoirs	Pumping facilities	Pumping facilities
Plants for water treatment	Plants for wastewater treatment	Plants for stormwater treatment
Delivery mechanisms	Sepctic systems	Green technology

- **Drinking Water Infrastructures:** Drinking water needs several destinations before reaching the end-user. Drinking water is mainly sourced from rivers, lakes, streams, reservoirs, and sometimes groundwaters. The infrastructure contains every step from the source, sanitisation, storage, pipelines, and other delivery solutions, which enables the public to reach clean, disinfected, and safe drinking water. In Table 10.1, drinking water is categorised as "lands near water sources." This is where the whole process starts. Then the water is sent to the treatment plants for sanitation and disinfection. After the treatment process, water is stored in reservoirs ready for distribution.
- **Wastewater Infrastructure:** The collection of wastewater has been one of the most critical public health issues throughout history. Throughout recent centuries, humanity has prevented significant amounts of waterborne diseases, thanks to the advancement of wastewater infrastructures (Ramseur, 2018). Currently, wastewater infrastructure has two main functions: collecting wastewater from households, industrial sites, and businesses and directing those wastewaters to treatment systems. Sewer pipelines and treatment systems are thus the infrastructure's two most important parts. Septic systems and pumping stations are different components of these central systems. Public and environmental health are significantly impacted by the quality of these two critical infrastructures.
- **Stormwater Infrastructure:** Stormwater infrastructure is the underlying system to control the rain, snow, blizzard or any other condition that causes excessive water accumulation on the roads, public sites, agricultural sites, and landscapes. Stormwater infrastructure can be categorised into Gray and Green based on their Environmental aspect. Gray Infrastructure contains mostly 'grey-coloured' systems such as pipes, channels, and canals. In contrast, Green Infrastructure can be described as up-to-date, environmentalist infrastructures that can help extract stormwater benefits. Green infrastructure for stormwater management includes rain gardens, artificial wetlands, permeable pavements, and natural highway bioswales (ASCE, 2021).

10.2 WHY IS WATER INFRASTRUCTURE IMPORTANT?

The quality of water infrastructure has a direct impact on public health. While everything is in order, it supplies people with healthy drinking water and helps to keep local rivers clean. If Water Infrastructure is not sustained and modernised, on the other hand, pollution will occur and cause illnesses (Hammer, 2017). Furthermore, Birkett (2017) states that contemporary civilisation heavily relies on the invisible functioning of human waste removal and disposal through wastewater systems as a critical infrastructure that assures the exclusion of cleansed drinking water and excretion from human waste. This isolation decreased the risk of joint waterborne disease infections experienced in London before 1857 during the cholera epidemic (Snow, 1857). As a result, for society's aspirations, global growth, and human health, adequately treated water supplies and wastewater services are critical (Birkett, 2017). According to the US Environmental Protection Agency (EPA) (2021), there are several economic, environmental, and quality-of-life benefits of adequate water infrastructure, including:

- Infectious bacteria, viruses, parasites, and toxic substances in water and waste are protected by adequate critical water infrastructures.
- A safe, trustworthy water infrastructure system and a well-thought-out long-term strategy are necessary to preserve growth and corporate investment in a city.
- Stormwater and wastewater control benefit the fishing, tourist, and leisure industries.
- More effective management strategies may significantly reduce water and energy use, lowering greenhouse gas emissions and less pressure on natural resources.

It is critical to maintaining the security of both users and systems. Otherwise, malicious actors may get access to this crucial data, disrupting water delivery. As a result, society is at risk of significant health issues and embarking on a very severe economic crisis.

10.3 KEY PLAYERS AND STAKEHOLDERS

Before addressing the cyber resilience issues that the water industry may experience, consider stakeholders in the industry.

- **Water Supply Services:** These institutions include those providing public, private, or cooperatively owned and managed water supply services ranging from water collection to controlling the chemical content of water, optimising the process of supplying water to businesses and final consumers, preventing and resolving problems in supply, if any (Global Water Partnership, 2017).

- **Private Actors:** In the private sector, many agents depend on the water supply to continue the business involved in the chain, from water production to its supply. Fruit and vegetable farming, textiles and garments, meat production, automatic manufacturing, and the beverage industry are important sectors that depend on water infrastructure (Manganello, 2019).
- **Regulators:** Since water infrastructure is critical for public safety, there is no consensus on how the state should supervise the sector, and there are different approaches from country to country. For example, in countries such as England and Australia, an agency exists separately from the institutions providing the water supply service, which has the duty of inspection and regulation, and this agency licences the water suppliers and inspects them. In countries such as France, Germany, and Uganda, there is no separate regulatory agency, and public sector asset holders oversee the service provider's performance under a contract. In the USA, some water supply institutions are public, subject to self-regulation and report their compliance with performance standards to the board of directors (Water Sector Regulation, 2020).
- **International Institutions:** The universal importance of water for human life is indisputable. Due to various reasons such as the climate crisis, globalisation, and increasing cyberattacks, international institutions' cooperation is vital to ensure the water infrastructure's safety and the water supply's smooth progress. UN-Water, the United Nations Environment Programme, and the Food and Agriculture Organisation of the United Nations are multilateral institutions aiming to sustain water resources. At the same time, an international partnership organisation is gathered as a Consultative Group on International Agricultural Research Institutes, which works on the agriculture and food sector of water. This organisation interacts with the private sector, academia, non-governmental institutions, and national and regional institutes.
- **Consumers:** Households and individuals consuming water outside of businesses are perhaps the most critical stakeholders. For this reason, households and individuals should interact with different key players and regulators of the water sector under stakeholder management and inform their demands and needs.

Water is an essential ingredient of human life. Therefore, it is crucial for the integrity of a state that water is clean and accessible to citizens wherever and whenever possible. For this reason, Presidential Policy Directive 21 (PPD-21) in the USA addresses the water sector among the 16 critical infrastructures necessary for the existence and integrity of the nation. It is essential to be able to identify the key players and stakeholders of this critical sector.

In the USA and Canada, there are structures called Public Water Systems (PWSs), which are classified according to the number of citizens they serve, the water source and the continuity of the service (EPA, 2022). American agencies divide these systems into three groups Community Water System (CWS), Non-Transient Non-Community Water System (NTNCWS) and Transient

Non-Community Water System (TNCWS). While CWSs are community systems that serve throughout the year in their region, NTNCWS provide continuous service to places such as schools, factories, hospitals and offices, although they are not community services. TNCWS, on the other hand, are systems that serve places such as gas stations and campgrounds that do not meet the definition of residential or regular customers and institutions. These water systems also have many components in themselves. The source of the water, the channels through which the water is transported, the areas where the raw water is kept and where the raw water is chemically analysed and purified, and the utilities where the treated water is stored, distributed and observed are examples of the physical parts of these systems. Otherwise, physical elements, cyber and human elements are also crucial for the system's functioning. The most critical cyber element is the Supervisory Control and Data Acquisition (SCADA) system. SCADA is a computer-based distributed computer system used to monitor and control the entire process of the water infrastructure connected to a central control room. Of course, experts from many different fields, such as engineers, chemists, microbiologists, security personnel, and public relations staff, who manage and analyse all these elements, also constitute the human elements. It should be kept in mind that specialists such as microbiologists and public relations staff are more likely to be found at more extensive utilities.

In a sector of public significance, such as water infrastructures, key authorities are established to monitor the processes' operability and protect them from prospective dangers. The US EPA is a significant agency established to clean, transport, analyse water, oversee water infrastructure, and support the Water and Wastewater Sector. It uses the framework developed in the National Infrastructure Protection Plan (NIPP) document of the Department of Homeland Security (DHS) to achieve its objectives. Furthermore, the Homeland Security Act of 2002, Homeland Security Presidential Directives 9 and 10, Presidential Policy Directives 8 and 21, Executive Order 13636, and the Public Health Security and Bioterrorism Preparedness and Response Act of 2002 (Bioterrorism Act) are significant federal authorities and directives that support the safety of water infrastructure. NIPP and Critical Infrastructure Partnership Advisory Council (CIPAC), on the other hand, are governance structures voluntarily that include private and public stakeholders (CISA, 2022).

The EPA, government agencies, and other federal agencies, along with the private sector, have traditionally shared the mission of protecting public health and the environment. In order to realise these missions interactively, a council called The Water and Wastewater Sector SCC, which includes water utility managers from many different associations such as the Association of Metropolitan Water Agencies (AMWA) and the American Water Works Association (AWWA), has been established. The Council uses information-sharing mechanisms called the Water Information Sharing and Analysis Center (WaterISAC). WaterISAC has extensive libraries, databases and training processes on potential threats to water systems and their resilience. In addition, director-level representatives of the following organisations also provide support for the safety and resilience of water infrastructure: US Department of Agriculture's (USDA) Natural Resources Conservation Service; Department of State; Federal Bureau of Investigation (FBI); Department of Health and Human Services (HHS); DHS IP; Department of Interior's (DOI) Bureau of Reclamation; EPA; Department of Defense (DOD) Department of Defense (DOD) Army Corps of Engineers (USACE); Association of State Drinking Water Administrators (ASDWA); National Association of Regulatory Utility Commissioners (NARUC); Association of Clean Water Administrators (ACWA); National Association of County & City Health Officials (NACCHO). There is also an intrastate network called the Water/Wastewater Agency Response Network (WARN), which was established to respond to threats and facilitate subsequent recovery (CISA, 2022). The WARN framework is also a critical volunteer-based structure that includes qualified personnel and technical equipment.

10.4 CYBER RESILIENCE IN WATER INFRASTRUCTURE

Due to ageing infrastructure, ageing staff, natural disasters, and even antiquated technology, utilities suffer significant difficulties. Operational, maintaining, and rehabilitating ageing infrastructure is getting increasingly expensive, forcing utilities to make the most of their limited funds and operating budgets (Wachal & Campbell, 2021). Moreover, Wachal and Campbell also state that the amount of information generated by modern metering infrastructure, system sensors, SCADA, and other systems outnumbers the staff's ability to examine, comprehend, and operationalise procedures.

In addition, climate change, water contamination, overcrowding, and old-fashioned infrastructure are driving water and sewage suppliers to adopt intelligent water systems that are dependable, efficient, and allow for real-time decision-making (Tuptuk et al., 2020). Hence, the isolation strategy that worked in older-generation facilities has become inoperable as intelligent systems in water facilities have increased. Furthermore, technological advancements have enhanced attackers' power and made identifying them even more difficult, as well as the attack's range of impact. For that reason, The Water and Wastewater Systems Sector is exposed to various threats, including deadly agent pollution, physical attacks such as toxic gas release, and cyberattacks (CISA, 2022). SCADA and financial and operational control mechanisms pose a high danger (Birkett, 2017). A cyberattack on vital water sector activities might have disastrous implications for human health and safety, jeopardise national security, and demand an expensive restoration (Germano, 2019). Securing private details, such as personnel records and user payment information, is indeed a responsibility of the water sector. Cyberattacks against water or wastewater utility operations or control systems can potentially have catastrophic outcomes. One of these outcomes is infiltrating the utility's website, compromising the email system and opening/

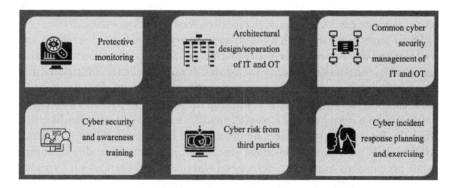

Figure 10.1 Recommended actions (Hassanzadeh et al., 2020).

closing valves, overriding alerts, or blocking pumps and other systems to disrupt purification and conveyance operations (Environmental Protection Agency, 2018). Moreover, installing harmful software, such as ransomware, that can disrupt corporate operations or process management is another crucial outcome of cyberattacks against water utilities. The report of the Department for Environment, Food & Rural Affairs (2017) mentions that to achieve a greater degree of cyber security maturity, it is vital to manage risks efficiently. To handle the cyber risk assessments, government cyber experts recommended several critical areas in which the industry should concentrate on its cyber security actions. In Figure 10.1, these actions are shown.

To explain the actions step by step, to avoid the growth of infections in IT systems and the resulting physical damage, OT and IT systems should be kept separate. While IT and OT networks should be maintained separately, security rules for both should be the same. The usage of sensors and software to give details on what is occurring within a network or device is referred to as protective monitoring. Monitoring helps detect harmful behaviour as a proactive. Activity logs, firewalls and anomaly sensors are checked. To illustrate, using the SCADA system in the water industry provides efficient monitoring. SCADA systems can provide live alarms for an immediate response and a comprehensive overview of all materials and tools for determining overall effectiveness.

Cyber incidents can target any member of an organisation. Thus cybersecurity should not be considered only the responsibility of the IT team. Therefore, employee awareness programs are considered a valuable strategy to raise awareness. AWWA's Risk Management Guidance for Small Systems (2021) states that employees should be able to identify a cyber risk, and in the case of a cyberattack, employees know whom to contact by training. The organisation requires predetermined plans and processes. These measures should be carried out immediately following an occurrence. These strategies and processes should be executed regularly so everyone understands their responsibilities. A predetermined response plan provides organisations to run as usual. The water sector cybersecurity risk management guidance report of AWWA recommends cybersecurity practices. One of the guidances is business continuity which contains a strategy for emergency response (West Yost Associates, 2019).

Third-party vendors, such as equipment providers, software vendors, and contractors, are increasingly providing access to corporate networks. This necessitates the parties' capacity to install software, make modifications, and connect their equipment to the host network on the systems. Policies must be made to mitigate this risk, such as limiting the number of persons with external access to a network and ensuring that devices linked to the leading network do not contain malware (Department for Environment, Food & Rural Affairs, 2017). Organisations must prioritise cybersecurity and take appropriate precautions to protect, detect and respond to cyberattacks (Germano, 2019). The actions led by the Department for Environment, Food & Rural Affairs can be examined under these headings. Separation of OT and IT systems, remaining in the same security rule and taking control of third parties' actions are considered protection steps. Monitoring is evaluated as a detection stage. In the last stage, conducting awareness training about cyber security, having a response plan, acting accordingly to the procedures during cyberattacks and exercising the procedures are actions of the response stage.

EPA is a federal government organisation in the United States charged with safeguarding human and environmental health. It is responsible for developing standards and legislation that promote human and environmental health. The EPA strives to enforce laws to safeguard the environment and society. Therefore, what EPA says is valuable to be considered.

It is assumed that no mechanical or software defence can defend water systems from all threats. As a result, improved security and the capacity of services to identify, respond to, and recover from physical and cyberattacks are required for this critical infrastructure because operators of water systems may compromise their capacity to manage the flow and quality of the water, as well as their ability to track the system's natural state (EPA, 2022). As a result, water admins must gain a better understanding of when their treatment techniques, motors, valves, tanks, and other devices are damaged, how to protect against an incident as soon as possible, and how to reconstruct so that public service can be continued in a secured and complete manner. Therefore, the EPA provides some tools to build cyber resilience. One such tool is the Threat Ensemble Vulnerability Assessment (TEVA) Sensor Placement Optimisation (TEVA-SPOT) tool. The tool's result-estimating module enables water services to evaluate health impacts, hazards, and vulnerabilities from contaminants (EPA, 2022). Utilities can secure their systems against malware cyberattacks, better address security crises, and run day-to-day operations using this technology (EPA, 2022).

Moreover, the Water Network Tool for Resilience (WNTR) is an open-source Python package that models and evaluates the resiliency of water supply systems. WNTR includes a versatile application programming interface (API) that enables system structure, operation adjustments, and modelling of disrupting occurrences and recovery activities (Hart et al., 2019). Moreover, the EPA prepared a document with its partners to explain how each organisation in the Water Sector CIPAC collaborates to improve water security and resilience, as well as the essential equipment and tools they have developed to assist them reaching their objectives (EPA, 2022). In detail, CIPAC was formed by the US DHS to encourage engagement between federal institutions and leaders from the critical infrastructure industry (Critical Infrastructure Partnership Advisory Council, 2022). CIPAC plans, coordinates, and implements programs to support the industry's cybersecurity and cyber resilience. These documents and sources provide information about the drinking water and sewage industries, especially in readiness, response, and recovery actions, and provide tools to help them enable and improve their efforts in these areas (EPA, 2022). Table 10.2 shows some of EPA's partnerships' activities to enhance cybersecurity and resilience.

Attacks on water systems may go unnoticed by the water utility or SCADA system administrator, but they can cause a complete network outage (EPA, 2012). Denial of Service, Spyware, Trojan Horse, Viruses, Worm, Sniffers, Key Loggers, and Phishing are all attacks on water utilities. Figure 10.2 below explains these attack types.

Water utilities can lessen their vulnerability to cyber threats with simple actions. These steps are:

- Defining assets that have to be protected.
- Creating functional subsystems.
- Placing in layered or graded defences to protect each one of the components.
- Regulating who has access to each group and how they communicate.

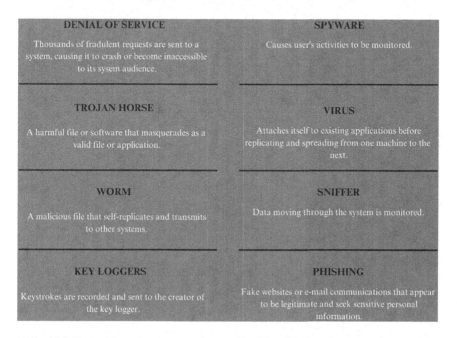

Figure 10.2 Types of most common cyberattacks (EPA, 2012).

Table 10.2 Goals of EPA partners (EPA, 2022)

		EPA Partners		
	US EPA Water Security Division	Water Information Sharing and Analysis Center (WaterISAC)	National Rural Water Association (NRWA)	Water Environment Federation (WEF)
Goals`	Through delivering new tools and exercises, it improves the water sector's security and resilience. In the following, the tools and activities that were used are detailed.	Provides knowledge and resources for preventing, mitigating, responding to, and recovering from all risks to water and wastewater facilities.	The national and state rural water association emergency response network provides personnel, equipment, and management services to the nation's 46,000 small and rural communities.	Integrates and develops the knowledge of water experts, raises awareness of water's effect and worth, and serves as a forum for infrastructure and service innovations.
	The Route to Resilience guides users through the phase of constructing resilience to all dangers via videos and a user-friendly design.	Members get 24-hour access to around 10,000 materials on a variety of water safety and resilience subjects through the online library.	Small and rural water system staff will benefit from NRWA Incident Response Education, which includes both classroom and on-the-job training.	Planning, Response, and Recovery in the Case of emergency the e-book assists providers in developing an emergency response plan for occurrences such as infrastructure breakdown, natural catastrophes, and man-made calamities.
	VSAT Web 2.0 allows water utilities to analyse risk and resilience from natural disasters and malicious attacks, allowing them to increase safety and resiliency while also complying with the America's Water Infrastructure Act (AWIA).	Semiweekly Security and Resilience Updates, half yearly Threat Analyses for the Water and Wastewater Sector, and ad hoc Alerts provide specialised information regarding risks to the water and wastewater industry, as well as recommendations on preventive and reducing measures.	Workforce Resiliency: With 4,000 hours of in-field training and 280 hours of classroom training, the NRWA Apprenticeship Program certifies water employee proficiency with an industry-led, nationally acclaimed, federally authorised certificate.	Safety, Health, and Security in Wastewater Systems is an injury-prevention handbook that includes processes and principles for developing programs and guaranteeing staff safety.

(Continued)

Table 10.2 (Continued) Goals of EPA partners (EPA, 2022)

	EPA Partners		
US EPA Water Security Division	Water Information Sharing and Analysis Center (WaterISAC)	National Rural Water Association (NRWA)	Water Environment Federation (WEF)
The Emergency Response Plan Template and Guideline enables water services in preparing an Emergency Response Plan that complies with AWIA and describes tactics, resources, methods, and processes that services may utilise to be prepared for and be responded to a natural or man-made disaster.	Monthly Water Sector Threat Briefings and the 15 Cybersecurity Fundamentals for Water and Wastewater Utilities are among the cybersecurity resources available.	Cyber Security Data Breach Insurance is a cutting-edge and one-of-a-kind program designed to safeguard utility customers who have experienced a cybersecurity data breach.	AccessWater.org is an online technical material repository that includes materials from WEFTEC and WEF Specialty Seminars, papers, e-books, technical reports, and fact sheets, among other things.

There are a few additional things that Water Systems should be aware of in addition to these. Utilities should implement measures to limit the number of people permitted access to systems. Updating software on a routine is essential. It is also harder to get beyond the utility's defences by employing solid passwords and anti-virus software.

As previously mentioned, in an environment where the proper operation and safety of water infrastructure are fundamental, it is critical to learn from prior experiences in order to be able to undertake more consistent and successful steps and take precautions regarding the cyber resilience of digitalised water infrastructure.

Cyber resilience is crucial in the water sector as the sector is responsible for providing essential services that directly impact public health and safety. The sector relies heavily on technology to support its operations, making it vulnerable to cyber threats that can disrupt services, compromise water quality, and jeopardise public health and safety.

The importance of cyber resilience in the water sector can be summarised as follows:

- **Protection of Critical Infrastructure**: Water infrastructure, including treatment plants, pumping stations, and distribution networks, is critical infrastructure. Cyber resilience measures help to protect this infrastructure from cyber threats, such as ransomware or malware attacks, which can cause physical damage, disrupt operations, and compromise water quality.
- **Maintaining Service Availability**: The water sector is responsible for providing essential services, such as drinking water supply and wastewater treatment. Any disruption to these services can have severe consequences for public health and safety. Cyber resilience measures can help to ensure the continuity of critical services, enable organisations to detect and respond to cyber incidents quickly, and recover from them effectively.
- **Protection of Sensitive Information**: The water sector collects and processes sensitive information, including personal and financial data, operational data, and proprietary information. This information needs to be protected from cyber threats, such as theft, espionage, or manipulation. Cyber resilience measures, such as access controls, encryption, and network segmentation, can help to protect sensitive information from cyber threats.
- **Compliance with Regulations**: The water sector is subject to various regulations and standards, such as the Safe Drinking Water Act (SDWA) and the Clean Water Act (CWA). Cyber resilience measures help water organisations to comply with these regulations by providing a structured approach to managing cyber risks and ensuring the confidentiality, integrity, and availability of sensitive information.

In summary, cyber resilience is critical for the water sector as it is responsible for providing essential services that directly impact public health and safety. Cyber resilience measures help to protect critical infrastructure, maintain service availability, protect sensitive information, and comply with regulations. The water sector should prioritise the development and implementation of cyber resilience measures to ensure they can effectively respond to cyber threats and protect their critical services.

10.5 CASE STUDIES

10.5.1 Case 1: Maroochy Municipal Sewage System

Maroochy has a municipal sewage system that uses 142 sewage pumps to manage more than 9 million daily gallons. A cyber incident occurred on the sewage system between 9 February 2000 and 23 April 2000 in the Shire of Maroochy.

Vitek Boden, a 49-year-old insider ex-advisor on the water project, carried out the attacks in early 2000 after being turned down for full-time work with the Maroochy Shire authorities. Vitek, an engineer, worked with Hunter Watertech for roughly two years as the site supervisor on the SCADA installation project until departing on 3 December 1999. One of the reasons why an OT system is more difficult to attack than an IT system is that it requires particular operational and internal knowledge of the ICS under management (Cohen, 2021a). To put it another way, a threat actor must know how to operate the equipment. That is why he was especially hazardous. He applied for a position with the Council at the time of his resignation. He was instructed to call back later to ask, and then in January 2000, he applied for a job with the Council again but was turned down. Vitek got access to computers that operated the Maroochy Shire Council's sewage system, changing digital data concerning 150 wastewater pumping stations and creating system failures. Therefore, pumps stopped operating, the connection between the central computer and the individual pumping stations was lost, warnings stopped going off, and even worse, one million litres of sewage-filled vast regions of the Maroochy sewage system. "Marine life perished, the stream water became dark, and the odour became unpleasant for homeowners," said Janelle Bryant, the Australian Environmental Protection Agency's investigations manager (Maroochy Shire Sewage Spill, 2022). Then, after looking into the data flow between the various pumps, it was determined that sewage pump 14 had transmitted the command to reset the investigator's change, but pump 14 was working perfectly. Therefore, it has been shown that the system's chaos is caused by a human hand (Abrams & Weiss, 2008). Police located a laptop computer with a digital copy of the control system software and a two-way radio transmitter in his vehicle (Levi, 2016). The steps for analysing this incident are as follows:

Identify: Since the necessary frameworks for cyber resilience were not used, the identify function did not work, and the necessary actions could not be taken during the incident.

Protect: There were no cybersecurity protocols, rules, or barriers in place, and the service contract's handling of the client's obligations was insufficient or ineffective (Hassanzadeh et al., 2020). That is why the protect function did not work either.

Detect: As previously mentioned, the detection was swift as sewage pumps could be visibly seen instantaneously.

Respond: The critical risk in this event was unauthorised access to the SCADA system, which allowed the malicious actor to spill untreated sewage into the surroundings. Because the hacker was a previous supervisor of the entire project, which controlled all pumping stations, the magnitude of the consequences may have been far-reaching. If the necessary frameworks and procedures had been implemented, a correct response could have been made, and the damage could have been avoided.

Recover: The effects of the sewage discharge were cleaned up. The procedure took many days and included the use of several resources. If the right protocols were followed, this process may be considerably sped up.

Lessons Learned: The attacker's harmful acts may have been stopped if the NIST protocols had been implemented. Given that the attacker was an insider, it would have been possible to restrict his access to the system.

10.5.2 Case 2: Florida, Oldsmar Water Utility System

On 5 February 2021, a plant operator in Oldsmar, with approximately 15,000 people on Florida's west side, observed his mouse moving about on his computer screen, activating multiple computer software that regulates the water being processed. The attacker boosted the sodium hydroxide level in the water supply to 100 times the average amount (Bergal, 2021). Sodium hydroxide, the primary ingredient in liquid cleansers, is used in treatment centres to regulate water pH levels and eliminate metals from drinkable water. Burns, intense pain, and bleeding are all possible side effects of sodium hydroxide toxicity. The steps for analysing this incident are as follows:

Identify: The supplier has conducted physical and cybersecurity risk assessments (CBS Miami, 2021). Therefore, critical assets, systems, and data had previously been identified, and a solid cyber resilience infrastructure had been established from the outset.

Protect: The Protect phase was also completed successfully, thanks to Oldsmar personnel operating per the necessary cyber security frameworks, and severe harm was avoided.

Detect: The intruder's actions were observed by an employee and not by the system itself, as it should be. The operator immediately reduced the sodium hydroxide to its average level when the hacker left the computer and informed his supervisor. The attacker appears to have gained unauthorised access to the target computer by exploiting the water treatment plant's TeamViewer software (Greenberg, 2021).

Respond: Although the operator responded instantly to the unfavourable situation, the system could intervene without changing the content of the water using its cyber security procedures.

Recover: It is unclear what steps the water utility staff took to recover the attempted attack afterwards.

Lessons Learned: City's water and other systems, according to experts, tend to be attractive targets for hackers since local governments' computer infrastructure is often underfunded (CBS Miami, 2021). The system should have acknowledged the intrusion as soon as it was noticed during the detection phase. The invader may be deactivated without an employee noticing if the proper cybersecurity processes were in place. After this occurrence, facility administrators decided to enhance their personnel's training. Furthermore, Honeycutt claims a lack of automation and process control (CBS Miami, 2021). It indicates that if setpoints were used to restrict low and high values, changes outside established boundaries could be stopped (Honeycutt, 2021).

10.5.3 Case 3: Key Largo Wastewater Treatment District

Salvatore Zappulla's term as former finance director of the Key Largo Wastewater Treatment District expired in December 2011. Later, during a normal assessment of the email system in February, Paul Christian, the facility's IT manager, became worried after noticing emails addressed to Zuppulla's email account. According to reports, Zappulla used legitimate district employees' login and password information to gain access to the district's computer network. Zappulla said that he had evidence of the insecurity of the local computers when questioned by authorities. Someone had previously accessed the water system remotely at that point and increased the sodium hydroxide concentration (Evans, 2021).

Identify: Considering how the cyberattack is carried out, it is seen that the procedures to protect the system's resilience against cyberattacks are not clearly defined, risk management is not carried out, and critical assets for the system cannot be determined.

Protect: The protection process could not be fulfilled since while the CFO accessed the system by entering his colleagues' passwords, there was no procedure in which user entrances were subject to a secondary authentication system.

Detect: During a routine check of email systems, the facility's IT manager, Paul Christian, discovered that the suspect had illegally sent information about the facility to his personal email using his colleagues (Jones, 2012).

Respond: After the IT manager discovered the leak, he notified the police, after which the CFO was arrested.

Recover: It is unknown what kind of security measures were taken after the incident.

Lessons Learned: Employees must keep their passwords updated at all times to minimise the dangers of identity theft (Hassanzadeh et al., 2020). Zappulla used this critical information to log in to the system from home, demonstrating the importance of two-factor security controls for securing access to computer systems. It was determined that the scope and frequency of routine security checks should be increased, as the threat was detected with the usual checks that should always be carried out carefully for systems, including sensitive and personal data.

10.5.4 Case 4: Bowman Avenue Dam

In a modest but alarming attack on critical national infrastructure, hackers broke into the dam's central server in 2013, presumably allowing them remote access. According to the prosecution, Hamid Firoozi hacked the Bowman Avenue Dam using a cellular modem to link the dam to the network and grant access to its SCADA system (Cohen, 2021b). Cohen also states that Firoozi was able to acquire information regarding the dam's state and operation, including water levels and temperatures, as well as the condition of the gate, which controls levels of water and flow rates (Cohen, 2021b). The steps for analysing this incident are as follows:

Identify: Because no precise information about the identification procedure has been made public, it is unclear if this stage was completed successfully.

Protect: Looking at the processes of the event, it can be understood that the Protect phase was not applied correctly.

Detect: Officials were alerted by the DHS about "unauthorised access" to the city's computer network. The attacker accessed and read data six times between August 22 and September 27, 2013, including usernames and passwords, according to a report maintained by the DHS that NBC was able to secure (Connor et al., 2015).

Respond: By chance, the dam's gate had been manually taken down for routine maintenance during the incident. If this maintenance had not occurred during the attack, the consequences could have been much worse.

Recover: What actions were taken for the recovery phase after the incident is unknown.

Lessons Learned: Failure to apply the above steps correctly and not following a specific framework or policy opens the way for immense risks. Fortunately, there would have been far more damage if the maintenance and incident times had not coincided. The DHS's warning to officials is the most favourable situation here. Moreover, Hassanzadeh et al. (2020) point out that the cyber incident occurred barely two months following the installation of an insecure web application. That is why the usage of unsafe online applications may cause an opportunity for attackers.

10.5.5 Case 5: North Carolina Onslow Water and Sewer Authority

In October 2018, Onslow Water and Sewer Authority (ONWASA) in Jacksonville, North Carolina, was attacked with ransomware, throwing customer-service services down. The timing of the incident had critical reasoning. It was a couple of weeks after Hurricane Florence (31 August–18 September 2018). ONWASA had a critical role in recovering from the devastating effects of Hurricane Florence. So the incident's timing was important (Antova, 2018). After the incident, ONWASA reported that they were attacked with malware named EMOTET. Emotet is a Trojan virus mainly spread through spam emails (malspam). Malicious scripts, macro-enabled document files, and malicious URLs are all potential infection channels. To look believable, Emotet emails may contain recognised branding. Emotet may use attractive phrasing such as "Your Invoice," "Payment Details," or maybe a pending shipment from well-known delivery companies (Emotet, 2021).

Identify: The identification phase of this attack can be considered semi-successful. Because there was a risk management strategy, ONWASA managed to keep water facilities working during the incident. Even though the computational operations were down during the hack, ONWASA kept all the plants and offices running. Also, customers could pay and use their credit cards by phone and in person (Sheridan, 2022). Keeping their facilities and plants open was vital after a hurricane. That shows ONWASA correctly prioritised their objectives and business needs.

Protect: In ONWASA's public release, it is stated that ONWASA had several layers of computer protection already implemented, including firewalls and malware/anti-virus systems (ONWASA, 2018).

Detect: The incident happened at midnight on 4 October. It was thought that the attack had been detected and prevented by the IT Department of ONWASA and a third-party cybersecurity firm. However, RYUK ransomware started attacking the machine and encrypting its contents on 13 October, possibly as a delayed-action attack. The utility's IT team tried to stop the ransomware by unplugging the system's network, but this last-ditch effort failed (Olenick, 2018).

Respond: The utility is coordinated its response to the ransomware intrusion with the FBI, the DHS, North Carolina state authorities, and various cybersecurity firms, according to ONWASA. The FBI investigated the event, according to ONWASA's public release (ONWASA, 2018).

Recover: "For several weeks, the absence of computational capability will impede ONWASA's timeliness of service," ONWASA said in a statement. ONWASA will rebuild its databases and computer systems. During the recovery phase, credit card payments will still be accepted over the phone and at a couple of the utility's predetermined locations (ONWASA, 2018). All other services must be performed manually until the system is restored.

Lessons Learned: ONWASA behaved responsibly and performed all steps correctly, preventing a disaster. Even though there was an unfortunate event of a delayed-action attack with RYUK ransomware, by separating the IT from OT, ONWASA kept the operations running. So the lessons learned from this case study show that keeping OT and IT separate, with multilayer security, can help prevent a cyber disaster.

REFERENCES

Abrams, M. & Weiss, J., (2008). *Malicious Control System Cyber Security Attack Case Study Maroochy Water Services, Australia.* Available at: https://www.mitre.org/sites/default/files/pdf/08_1145.pdf.

American Water Works Association, (2021). *Water Sector Cybersecurity Risk Management Guidance for Small Systems.* Available at: https://www.awwa.org/Portals/0/AWWA/ETS/Resources/Technical%20Reports/WaterSectorCybersecurityRiskMgmt.pdf?ver=2022-03-17-102456-127.

Antova, G. (2018). *What the Onslow Water and Sewer Authority Can Teach About Responsible Disclosure.* Securityweek.com. [Online] Available at: https://www.securityweek.com/what-onslow-water-and-sewer-authority-can-teach-about-responsible-disclosure [Accessed 17 April 2022].

Bergal, J., (2021). *Florida Hack Exposes Danger to Water Systems.* [Online] Available at: https://www.pewtrusts.org/en/research-and-analysis/blogs/stateline/2021/03/10/florida-hack-exposes-danger-to-water-systems [Accessed 15 April 2022].

Birkett, D. M., (2017). *Water Critical Infrastructure Security and Its Dependencies. Journal of Terrorism Research,* 8(2), 1.

CBS Miami, (2021). *Miami-Dade Water & Sewer Does Risk Assessment After Florida Water Plant Hack.* Available at: https://www.cbsnews.com/miami/news/miami-dade-water-sewer-risk-assessment-oldsmar-hack/ [Accessed 30 August 2022].

Cohen, G., (2021a). *Throwback Attack: An Insider Releases 265,000 Gallons of Sewage on the Maroochy Shire.* industrialcybersecuritypulse.com. 4 November 2021. Available at: https://www.industrialcybersecuritypulse.com/throwback-attack-an-insider-releases-265000-gallons-of-sewage-on-the-maroochy-shire/.

Cohen, G., (2021b). *Throwback Attack: How the Modest Bowman Avenue Dam Became the Target of Iranian Hackers.* [Online] Available at: https://www.industrialcybersecuritypulse.com/throwback-attack-how-the-modest-bowman-avenue-dam-became-the-target-of-iranian-hackers/ [Accessed 16 April 2022].

Connor, T., Winter, T. & Gosk, S., (2015). *Iranian Hackers Claim Cyber Attack on New York Dam.* [Online] Available at: https://www.nbcnews.com/news/us-news/iranian-hackers-claim-cyber-attack-new-york-dam-n484611 [Accessed 16 April 2022].

Critical Infrastructure Partnership Advisory Council, (2022). *Cybersecurity & Infrastructure Security Agency.* Viewed 31 March 2022. Available at: https://www.cisa.gov/critical-infrastructure-partnership-advisory-council#:~:text=The%20U.S.%20Department%20of%20Homeland,critical%20infrastructure%20owners%20and%20operators.

CISA, (2022). *Water and Wastewater Systems Sector.* Viewed 24 March 2022. Available at: https://www.cisa.gov/water-and-wastewater-systems-sector.

Department for Environment, Food & Rural Affairs, (2017). *Water Sector Cyber Security Strategy.* Available at: https://assets.publishing.service.gov.uk/government/uploads/system/uploads/attachment_data/file/602379/water-sector-cyber-security-strategy-170322.pdf.

Emotet, (2021). *What is Emotet Malware & How to Protect Yourself.* Malwarebytes.com. [Online] Available at: https://www.malwarebytes.com/emotet [Accessed 17 April 2022].

Environmental Protection Agency, (2018). *Water Sector CyberSecurity Brief for States.* Available at: https://www.epa.gov/sites/default/files/2018-06/documents/cybersecurity_guide_for_states_final_0.pdf [Accessed 27 March 2022].

EPA, (2012). *Cyber Security 101 for Water Utilities.* s.l.: s.n.

EPA, (2022). *Information About Public Water Systems.* [Online] Available at: https://www.epa.gov/dwreginfo/information-about-public-water-systems [Accessed 4 April 2022].

Evans, J., (2021). *Someone Tried to Poison Oldsmar's Water Supply During Hack, Sheriff Says.* Tampa Bay Times. Available at: https://www.tampabay.com/news/pinellas/2021/02/08/someone-tried-to-poison-oldsmars-water-supply-during-hack-sheriff-says/

Germano, J. H., (2019). *Cybersecurity Risk & Responsibility in the Water Sector.* American Water Works Association. Available at: https://www.awwa.org/Portals/0/AWWA/Government/AWWACybersecurityRiskandResponsibility.pdf.

Global Water Partnership. (2017). *Water Supply and Sanitation Services (B2).* [Online] Available at: https://www.gwp.org/en/learn/iwrm-toolbox/Institutional_Arrangements/Water_Supply_and_Sanitation_Services/ [Accessed 24 May 2022].

Greenberg, A., (2021). *A Hacker Tried to Poison a Florida City's Water Supply, Officials Say.* [Online] Available at: https://www.wired.com/story/oldsmar-florida-water-utility-hack/ [Accessed 15 April 2022].

Hammer, B., (2017). *For Clean Water, We Need to Invest in Infrastructure.* National Resources Defense Council. 17 May 2017. Available at: https://www.nrdc.org/experts/becky-hammer/clean-water-we-need-invest-infrastructure#:~:text=Water%20infrastructure%20directly%20affects%20our,that%20can%20make%20people%20sick [Accessed 24 March 2022].

Hart, D., Klise, K., Bynum, M., Laird, C. & Seth, A., (2019). *Water Network Tool for Resilience (WNTR).* (Version 2.0). (Source Code). Available at: https://www.osti.gov/doecode/biblio/3818.

Hassanzadeh, A., Rasekhb, A., Galellic, S., Aghashahid, M., Taorminae, R., Ostfeldf, A. & Banksg, M. K., (2020). *A Review of Cybersecurity Incidents in the Water Sector.* Journal of Environmental Engineering. Available at: https://arxiv.org/pdf/2001.11144.pdf [Accessed 30 August 2022].

Honeycutt, P., (2021). *Security Incident at Oldsmar Water Treatment Plant and Lessons Learned*. Logical System. Available at: https://www.logicalsysinc.com/wp-content/uploads/2021/03/SecurityIncident_OldsmarWaterTreatmentPlant_LessonsLearned.pdf [Accessed 30 August 2022].

John, S., (2017). *5+ Types of Water Infrastructure*. Simplicable. 3 April 2017. Available at: https://simplicable.com/new/water-infrastructure.

Jones, M., (2012). *Report: Hacking Lands Florida Wastewater Official in Hot Water*. Government Technology. Available at: https://www.govtech.com/public-safety/report-hacking-lands-florida-wastewater-official-in-hot-water.html [Accessed 30 August 2022].

Levi, R., (2016). *What the Maroochy Incident Taught Us About Cyber Warfare*. Medium. 7 February 2016. (Blog). Available at: https://medium.com/curious-minds/what-the-maroochy-incident-taught-us-about-cyber-warfare-4a1abd6abcfc.

Manganello, K., (2019). *Which Industries Use the Most Water?*. Thomasnet.com. [Online] Available at: https://www.thomasnet.com/insights/which-industries-use-the-most-water/ [Accessed 24 May 2022].

Maroochy Shire Sewage Spill, (2022). *Repository of Industrial Security Incident* Available at: https://www.risidata.com/Database/Detail/maroochy-shire-sewage-spill.

Olenick, D., (2018). *North Carolina Water Utility ONWASA Taken Down by Ransomware*. Scmagazine.com. [Online] Available at: https://www.scmagazine.com/news/critical-infrastructure/north-carolina-water-utility-onwasa-taken-down-by-ransomware [Accessed 17 April 2022].

ONWASA, (2018). *Media Release*. [Online] Available at: https://www.onwasa.com/DocumentCenter/View/3701/Scan-from-2018-10-15-08_08_13-A [Accessed 17 April 2022].

Ramseur, J. L., (2018). *Wastewater Infrastructure: Overview, Funding, and Legislative Developments*. Available at: https://sgp.fas.org/crs/misc/R44963.pdf [Accessed 17 April 2022].

Snow, J., (1857). *On the outbreak of Cholera at Abbey-row, West Ham*. [Online] Available at: https://www.ph.ucla.edu/epi/snow/abbey_row_outbreak.html

Sheridan, K., (2022). *NC Water Utility Fights Post-Hurricane Ransomware*. Dark Reading. [Online] Available at: https://www.darkreading.com/endpoint/nc-water-utility-fights-post-hurricane-ransomware [Accessed 17 April 2022].

Tuptuk, N., Hazell, P., Watson, J. & Hailes, S., (2020). *A Systematic Review of the State of Cyber-Security in Water Systems*. s.l.: MDPI.

United States Environmental Protection Agency, (2021). *Things Local Officials Should Know about Sustainable Water Infrastructure*. Viewed 24 March 2022. Available at: https://www.epa.gov/sustainable-water-infrastructure/things-local-officials-should-know-about-sustainable-water.

Wachal, D. & Campbell, C. (2021). *Digital Twins Bring Value to Water Utilities*. 21 May 2021. Available at: https://www.esri.com/arcgis-blog/products/arcgis/water/digital-twins-water-utilities/ [Accessed 29 March 2022].

Water Sector Regulation, (2020). Public-Private-Partnership Legal Resource Center. [Online] Available at: https://ppp.worldbank.org/public-private-partnership/sector/water-sanitation/laws-regulations [Accessed 24 May 2022].

West Yost Associates, (2019). *Water Sector Cybersecurity Risk Management Guidance*. American Water Works Association. Available at: https://www.awwa.org/Portals/0/AWWA/ETS/Resources/AWWACybersecurityGuidance2019.pdf?ver=2019-09-09-111949-960.

Chapter 11

Conclusion

Humankind has been faced with crimes since its existence. The phenomenon of crime, which has developed and changed over the years, has been defined and posted in many different ways. When it is asked, most people define crime as acts that break the law. The Declaration of Human Rights states that "Everyone has the right to life, liberty and security of person." Therefore, in international laws, people have the right to defend their security. The 21st century has brought an era with the digitalisation trend to the new danger that humankind requires to defend themselves. This new threat, which is encountered in all areas of life and whose importance increases day by day, is cybercrime. Various governments and companies are taking many measures to prevent these cybercrimes. Aside from the variety of measures, cybersecurity is still a huge concern for many. Cybersecurity is the practice of protecting systems, networks, and programs from digital attacks. Cyber resilience, on the other hand, is the measure of an individual's or enterprise's ability to continue working as usual. At the same time, it attempts to identify, protect, detect, respond and recover from threats against its data and information technology infrastructure. Nowadays, with the increasing impact of technology in people's lives, information security is exceedingly important. Cybersecurity plays an essential role in the field of information technology. Information security has become one of the biggest challenges of our time. That is why one of the most valuable things is knowledge of cybersecurity. With the increasing use of technology, a large amount of digital information emerges individually and institutionally. The protection of digital information requires just as much importance. Multiple cyber methods compromise digital information. On the other hand, cyberspace can be defined as a worldwide territory in the data ecosystem, the interconnected IT infrastructures including the Internet, telecommunication systems, computer networks, and embedded processors and controllers.

Critical infrastructure sectors are those whose assets, systems, and networks, whether physical or virtual, are deemed so important to nations that their incapacitation or destruction would have a crippling effect on national security, national economic security, national public health or safety, or any combination of these. Each country might define their unique critical

Table 11.1 Number of Cases per Country

Country	Number of Cases
USA	26
Germany	4
Global	3
Ukraine	2
Australia	1
Belgium	1
Brazil	1
Canada	1
China	1
France	1
India	1
Iran	1
Japan	1
Netherlands	1
Saudi Arabia	1
South Africa	1
Spain	1
United Kingdom	1
Total	49

infrastructure. In this book, we compiled nine critical infrastructure sectors: Emergency Services, Energy, Finance, Food, Government, Healthcare, Telecommunications, Transport, and Water. The continuity of services in these sectors is vital for the daily lives of societies and economies. This study introduces 49 case studies from various parts of the world. Twenty-six case studies are compiled from the United States, offering the country the largest number of cases by far. This regional bias mainly resulted from language bias, as we could only investigate sources shared in English. Furthermore, one might also argue that American sources are more transparent about cyberattack reporting, as we know that many countries or companies might prefer to keep these attacks secret since they regard these incidents as extremely critical. Table 11.1 summarises the number of cases and their locations

This book investigates Cyber Resilience in Critical Infrastructure by paying attention to recommending a national-level cyber resilience framework for all nations to use. Furthermore, we present sectoral analysis and case studies for each infrastructure by going through an in-depth analysis. As military tensions grow in many parts of the world, nations are alarmed and focused on their national cyber resilience, especially the reliability of their critical infrastructure. We believe this book will be a popular reference and guidebook for a wide range of readers worldwide, from governments to policymakers, from industry to the finance sector and many others.

Index

Printed in the United States
by Baker & Taylor Publisher Services